A Journey's Way Back Home

- BOOK ONE -

THE MEADOWLANDS

TRILOGY
A WHOLLY OWNED SUBSIDIARY OF **TBN**
PROFESSIONAL PUBLISHING MEETS POWERFUL PROMOTION

Trilogy Christian Publishers
A Wholly Owned Subsidiary of Trinity Broadcasting Network
2442 Michelle Drive
Tustin, CA 92780
Copyright © 2025 by Allen W. Leafgreen
Unless otherwise indicated, all Scripture quotations are taken from the King James Version of the Bible. Public domain.
All rights reserved, including the right to reproduce this book or portions thereof in any form whatsoever.
For information, address Trilogy Christian Publishing
Rights Department, 2442 Michelle Drive, Tustin, CA 92780.
Trilogy Christian Publishing/TBN and colophon are trademarks of Trinity Broadcasting Network.
For information about special discounts for bulk purchases, please contact Trilogy Christian Publishing.

Trilogy Disclaimer: The views and content expressed in this book are those of the author and may not necessarily reflect the views and doctrine of Trilogy Christian Publishing or the Trinity Broadcasting Network.
Any resemblance to real persons or other real-life entities is purely coincidental. All characters and other entities appearing here are fictitious.
10 9 8 7 6 5 4 3 2 1
Library of Congress Cataloging-in-Publication Data is available.
ISBN 979-8-89333-713-6
ISBN 979-8-89333-714-3 (eBook)

A Journey's Way Back Home

- BOOK ONE -

THE MEADOWLANDS

ALLEN W. LEAFGREEN

TRILOGY
A WHOLLY OWNED SUBSIDIARY OF TBN
PROFESSIONAL PUBLISHING MEETS POWERFUL PROMOTION

～ DEDICATION ～

Dedicated to my mom, who inspired me with her poem "The Angels."

ACKNOWLEDGMENTS

First of all, I thank the Lord for such a wonderful gift to allow creativity to flow through me. At times, enhanced words came from the Lord, challenging skills that I thought I didn't have for such an entertaining theme, and I prayed. Using tools such as a thesaurus, I searched to broaden my capabilities with fresh ideas for descriptive analogies with the creative writing skills that I had developed in my junior year of high school. The most exhilarating part was how it stimulated all my senses and opened new horizons for my mind during that school year. 1980, to be exact.

On September 28, 1995, at the age of thirty-two, I was struggling. I was trying to figure things out on my own, and I was failing. A couple of months ago, while serving as the door greeter for Wednesday's night of kindness, my mentor, Mike T., asked if I knew Jesus during an evening service. He went out of his way to make me feel welcome, and that night, I accepted the invitation and came to know the Lord. Through his discipleship, over many heart-aching nights and late-night phone calls, we untangled messes and a deeper understanding of who I am now in Christ Jesus compared to the understanding of a once thirteen-year-old boy perspective of who God had become to me.

So here I am, with newfound confidence, guided by Psalm 3:3 as my life verse, which pulled me out of dark times. Using the Word of God, Christian fellowship, accountability, and countless church services as my tools, I took on the battlefields of life, stepping into what I thought would become of this new creation in Christ, shielded by His grace alone.

Over time, the tools began to lose their edge. It only takes a moment in time to get derailed, and my faith pretty much began a course parallel to the parable stated in Matthew 13:1–9. It doesn't take much to figure out the analogy: I had become miserable.

Yes, I've experienced enough creative living and made my share of descriptive messes. It didn't happen overnight. Nothing under the sun is new; thank God for Romans 8:1. On December 19, 1997, I rededicated my life to the Lord through excessive Bible reading, praying, and quiet evenings as my artistic style came back into existence. Now, after many years have passed (2022), I have designed my style to reappear throughout *A Journey's Way Back Home*, such as in the prologue and throughout the pages of what started out to be just a rebirth and reminiscence over poems, finding a way to interact between them and giving them new life. Through scenes of different compositions leading from the great entry, his trial, persecution, crucifixion, and resurrection. Blossoming with the help of daily readings, contemporary Christian music, and a strong desire to search out His Word, using concordance, and looking up scriptures that applied to an idea.

Throughout this series, I was inspired by scriptures that expressed life-giving passages wherever the Lord led, jotting down ideas coming in the middle of restless nights, a just guide adventuring back into these writings. I had strong influences from J.R.R. Tolkien, C.S. Lewis, Stephen R. Donaldson, Ted Dekker, and the fantasy-fiction and adventure genres, with a touch of VeggieTales to inspire what has become several books, along with a certain twist of poetry to round out the edges. Imaginary beings in a biblical setting to glorify the Father and Son.

These characters develop virtues, values, and principles in historical settings throughout the Bible. A developed, strong-minded individual with a wealth of head knowledge about the Bible, yet still distant from truly knowing the Way, the Truth, and the Life in Christ Jesus. Gifted, lovable, and admired by many, he comes to the Lord in an unimaginable way, even attempting to witness to a homeless person, only to fail miserably in more than one way. Through these stumbles, he will learn valuable tools, be equipped with the spiritual gifts granted by the Lord, and experience surprising Christian fellowship. However, along the way, he will confront dark principalities that must not be underestimated, for they are formidable forces. Without Jesus, I even hesitate to speak their name; it is what it is. Praise God for the power of Jesus' name.

I have set it up so that the scripture references are located on the back pages of the book. Wherever you find "(1)" or any such number, just head to the Appendix, and you will find the corresponding Bible quote.

I am pleased with this accomplishment so far. Even though it was a stress reliever and many hours of enjoyment stimulating the mind and soul, I have faith that this work will enlighten a wide range of readers. The work is not completed in me, but there is a river flow of ideas to close out the series. With the Lord's help, it can stand on its own solid ground, deep-rooted, and be a blessing to those of adventure.

—Allen W. Leafgreen

~ CONTENTS ~

Introduction	13
Prologue	19
Chapter One	21
Chapter Two	69
Chapter Three	101
Chapter Four	135
Chapter Five	165
Chapter Six	175
Chapter Seven	201
Chapter Eight	239
Chapter Nine	251
Chapter Ten	259
Appendix	281

— Introduction —
THE CROSS

A Journey's Way Back Home
(1)

You say that the long and narrow road has become more than you can bear, and the weight that you have placed upon your shoulders, you choose no longer to sustain. Tired of all the burdensome load and need a helping friend. Instead guided by deadfall's lead and confined in a prison of loneliness at the end. Then let the light point in the direction, following our Father's will, to your journey's way back home.

His love and understanding, mercy and grace. His heart's cry of compassion, a devotion to seek and save the lost. His many words of encouragement to mend each one's broken heart, reassuring each of us to finish what we started. Spoken words saying that we would do far greater things than He; if only we would take a step in faith, follow, and believe. Tell me how you intend to just let go when He has done so much for you and others in your life. I have seen the seeds you have sown and watered with the word to spring what was dead, giving it, in Christ, new life. Christ was your reflection when showing them love to edify their weary souls. Many healed from their sickness and were released from their bondage. Do not abandon or let the thief of life steal from your mind's intuition. A wounded heart needs a fervent prayer so that you will again open up your eyes and conceive. Pick up what you now call baggage. He is waiting for you to take heed. Follow Him on your journey's way back home.

You say that the long and narrow road has become more than you can bear. And the weight that you have placed upon your shoulders, you choose no longer to sustain. Tired of all the burdensome load and need a helping friend. Then let the light, once again, point in the direction of your journey's way back home.

His kindness and comprehension, His mercy and grace, His heart that cried with devotion, always with a prayer. In God's trust and guidance of a greater love that led the journey's way. His compassion and concern, while others opposed in His hometown, treated Him as a common fool. Those eager, who thirsted and hungered for His word, He healed them from their infirmities as the truth set them free. Forgiveness is given to those who, while writing words in the sand, have not sinned; let them cast the first stone. His hand wiped away His written chosen words, and it is the same today. He remembers our sins no more.

You say you're wounded, tired, and do not understand, and you wander around aimlessly, in your own selfish ways. Just lay down your life for others, like you once did before your home, once cleansed from a destructive spirit, now sees your weakness and has returned several strong folds more. You do not have to be subject to them; only you can call upon the Savior. Just keep searching, and He will be attentive to your journey's way back home.

The Lord prayed in Gethsemane's Garden for His Father's will to be done. God, our loving Father, took His Son by the hand to where His battle would be won. By the Father's will to a journey's way back home.

God's love and understanding, mercy and grace. God's heart and devotion to save the lost. For God so loved the world that He gave His only Son, that whoever believes in Him, their final battle would be won. God's compassion and concern, for those not to perish but to have everlasting life. The Lord's many encouraging words to His disciples, God would finish the good work that had been started in each one of our lives. A new covenant with the Lord, with fervent desire. He said, "This Passover with you I share before I suffer. Yes, I am among you as the one who serves and a friend. Each of our lives will be scattered, but I will remain amongst you." Another day closer to the place of the "skull" and a journey's way back home.

You say that the long and narrow road has become more than you can bear. And the weight that you have placed upon your shoulders, you choose no longer to sustain. Tired of all the burdensome load and need a helping friend. Then let the light point in the direction to remind us of His love, to His journey's way back home.

Early in the midnight watch, after the true "Lord's Prayer," this man, a Nazarene, was betrayed by a person that He loved with a gentle kiss upon the cheek. You know, the one who dipped the bread.

"Although my friend of the 'stone pillar' would defend me 'until death's end,' he scattered and ran with My disciples down a path of misunderstanding and confusion for a moment's time in My life."

Taken and scuffled off by the guards, placed on trial for all that He believed. Passage down a path of disbelief as a rooster crows in the silence of night's cover.

"I hear a friend weep bitterly, and it saddens My heart for he needs physical comfort, forgetting the spiritual comfort I taught him as he is lost in a whirlwind of mistrust. Peter... although many precious tears have fallen... I am with you. Understand I am in the Father's will. To a journey's way back home."

THE MEADOWLANDS

You say that the long and narrow road is more than you can bear, and the weight that you have placed upon your shoulders, you choose no longer to sustain. Tired of all the burdensome load and needing a helping friend, then let the light, once again, point in the direction of His journey's way back home.

Blindfolded from the light, mocked and ridiculed, struck and beaten, this man, Christ. Dressed in the finest robe, trashed with words that could kill the inner soul. Set upon Him a crown of thorns, falsely accused, not speaking a single word. A public demand, a verdict set, one man washes his hands clean. Another guilty man set free. Our Lord is to be crucified. Some are in tears; others just watch and pray. Outside of Jerusalem's gate, a place once filled with praises, "Blessed is He who comes in the name of the Lord!" now sings a song of hate. Death and threats lead the way to a place called "Golgotha." A trail of blood, now a reminder down the same road that was once scattered with good seed.

A man along this way, compelled, singled out of the crowd, watching in disbelief, now interacts with the Man to help bear His cross. Jesus' body, rendered full of stripes and fresh flesh torn, now bears the weight of the cross beam; with the help of another, it now can be endured. In the distance, Calvary. Confusion sets the atmosphere in each one's mind as Jesus faces His destination, by our Father's will, on a journey's way back home.

A great multitude of people followed behind Him, desiring to draw near and comfort our Lord. The Roman soldiers, cold in their hearts, push all those who care away, for a soldier's commission is only to lead Him on. Approaching Calvary, Jesus ponders in their direction, none of His pain a concern. Laying down His life for each and every one of them. He is joined by two thieves, their destination known. For even the prophets of times past had already known. On the hill of Calvary, they join Him to be crucified.

A determined soldier mocks Him face to face as each fatal word is spoken, driven deeply into a loving heart. "He is the Christ, the chosen of God. He came to save others, yet He cannot save Himself." Laughter becomes overwhelming, overflowing the pain cry of our Lord to the centurion, another man. Now set upright, in God's timing, another nail driven into His hands sets History into place. All is set for a journey's way back home.

The two thieves are now established into their attitude, grumbling, each one worried about their own dismay. Our Lord, in prayer, giving praise, understands He cannot withstand this trial alone. The thieves begin to listen in as Jesus calls unto God, asking God to forgive each of them, "For they do not know what they do." The angered thief to the left ridicules, only to steal what was already given to him. In rebuke of the one's chosen weakening words scattered, the other criminal returns with a repentant heart, asking forgiveness. Jesus turns His head toward a rugged, broken man in acknowledgment, encouraging him with these words: "I will see you in Paradise," after a journey's way back home.

The guards pay no attention to their worthless talk and try to find ways to keep themselves amused, for this has become another monotonous event for their callused inner souls. Each hour passes by them, and all have missed the whole point of a man who could become their Savior and give life-changing events to each of them, and instead take another man's life as they toy around with His worthless clothes and make up games to see who will own this ragged raiment, to them worth more than the price of gold. A soldier's lost way, their crossroad, to a journey's way back home.

There were so many distractions in His agony, with many discouraging words. He could have died in deadened silence, knowing His struggles would be at an end. Even in His pain on a blood-clung cross, Jesus still ministered to all He loved, showing His mercy and love to a place of greater love. He brought comfort to each of those who mourned before His cross, letting them know the Father's will was in dire need to be done, as the multitude gathered around, not understanding the Father's will of true love. From this day forth, lives would be changed, redeemed by His blood and water that flowed. A mediator sent for each of us, to bring a fresh new breath of hope. Closer to the love of our Father because of His journey's way, a journey's way back home.

As the long and narrow road comes to a path's end, forget about that hindering attire that you have passed along the way. When all fixations seem to be hard to discern, look forward to Him, reach forward to those things ahead, and remember each footstep taken already is taken by Him. A path once narrow now is widened in-depth by our Father's will because each set goal has been given, willingly, over to Him. Taken in the footsteps of faith as we shine in His light, there is a new journey, hope, and understanding of life when we follow in our Father's will. Wherever in your journey, taken from the beginning to the very end, there will be a faithful companion nearby, one to guide you on a journey's way back, a journey's way back to Him.

~ PROLOGUE ~

Did not our hearts burn within us while He talked to us on the road and opened the Scriptures to us? Let us once again open our hearts, and the peace of God rule in all understanding. For He satisfies the longing soul and fills the hungry soul with goodness, as the Scriptures preach Jesus to all.

Does your soul melt because of trouble? He calms the storm within us so that the waves are still.

My heart is broken as I ponder on Your spoken word. Letters in red from You.

"And ye shall know the truth, and the truth shall make you free" (John 8:32). "If the Son therefore shall make you free, ye shall be free indeed" (John 8:36).

Where is Your word that I have hidden in my heart? My soul melts from heaviness.

Let me once again run the course that once enlarged my heart…

— CHAPTER ONE —
ANGELS

    A strange sensation, an aspect never felt before, of plunging into the great abyss. The circulatory flow of a current at this time is unrecognizable, caught between floating in the atmosphere's wind currents and then the essential contact with the ground. There is no sense or form of a human body existing, just matter, as crazy as it seems. Singled out in solitude with the absence of personality traits, I need to be digitally programmed again, as all sense that has been acquired is now lost and strung out between here and beyond. Where are all the friendships acquired that started the day in the spring fragrances, lost in eternity? Nothing makes sense, for there is no clarity between here and there. Then, as the cluttered clouds start to clear into the misty froth, my identity begins to form. A body of mystical substance with an indefinite shape appears before my indistinct structure in the silhouette of a figure with wings.

    I hear the angels sing. I'm the only one who hears them. I feel the angels surround me. The Lord's presence is near. I hear the music so divine, like the chimes blown in the wind. In awe of the senses of the mind, it's not a singing I have ever heard before. It seems to fill all my senses of being. I feel like I am in the presence of a holy God. Peace and love fill my soul. I feel my spirit soar as the Lord wants me to be still and listen. It is a place of love that I don't want to leave. For some reason, God did this for me alone. I do not comprehend or understand, but I feel the Lord in my heart when I hear the angels sing. I'm submerged in the constant falling into the comforts of their arms, caressed and gently set in a placement of contentment, the enjoyment of their amenity. My beating heart is set to rest deep into the heartland.

Reflections

The image of a mirror, just a slanted piece of glass but so capable of displaying the inside truth of a man, but in due time. For now, that is irrelevant and worthless in the questioning of time itself. As their images project the absolute truth of a feeling that cannot be described by the poets in chosen words, my mind ponders on the thoughts as clarity begins to shine forth in an overjoyed feeling, but this is not just a feeling.

There is a tug on the heart, like a hug that flows from one person to the other in a cycle of joy receiving and transferring amongst us. Subconsciously, unconsciously drifting. Erratically in and out between the two in differences that are astounding to jest the mind alone. Consciously adrift on a life raft of forgetfulness of a carefree day. Sculling with oars of life downtrodden floating down that same lazy stream of just being and the fragrant smell of something as simple and complex as H_2O. The senses of a repressed mind, emphasizing past events, are triggered by anything once surrounded in images of any one thing done in Adam's water or maybe even wine, drunken in the spirit of things once sought and in this life of soberness. In the broadness of an accommodating mindset, constantly drifting. Alone. On the water's edge. As the water reflects a face, so a man's heart reveals the man. Forgetting those things that are behind and reaching forward to those things that are ahead. Pressing forward to the goal of the upward calling of God. Having this mindset... or do others think otherwise? God will reveal even this. In the midst of it all, I question: is this my true existence, or am I only beginning to transform into who I am meant to be?

These emotions or lack of emotions...now, in present time, there is a sensation I have yet to cultivate or implant in my mind; a sense of reality or lack of, who's to say? I have not passed on, for my heart beats an accompaniment, a musical symphony's beat, in a rhythm that has allowed my mind to wander in this attitude of thoughtfulness or thoughtlessness. Again, who's to say? I know what I'm dreaming: an unconscious, oblivious, and ridiculous rapid-eye movement as it races for a period of time. Is it intellectually or imaginatively? A gentle breeze starts to bring clarity and reflections of an image embedded and untarnished. Does not a refining pot for silver and gold refine a man's value by what others say of him? I cannot contain all that has made entrance to my mind's flow of this existence. Scenery, sounds, and impressions have flooded the inner waves of my nerves and impulses, an ordinary life flow. New directory circuits of activity breathe new imagery. A place only recognizable by the tablets of my mind's memory of a place in time that I have only visited on the pages of a life-giving book, written in red to emphasize the character of the Lord and Savior. Presumably, I have turned to the next page as if I entered this realm. I am there, through the life passageways of this life-giving book. Is it just another thought or my existence? Have I become a being or just another logical reflection in my own captured mind?

(2)

The prophets of old foretold of this man's predestined destination and are now brought to pass. This man was taken away, so how can one sense the emptiness inside while hope fills the inner soul of my heart? And looking through eyes of desperation, so clear in faith and belief, or is it my artistic perspective of this man?

THE MEADOWLANDS

Words that will soon be written in the flowing crimson blood He will shed. Though the image has settled in my recognition, it has not quite reached my heart. Is this how guilt is perceived, without proper representation? A gentle spirit now rests and hovers over this scientific mind of reason, murmuring softly in endearment for a compassionate man. Previously depicted many times through the capturing bond of love on paper, in pastel and charcoal, these renderings limit any true impression of a man fulfilled in His life's calling and poorly represent His spiritual awakening.

A sudden flash of inspirational aurora. The contour appearance of lights glittering, outlining His face just recognizable to the particular, known by Him and is known by those who proclaim their love for Jesus, their Savior. The comfort of a man filled with passion speaking the words of life as they walk by His side with the burning desire of a coming day, proclaiming, "You are the Christ!" Words of joy now overflow as a bumble bee soaring to nest on the nectar of life…

And a song of joy takes flight…

> Your tender mercies
> are from heaven above;
> a breath of passion
> from a promising word.
> Let each new day with
> a burning desire for hope,
> be ignited in the depths of my inner soul.
> Listen to each heartbeat of sacrifice,
> an offering to the Lord, my God.
> Take not this word from my lips
> the words of life to which I love.
> As I sing praises to magnify your name,
> I shall walk and keep Your liberty
> and will not be ashamed.

> I delight myself and lift my hands
> to a living and eternal God.
> Who provides and encourages my life
> to talk about the Good News
> to others of the one whom I love.
> Although life is filled with many questions
> that I cannot give the answers to
> I meditate on the promises
> and His word.

After all these heart-flowing words and in the twinkling of an eye, this man, Christ, is delivered.

So, my question to myself as I speak out loud—or at least I think I said it out loud—who's to say? But that doesn't matter here or there. My question is, "Did I just witness a bee singing a song or a hymn?"

I'm like a casting shadow just over the horizon, witnessing a developing scene where this man is being delivered into the hands of religious men and seized by the Roman soldiers of a biblical era. The slyness of a betrayer looking over his shoulder, the one who walked along the sides of a brook, a stream's banks, flowing by the tree of life, and drank of the living water Jesus provided. He entered the hearts of twelve beloved men, now minus one. Descending into the abyss of a fog bank approaching and then into nothingness as this man is no more. He's of no significant value, divided by circumstantial evidence of substantial falsehood or of believing or not; you choose the side that you stand by! My mind goes vacant but yearns for the comfort that will lead me from this unconscious darkness.

(3)

As Moses lifted his hands as instruments, did not the Red Sea part? Delivered…

I am delivered out of the hands of the cruel man into this darkness. I am a wonder to many and hidden like a common thief of the night. I hear angered words spoken forth for those who revolt against them and, being greatly disturbed by the preaching of the risen Lord, are now placed in the custody of man. The many twigs and leaves that lashed out at me have now left scars of the foreshadowing things that will become of this man, Jesus, who is handed over. Pursued….

Am I being pursued? Why must I wait here in Your silence? I lay hidden in the underbrush, watching some of His disciples being prosecuted for the one they trusted and would deliver them, but from what? He rides on the heaven of heavens which were of old. Indeed, is not His strength in the clouds? Give me the physical strength of Samson… so that it will happen when their hearts are merry that I may perform.

David's devotional heart, "The apple of your eye," and the leadership of Joshua; with them, no man shall be able to stand being strong and of good courage. To wherever I go…!

Disrupted in the darkness, the dust settles down from the pits that swallowed them in the guardianship of an appointed timing of the Lord. Now… My heart is content as I walk on a path in which He made His presence known and whispered my name. Where shall I go…? For there are no atheists in foxholes. I listen to His spoken words, *"Go stand in the counsel and observe as My name is being glorified to the people, all the words of this life; it is the Spirit who gives life."*

"As the night's cover ends and the dawn of light rays appears, many quoted scriptures shall come to pass, this very night by many of His disciples for what they believe, as the light has been taken away from their once normal livelihood of Peter and John. Be still and listen!"

In the thicket cover of the woodlands, piercing through the many sights and sounds of my surroundings, I come to the realization that I have come into existence. Almost to the point of being educated first before being thrust into this point of time. Should I be able to recognize the voices in the so-near distance as I begin to close into this captivated space to the sounds of a familiar voice given to my newly birthed senses?

(4)

A familiar voice with intimate spoken words pulls at my heartstrings as it reminisces about past precepts' proclamations, but I only hear audible patches of frequencies with the choppiness of broken conversation.

"Be it known unto you all, and to all the people of Israel, that by the name of Jesus Christ of Nazareth, whom ye crucified, whom God raised from the dead…" (Acts 4:10).

"This is the stone which was set at nought of you builders, which is become the head of the corner (chief cornerstone)" (Acts 4:11).

"Neither is there salvation in any other: for there is none other name under heaven given among men…" (Acts 4:12).

My mind races and my vision scans those around me, and then I see him. Dancing around, praising God, for he is the one Peter and John healed and is the witness of God's miracle upon him. The murmurs from the council and boldness in the air as one whispers to the other that "they had been with Jesus, for aren't these men of common understanding?"

"Do not speak forth His name again," says a whitewashed, shrewd man who believes he can fathom God's words of life, only to be denounced by the saints, "Whether it is right in the sight of God to listen to you more than to God you judge."

(5)

Whom shall I fear in this city, as the assurance of God prevails deep amongst the congregation gathered? There is testimony in Your healing, signs, and wonders. For God has scattered the bones of those predestined by Your Hands to those who devise deceitful matters with threats, giving us confidence and courage to speak forth the name of Jesus and the word of God. Shaken and filled with the Holy Spirit, boldness fills the air.

(6)

"Shaken... Jolted in a new direction. Settled in. I will do a new thing. Now it shall spring forth. I will make a road in the wilderness and rivers in the desert. Be still and listen."

SALT AND LIGHT

Has this audible voice always been so persistent in my conscience? It's not a bad thing, but it definitely will take some time to get used to. A spiritual guide, in such an amplified but subtle voice that cannot be mistaken for my own, or is it just thought impulses? Goodness indeed, but from God? The other thing in question is the means of some sort of transportation malfunction; it is not normal, tossed between here and there. The rays of the dawning light projected in the eastern skies absorb and are now affiliated with the canyon walls from below, shining magnificent light pastel colors across the many miles of an existing canvas. Looking over the edge, the hand of the Lord came upon me and set me down in the midst of the valley. There were many there in the open valley. Dry bones, very dry bones.

"Be still and listen..."

"I will cause breath to enter, and they shall live. Follow Me, and I will make you fishers of men."

Great multitudes followed Him from Galilee and beyond. Healing...

Seeing the multitudes, He went up a mountain, and when He was seated, His disciples came to Him. Preaching...

"Blessed are they which do hunger and thirst after righteousness: for they shall be filled" (Matthew 5:6).

Teaching...

"Ye are the salt of the earth: but if the salt have lost his savour, wherewith shall it be salted? it is thenceforth good for nothing, but to be cast out, and to be trodden under foot of men" (Matthew 5:13).

"Let your light so shine before men, that they may see your good works, and glorify your Father which is in heaven" (Matthew 5:16).

And how to pray…

"…for your Father knoweth what things ye have need of, before ye ask him" (Matthew 6:3).

"For he taught them as one having authority, and not as the scribes" (Matthew 7:29).

Sending… as He sends out His twelve disciples.

"…Let your peace come upon it: but if it be not worthy, let your peace return to you. And whosoever shall not receive you, nor hear your words, when ye depart out of that house or city, shake off the dust of your feet" (Matthew 10:13–14).

"Be still and listen… You're not ready and are not listening, for there will be persecution."

"But do not fear those who kill the body but cannot kill the soul. I will take care of the rest needed to be taken…"

Taken by the seventy-two who took flight scattered in pairs and throughout all of Jerusalem to proclaim the truth, the faith of a mustard seed can move a mountain and send radiant rays of light into the depths of a barren cavern. To begin a refreshing new start and the renewal of our minds. For God does not see us from an outer appearance but looks directly into our hearts. To be a friend who always loves a brother in burdens and covers him in prayer. To heal the needy and poor. For nothing is impossible with God! And here I am, witnessing and proclaiming His name?

Each footstep taken is one that has been taken by Him down this same beaten path that is now covered in prayer and has transited into the passages of my mind, becoming a disciple of this spoken word? Or maybe my influences are trying to distract me into a voice of reasoning, redirecting from this undetermined madness?

The voices of murmuring begin to disperse into many directional outlets from the outer and intercity way, climatical destinations to attend and preaching the good news to all who shall listen. The scenery is one of destitution to the maidens who take their vases or vessels to the local town well, drawing water for the men in the village and the livestock that will nourish their fragile livelihoods. Shuffling around in an unsettled spirit, the dust begins to settle as all eyes are cast upon these two strangers who approach. One in the body form of myself, where, for the first time, I have felt and have the senses of a human form indeed. Putting head knowledge over intentions of the heart can, at times, keep you out of trouble, but if you are only going through the motions to try and speak life into those who feel hopeless, it is a road to disaster.

I am going into this with the wrong perspective, treating this as an act or a scene in a movie, trying it to pass into realism to draw my audience into the atmosphere where they, too, are witnessing the events and becoming emotionally attached to the projected characters. How hard can this be, anyway?

"Oh, look over there lurking in the shadow of a barren hut. Let's go. Hmmm, what was that about salt? Oh, now I remember."

Approaching cautiously, we appear before with an uneasy spirit hovering over us; my spirit says, "This won't turn out well; oh well, God has our back." Descending without prayer over the anxiousness of my finesse. Here goes. "My friend, for the good, He works out all things for our good..." Thinking to myself with words of encouragement and confidence like all of the school assessments in my Lecturing 101 class, I do it in the form of Abe Lincoln in the Gettysburg Address:

Many times throughout my early days
I have walked this same path for a positive affirmation.
And many times, I have pondered on nature, never realizing
the beauty of God's creation.
For I have, in my recent past, taken steps in faith
toward a misleading crossroad away from the truth
believing it to be a blessing in disguise.

Only in my sorrow to find out my chosen step took me
to a path of selfishness and blind compromise.
For if it was only me alone mislead,
that I could understand,
but to the many searching eyes of lost souls.
Have I prevented them from seeking
For those answers
that would release them from the night?
But I am forgiven of my carelessness
and given another chance,
to be their salt and light?

The response isn't as promising as I thought it would be; maybe I didn't put enough emotion or the right emphasis, at least not to the standards of the Lord in His compassionate heart of understanding. The squinting of the eyes is the first cue that I am not on the grounds of hope in this man's life. I am not taking what is wrong to make things right as I am now at the end of my life rope. And he knows it as he ponders upon me, and boy, he sure did a whole lot of pondering until the end, when he replies with a snarl, "What's that got to do with me?!" And the cane, oh, let me tell you about the cane. He whacks the bejesus out of me, and the ridges and tree knots, well, that's a whole other story. He must be possessed because he moves with blinding speed; not only is he beating the heck out of me, but he strips me down naked, buck-naked, I'd say.

When I come to, well, he has left his torn robe as I believe I blessed him with my robe. I guess I could have used that second robe after all. And what about my comrade? We parted two by two, like Noah's Ark, so why am I the only one standing? That's if you want to call it that. In the distance, I hear a voice whisper my name.

"You weren't ready, be still and listen… This soul can only be received by a fervent prayer!"

The Vision
(7)

"Be still and listen...

"Having eyes, do you not see? And having ears, do you not hear? And do you not remember? How is it you do not understand? Why do you reason? Is it not written on your face and placed on your heart? Is your heart still hardened? Follow Me! Whoever comes to Me and hears my sayings I will show him who he is like! He is like the man building a house and laid the foundation on the solid rock. And when the flood beats against that house, it cannot be shaken, for it is found on the rock! Have you built your house on the rock?"

"You know all things. So, why, Lord, are You not at my heart's door? Lord, help my unbelief. Have I not searched out Your word, analyzing it, sometimes in disbelief and sometimes with hard sayings and foolish things, like a donkey talking?"

"Have you considered Caleb or Gideon? You have prayed for the strength of Samson and the leadership of Joshua; this I will not give. Each one of them glorified Me in ways of their good character and matured in their weaknesses. 'Those are not your strengths. For they shall soon be cut down like the grass, and wither as the green herb. Delight thyself also in the Lord'" (Psalm 37:2, 4).

"'Commit thy way unto the Lord; trust also in him; and he shall bring it to pass' (Psalm 37:5). Rest and wait patiently for Him. The steps of a good man are ordered by the Lord, and he delights in His ways. 'For I know the thoughts that I think toward you, saith the Lord, thoughts of peace, and not of evil, to give you an expected end'" (Jeremiah 29:11).

"Give us a clear vision that we may know where to stand and what to stand for because unless we stand for something, we shall fall for anything."

"Where there is no vision, the people perish."

GIDEON
(8)

"Now, back to you, sending yourself off with the seventy-plus one.

"You know, if you 'pondered' at Gideon through my word... you would not have gotten beaten down or swarming with the dust bunnies that you gathered in areas we would rather not mention. Just saying! So, be still and listen... Our fathers have told us of the deeds done in their days, In the days of old when our soul was bowed down to the dust..."

"Not funny!"

"You're not being still... now listen.

"Our bodies clanged to the ground; yes, I had to go there to prove a point. I drove out the nations with My right hand, for they did not gain possession of the land by their own sword, nor did their own arm strength save them. But it was My right hand and the light of my appearance; I saved them from their enemies."

Regarding Gideon, the Lord is with him, a mighty man of valor, swarming in the midst of numerous locusts of men and camels of warfare. Swarming...

Swarming round and round as my head begins to swell and my breathing is shallow, I overlook the depths of a valley with a multitude of soldiers gathering as the sands of the seashore. For God knows the secret of our hearts and the longing to perform for His glory to shine upon us.

"Be still and listen...

"Well, you shall perform soon, but for now, you can't move because you're a loaf of bread. To be exact, a barley loaf of bread in the night."

"What?"

"I know. Be still and listen... Yes, I'll let you know when you can 'roll,' but for now, I am foreshadowing all that shall come to pass for Gideon. This is where you learn patience. Listen and observe...

"Gideon. Go in this might of yours; have I not sent you? Do not look at yourself as the least in your household. You are a mighty man of valor. Peace be with you, and do not fear! Your loyalty I have seen in your heart... for I am with you, for it is greater to know this as the same assurance given to Moses and Joshua."

"Hey, I'm a loaf of bread. How am I supposed to interact with Gideon?"

"Listen... You're a loaf of bread so that you will remain still and see with your eyes and hear with your ears to stay productive. Now watch... Gideon. Go build an altar and call it 'The Lord is Peace.'

"Now he will be faithful to Me, my sourdough friend, but Gideon will go in the cover of the night because he is worried and fearful of what others will say of him... Are you listening, Pumpernickel? He lacks the confidence to listen to how he wants reassurance that I have called him to proceed. Even this night before night ends, Gideon shall place his household in order, casting down all principalities that exalt themselves over the Lord, God Almighty. And to make Gideon's name known amongst all who worship another.

"Gideon, have I not sent others the spirit of the Lord... to all who call on His name?

"As one man calls on the Lord and is encouraged, one might understand his asking for one sign out of faith to proceed. Gideon shall make several requests showing his weakness of faith. Wavering back and forth like a reed being blown in the wind. Listen to Gideon's insecurities speak forth...

"If you shall save Israel by my hand as You have said, look..."

"Look... Ooooo, I know this part. Gideon just does not get it. Hey, can't I be the fleece? I'd rather be the fleece. At least I could interact and take action by holding water and then getting twisted by the hands of Gideon. I am not sure if it is because the oven is being preheated for my spirit of readiness or if the Lord is at His boiling point due to my comical gestures in this matter of me being bread. On the rise, to rise and be proof of God's existing help to mankind? Should I continue with these puns? I think not."

"*Be still and listen before I turn you into a twisted pretzel!*

"*As water being poured from a fountain, we are blessed by being servants while washing his disciples' feet; so has Gideon done from his fleece an overflowing from the heart. Go forth; you shall revolt against the Midianites. Although insecurities overshadow his steadfast traits of being humble, caring, and teachable, I will bless him.*"

"Wow, there are many here to follow the leadership of Gideon, but You're going to shake some of them off like a dog shaking off the fleas. I find it hard to believe in my thoughts that I, too, can have conversations with a loving God, but why? I have not called upon His name other than mere suggestive slang in the remarks of, 'Oh God' or remarks similar to this phrase in a phase in my past life."

"*Yes, some will be fearful of the enemy's loudness, laughter, and lack of confidence in themselves and being in earshot distance of their camp by seeing the Midianite's numbers.*

"*Gideon's are still too great for My glory to be known that the land will yield its harvest and all the ends of the earth will fear. Yet another test of faith by Gideon as he listens to My request not to conform to the pattern of this feat but be transformed by the renewal of his mind so that he will be able to test and approve that My will is good, pleasing, and perfect. Gideon does not think of himself more highly than he ought to but with humbleness according to his faith. I have planted a seed in him to not lack in zeal, keep spiritual fervor, patience in affliction, and be faithful in prayer. And as a dog laps water with his tongue, these men who have chosen this way to drink water shall be reduced from Gideon's care, and the remaining 300 shall proceed for My glory.*"

"Forgive me for asking, but it sounds as if Gideon already has these attributes. Does he still lack confidence? But what do I know?

I am just a pretzel. So, a pretzel I shall be!"

"Silence, you are a grasshopper in your own eyes if that is the way you perceive yourself. I have planted those seeds to be nourished and watered by each circumstance I set at Gideon's hand. Now...

"Gideon, arise and go pursue the Midianites, for I have placed them in your hands, but if you are still fearful, you shall not go alone but with your companion. Go down outside their camp to listen to what they say so that you can be strengthened.

"And now... you are a loaf of bread rolling.

"More like tumbling, like a tumbling tumbleweed. Roll on, dude...

"Dude..."

"What the...?"

I thought bread had a hard outer crust and a soft, cushy interior. Umm, mph. It is like having your legs kicked out from under you, that is, if I had legs, and the sensation of your belly rolling, churning. The mind is a strange thing; I am not sure if the cause is motion sickness or loss of directional mishap. These unexplained thoughts have found a way into my now-so-twisted mind. "Inspirations of Spurgeon's Overture" enter the passageways; never heard of it, but what do I know? I am a loaf of bread, for cryin' out loud. Here it goes; a voice whispers and inspires me to vocalize my voice as in song. Geez, can you make this any harder? Freefalling from an unbelievable height, I take flight!

I could, but it is your time to shine like butter on a roll...

And as I roll, like a buttered roll...
For all to hear and proclaim the name of the Lord, God almighty.

Inspirations of Spurgeon's Overture
So, it happened to Gideon on this night,
The Lord's will to improvise.
When the Midianites gathered for sleep
With cold, cold hearts and unsound mystique

ALLEN W. LEAFGREEN

The dreamer had dreamed the dream this night.

So, it happened in the stillness of the night,
While communicating together by campfire light.
He told a friend,
In the midst of the dim moonlight.
About the dream he has dreamed this night.

So, it happened during a weary watch
At that same specific moment in time.
Neither did they know, to the stealth's delight, to his surprise.
Overhearing!
For it must be Gideon!
That the dreamer dreamed in the dream this night.

So, it happened beyond the shadow's composition,
Through illuminated wisdom and discerning intuition,
That the Lord placed His hand upon Gideon for his reassurance.
The dreamer confined without interference
Shall come to pass the dream the dreamer dreamed this night
Completed with a tumbling loaf of barley bread.

And as the tent collapses, reality kicks in, or my reality for this chosen frame of mind; it happened all in the Midianites soldiers' dream. So, was I implanted in this soldier's dream, or is it one of my own, broadcasted between here and there? It is hard to say and quite confusing. With all in motion, literally, as my mind spins out of control trying to cling onto any type of direction given and then, "*Ump-umph.* Geez, can you be a little gentler, please? Okay, dismount, finally level ground," as my legs pop out from their dough pockets like popover rolls finishing in the oven, I can walk again.

I hear Gideon cry out, "This night, this time, arise now, for the Lord has proclaimed this battle won." Dividing his chosen anointed forces in formation equals setting plans in motion. He shouts out to all, "The sword of the Lord and Gideon!" At the beginning of the middle watch, when all are resting at the post, the trumpets blare, and the pitchers crash amongst the ledges. Every man's sword against his own companion's confusion sets the night. Looking at the reflection in the watering hole, I see I am back to being my loveable self again.

The Pen and Heart of David
(9)

Hmm-mmph. My loveable self, confusion once settled deep within me, now a reflection of change. Where did I hide that pure, peaceable spirit flow, willing to yield at times, gentle and full of compassion? Am I blind? A fool who raged? Am I no more chosen to my nature of character, to brotherly kindness so that I shall not be barren or in danger of being unfruitful to others? How miserable of a person would that be? Thanks be to God, who has rescued me from my mind! He who searches the heart knows the mind and freely gives all things. Thank God for this "sweet wind of change." There goes that bumble bee taking flight with a song at heart; it has to be his musical buzzing and flapping of his wings, and his flight is so close to my ears. Should I swat at him and make this pesky bug go away? The bee is in mid-musical strumming and humming,

There is a strong wind blowing,
coming across the sky,
changing direction.
Fulfills my heart's desire,
touched by his love,
hearts beat overflow,
wrapping around

ALLEN W. LEAFGREEN

*this sweet wind of change.
There is hope and future,
there has always been
but sometimes we search in wrong places
when we need to be looking for Him.
Faith as a little child,
trusting He is always near,
follow and believe.
In the promises of His word
and this sweet wind of change.
Hearts that have been broken
now mended in love,
His mercy, understanding
and tender, amazing grace.
When my heart needs protection
and a safe place to abide,
from heartache's pain.
He is a shield for me
and becomes my strength.
To the struggle from fears,
wrapped in a world that allows no change,
I am in need of Him to stand my ground
and this sweet wind of change.
There is a strong wind blowing
coming across the sky,
changing direction.
The Lord will fill our hearts' desire
our heartbeats overflow.
I can see love given in Christ,
as no spoken words are needed,
I can feel Your love
in this sweet wind of change.*

THE MEADOWLANDS

"Hmmm, silence is not my friend. Am I lost here in my own thoughts? Or have I quieted my own enemy within? What is man that you are mindful of him, Lord? Do not let me settle here in my own stillness. You know my foolishness; contempt has broken my heart, and I am full of heaviness. Does not Your Word say, 'And your heart shall live that who seek God'? (Psalm 69:32). You have made all things known, but there is darkness overshadowing the light of my dawn!"

Once again, the sound of a bubbly bumble bee takes flight in a transformation of instrumental notes in the beating of his wings and gives into flight, with words of wisdom penetrating the air.

Who shall ease the burdens
that are like heavy weights upon a weary soul?
May the Lord answer you on the day of trouble.
Cry out to the Lord, our God,
for he wants peace to be with you.
He does not forget the cries of the humble.
Give into prayer,
bringing words of encouragement
when hope seems to be gone
and all is in despair.
The Lord shall always be your comfort.
Just have faith, knowing He really cares.
Trust in the Lord:
He will be your strength in weakness
and shelter He shall provide.
Under the feathers and wings take refuge,
the truth a shield
and a strong tower for those
a place to abide.
For when your heart melts because of trouble
and trembling which causes distress

and when situations seem innumerable,
then cast your burdens upon Him
and 'Fear not'
will be the Lord's request.
For there is a song of praise and worship
that is deep down inside my soul.
Ignites a flame that burns with desire,
for the love of my Lord this night.
There is peace in His commandments
hidden in my heart
that will cleanse a man of his ways.
But You do not desire sacrifice or offerings,
only to come daily to His amazing grace.
Of the one written throughout the Bible.
To those who seek God,
your hearts shall live.
From the birth of sin
to the resurrection
of His Son's salvation, which Jesus gives.
Even before His death upon the cross, Jesus proclaimed,
'I am the way, the truth and life.'
For God so loved the world and all of us,
God gave his only son, for this is God,
our God forever.
He alone will be my guide.

"Has this been written in my heart, or is it just all in my mind? I mean all of this! I salute the being of this bumble bee in flight!"

"Be still and listen..."
(10)

"I have declared the former things from the beginning, and suddenly, they have come to pass. From this time, you will hear new things, even the hidden things. I have tested you in the furnace of sorrow. Come near to Me. I have not spoken in secret from the beginning; from the time that it was, I was there. I am the one who teaches you and leads by the way you should go. From this time forward, I shall give you a longing for fellowship amongst the brethren, for iron sharpens iron."

The last sounds of Gideon's trumpet blow, proclaiming his way to victory and ringing in my ears, while that whispering voice that had been placed in a silent call, a longing for companionship has receded in my mind, in my heart, and in my soul so that I may come to you in joy and rest in your company and the company of others.

Into the Company and Companionship of others
(11)

"Listen...

"Go into this time, for it is a time, the time when Samuel went no more to see Saul until the day of his death, although Samuel mourned as the Lord regretted that he was granted to be king.

"The consequences for those who are disobedient are like these: a distressing spirit hovers over a man once anointed in oil and given a kingdom, only for it to be torn from him by the tearing of Samuel's robe. Then enters

a man, a man who sought after My own heart. For nothing restrains the Lord from saving by many or few to accomplish great things based on what is seen, but small opportunities prepare for bigger battles..."

The battle belongs to the Lord at this appointed time, but for now, this is where it all begins...

It begins in the time of spring, as the sweet smell of the whole wheat grass brings a strange sensation of hunger pains. Suddenly, I have a craving to eat this stringy substance, and the weight of my coat is enormous and burning. Is this all in my mind, or is this not what I have in mind? I'm a four-legged beast of a thingy.

A thingy... Well, not quite a man of equal but a companion and acquaintance to this mighty man of valor. With this sweet counsel of togetherness, I walk into the house of God.

"I shall bless your time with David, even as a four-legged sheep. The battle belongs to the Lord... in the mind and onto the fields of life's course. So goes for Saul, as a spirit of infirmity still haunts him and of the decisions that he makes, but for this time, My presence and appointed time has come for Saul to call upon his armor-bearer to relieve the sounds of the clanging metal and the taunting of battle cries with his instrument of relief. For now, it is not a time for companionship but a championship as all is gathered. "

The awareness has settled the humbleness in my heart; for now, I shall become one as dependent on all my aspects of life as this four-legged creature that I have become. Is this my new promised land given to Moses during the Exodus, a land flowing with milk and honey? It sounds appetizing. Perhaps it's a craving for an endless supply of hay, or even barley if it's within reach—or should I say, hooves first—toward the approaching stranger, who I'm certain will make himself known during this unfortunate transition.

"Hey David, gather your four-legged friends and come here at once. Saul has need of your presence. I am sending you with provisions for your brothers and Saul, loaded here on the donkey. Hurry along now...!"

THE MEADOWLANDS

This is the man with eight sons, Jesse, a man of integrity visited by Samuel himself, for the Lord does not see as man sees but looks at the inward appearance and of the heart. The heart of David was anointed by His choice. Even if he is youngest, from that day forward, the Spirit of the Lord came upon him, and now I, myself, stand here before David as one of the many sheep that he attends daily. For this is the day that the Lord has made. Who has covered the heavens with clouds and prepared the rain for the earth? The mountains rise past the horizon gates at the dawn of a new day. Arise! I have to ask myself what in the hea—oh, what in heaven's name was I thinking? I better not go there, but where is this information that ponders throughout the thoughts of my mind coming from? Cool, I guess. Is it like being invaded in a good way?

The sturdiness of David's voice, demanding but gentle, announces, "Arise all and hurry along. I must be off; Jacob shall lead you this morning. This way. That means you too, Aly, yes, you." He makes direct eye contact with me and rolls his eyes. "Thanks for assisting my sheep, Jacob, but you will be without the boys; they are in bad standing and can't be found at the moment. Maybe Jesse can give you the rundown and details of the matter; he is flustered and not making much sense, saying that it is a good story of mischievousness and it's not the time to tell it. Thanks again. You are always a good friend."

Jacob, straightforward and with a happy-go-lucky attitude, says, "Always, whenever I'm needed. I will only take them into the open meadows west of here, and I have my sling and staff; all will be fine, David. Take care. Come on, Aly!"

Hey, that's me, and I have a name, too, Aly; I'm liking it! I'll let you slide on your rudeness, Mr. David, in the process of ignoring Jacob. No worries. I'll gather the others so we can be off. I'll pack light as I make my way over to David after rounding up at least four of my comrades, who follow me with ease; well, I did have to take a nip at the fifth one lagging in the grain. Not the best shepherding skills, but it got him going. Jacob is just standing there with a smirk in disbelief. I stand in front of David with my big brown eyes gazing into David's.

"Come on, Aly, you're making this hard on you and me; I'm not kidding around; don't make me have to use this!" says David as he reaches for his staff or shepherd's crook of a thing.

Jacob comes over to embrace him over the shoulder. "Let me take care of Aly and be on your way now."

As Jacob begins to walk away, he gives Jesse a glance of recognition, a man who is on his last thin thread of dismay and mutters out loud, "Oh, the three of those boys done did it now, just you wait, just you wait and see."

Jacob smiles, shakes his head, and says to himself, "It is probably for the best that I don't know! Now come to me, Aly!" Not listening to what Jacob is saying, I follow behind David, begin to feel a slight tugging around my chest, and my motion stops immediately. Hey, no need to use that thing; I'm already mentally scarred by a past reference flashback. So now what? I watch Jacob moving in one direction, knowing that he has one over me, and David moving in the opposite direction, with a donkey loaded down with who knows what. When they approach the crevasse of two monumental stones that honor each who passes through, home from journeys' end or the farewell of companions in swaying motion, they disappear out of sight, and all are welcomed.

The Forest of Desolation Souls

Jacob, I worry about Jacob; he is no bigger than the stick that he carries but a happy little guy. He's watching very closely; he must have eyes in the back of his head as he calls for me. "Not today, little one; David has been summoned." Gone? Funny you should say, Jacob, and so is my confidence in myself, overwhelmed, as my spirit fails me. My eyes flash back to Jacob tending the sheep in a caring way, and I think that this is more than likely the act of David watching over his herd, but why, Lord, am I feeling on the edge? It's nothing that Jacob has done. You know the path I walk—glancing to my right, pondering to my left—while they secretly set a snare for me and the others of the flock. Does no one care for my soul? Has Your security failed me and others?

My voice cries out for Jacob, yet I am but a harmony of sheep voices. To my amazement, Jacob has already assumed the stance of a military man in battle, as the intentions of a battle cry unfold. I am in the midst of unsettled sheep pacing back and forth, being bunched up in a corner of protection. The ear-piercing screeching sounds unlike any other calls in nature in their voices, and their wingspans are the length of Jacob; the eagles have their sights set on warding off any misfired shots of Jacob's sling. The two eagles circle around in pursuit, trying to isolate one of their ground prey. The little lambs are in the field of game for the navigational fowl as their ewes rush them inside a close circle of love.

My own vision is a blur as I have singled myself out into isolation because over-anxiousness has set its course to my destination. I look over my furry shoulder of wool with all these legs in a panic motion. Then it happens; "Hey, *umphh!*" I say as the circular vision of trees goes round and round. As I lose sight of all things, even the action pack display of courage of Jacob's swiftness and accuracy, I take a fall that is like the span of my life, or is my life at hand? But then contact is made, just tuck and roll, baby, then dismount, voilà. My path becomes familiar, up or down, right in front of me, a path that has been well trotted upon. Familiarity has placed my heart in the pursuit of shelter, but in which direction shall I go? And as the dust settles, so do I, as my mind has purpose and clarity about the upward calling of God.

Well, I know it is not God, but I am relieved when I hear the voice of Jacob calling my name, "Aly, Aly, all is well. I've lost none of my own. Return to this saddened shepherd, for I cannot rest this body till all are retrieved."

I start to answer his plead, but I stutter and step, shaking like bacon sizzling away in the pan, ready to be turned, but I shall not turn. I continue down the beaten path, running fast and far away from the howling of Jacob. Nothing to do with his accounting of the sheep. And as my blood pressure is put back into order, a new voice, or should I say, many voices, emerge from the forest wall; they whisper my name lightly, "Aly."

"Come, Aly, come seek the shelter you desire. Let peace return to your soul to feel warmth and safety, covered in this haven where even the light is tamed. We will not let the thorns or briars cling or tangle in the whiteness of your woolly coat. Whom shall you fear? Come join us. We do have a narrow path for you to prance on, and we let the light shine onto its entrance, entrancing so you will not be mistaken about which way to go, Aly. It will lead you into the thickness of our recessing lounging place out of harm's way. Trust our guidance, and we shall bring you to your home destination."

And then, out of a trance, my inner voice is screaming, "No! No! Do not go over the hills and through the woods unless into the wolves' mouths you want to go; they nip at your ears and bite your nose, and you have no breath no more! Oh, I don't like that; it could happen," I hear myself speak forth aloud.

Then, as if nothing ever were spoken by this barking thicket before me, there was silence. Then a barraged uproar of *"No, no, no!* We will not let any infliction on you. Many have entered and embraced our comfort, and most have chosen to stay; there is a commonwealth of people who will nourish you out of sincerity; come see. The ones who chose not to resign here have given a name of eradication of their souls. Hurry, time is wasting away, for Jacob is near, extremely near!"

The whisper settles, "no more, no more," directly coming from the Lord, while the whispers of the woodlands grow lifeless as if the pleas of their cries have surrendered to reality. The Lord's thunderous voice snaps all doubt aside as He shouts with all His might, *"I will not leave you or forsake you. I am always with you. Jacob will not disservice you in these troubled circumstances that were predestined to happen, and you're being called to return to David, your shepherd of joy. He is essential to him and others who shall enter in this pursuit of challenged integrity."*

Back into the Arms of David, Well, Maybe...

The familiar, packed-down soil of a well-trodden path smooths beneath my quickened stride as urgency propels me further from the confusion I've left behind. In the near-yet-distant light, I see a faint image of a donkey and man walking in the assurance of life, very, very faint whispers of a voice singing in unison with nature, as I hear the voice of David magnifying the Lord. David, my friend and my shepherd, sings, "He makes me lie down in green pastures, He leads me by still waters…" Oh, the green pastures that lead to David. Wait a minute, how shall he react? Jacob's arms are where I am set to be, but now, like a vagabond, I am a wanderer, slinking through the meadow, trying to stay hidden. It's an open field; in this challenge, one must be creative, highly creative, distorting the body in areas and shapes that cover you not, but quietness is in my favor, unnoticed, crouched behind this pebble of a rock, and the voice of David singing a song of hope to fill up these blue skies! Just past the turning of the road, I run as fast as my legs can carry me into a tree line of saplings and turn my head to look. I listen in but don't see…

"He restoreth my soul: he leadeth me in the paths of righteousness for his name's sake. Yea, though I walk…" (Psalm 23:3–4).

… right into a tree with a big ole thud while looking over my shoulder to see if all is clear; who knows how it was overlooked, but I just can't get past the looking over the shoulder's painful routine. Did I blackout from exhaustion or from the new knot, not of my wool, I kid you not, but protruding from my head? Probably the latter, but anyway, all fours are pointing up with all exposed, so the world can see my gender as I look up. I see David and the donkey, of course, with a big ole grin on his face.

The gap now set in my lower roll of molars is intrusive, but it doesn't seem to be noticed by David.

"Hey, Aly, how'd you get here? This is no place for you to wander about; get over here. You clumsy walking robe. How many times have I told you? You can't always be at my beck and call!"

Hmm, I wonder if David has a sense of understanding of the behavior and body language of a sheep. I'll shrug my shoulders. Not bad for just a trivial gesture that he has seemed to pick up on.

"What? Oh, you don't say, Aly? Well, we're too far into my quest to turn around, and I could use a listening ear as company, my good friend of mine. Let's roll!"

Oh, if you only knew David, I'll catch you up to speed on that one later. But for now, I am safe in the hands of one of my people!

I could get used to this sheep thing with these four legs and the sounds of a rhythmic pitter-patter as I walk; I can't wait to get on cobblestone and hear what that sounds like. I have a strong desire to listen to all David has to say to me; such a warmth that goes deep into my furry soul, and it's not from this extra coat. I have a longing to be comforted by him. My vision is a whole lot better than before; I guess there is a transitional phase I had to go through, but I see things very clearly, and I know David has my back, literally. What the heck is that smell? Did David eat beans or something? Then David, with disgust written all over his face, stops in mid-sentence…

"You anoint my head with oil…"

I think to myself, *Oh, it's not oil you're being anointed with, buddy, just saying, hey...!*

David speaks forth a new proclamation!

"Hey, okay, which one of you did that? Don't give me that look, you stubborn ole mule!" he said, waving his hands around, trying to filter the air from the smells of rotten cabbage. So, rolling my head around with tears swelling up in my eyes by getting a snout full, I look toward the donkey and say, "No duh... Sherlock!" (For the record, this is our first conversation, and it probably won't be our last. A new thing or world is opening before me as we speak; literally, just saying.)

At first glance, it seems that this mule has just winked at me while grinning and giving me that *what are you going to do about it* look as he takes full credit for this leakage.

"It wasn't David, it was me. And watch out for that snake crossing over; it's not poisonous, but...!" I look down to the ground to see what the donkey is talking about. *Oh, you.* Out the butt, rounds of projectile come flying out my tuchus like shooting off a clip from, I don't know, some kind of weapon or another? Sorry, I mean out my derriere or whatever you want to call it! As if it would even matter, I gaze around from side to side with my awesome peripheral vision, for my eyes kind of bug out, so to speak.

"That wasn't very sociable, excuse me!"

The donkey gives me a rude once-over and says, "For what? When you gotta go, you gotta go; that's that, thank you very much. Good day and cheerio. *Hmmmmph!*" Either David has learned to be a ventriloquist, or my mind just checked out for the day! But it was a groggy voice and sounded as if it came from the donkey.

I come over to nip him on his shoulder and say, "Excuse me, are you talking to me?"

His head goes in a full circle and then snaps to a point. He's irreverent and straight to the point in his attitude of *You're bothering me; go away, kid.*

"I did, but not now!"

Trying to get this character to calm down a little, for he is so intense, I say, "Oh, well, what is your given name, may I ask?" This small talk conversation isn't getting any easier with his answers.

"You just did, and my surname is Ebenezer; that is when David is upset because I will not budge when something doesn't seem right or safe either or, yep, that about does it. But he calls me Mr. Ebb most other times."

With a look of confusion, David looks at us and says, "Boy, aren't you two a pair? Good to see you're on good terms this day that the Lord has made; we still have quite a way to go." Distinguishing characteristics have set a new grip on the comforts of a beaten path as the journey begins.

THE MESSENGER
(12)

"Go forth and listen… Aly, I will send my messenger ahead of you. She will prepare the way for you. There is someone shouting in the desert, one of great stature and strength. From the mountaintops, as the earth shakes, he proclaims with envy and fumes at the top of his lungs, who is your God. She will march through the wilderness that will lead into a great valley and confirm my promises are yes and amen. I have given you my word, and the company I have sent shall proclaim it. Go find the messenger."

And in the near distance, approaching the three at a quickened pace arises a messenger, small and furry, springs back and forth out of a patch of the fragrance of a mid-morning meadow, quickly pouncing without a care in the world. Well, that is until now, for a great disturbance has been declared and needs invincible divine attention to this given message. With steady speed, she zigs-zags down a beaten road where she encounters a donkey, sheep, and a person that she recognizes even from his backside, swaying back and forth in the gentle breeze of life.

"And that's David; oh, how I adore David, the way he cares for his father's sheep and the music he makes while he practices his vocals praising our God, in spirit and truth!"

Her nose is a-wiggling and twitching to the rhythm of her thought pattern, keeping it to herself, not wanting to speak it out loud in fear that this self-proclamation would be set into a motion of truth. Her thoughts sometimes get the best of her. *There's nothing that I wouldn't do for him, but I am the least in the kingdom. A rodent of a rabbit at that, being shoved out of the cabbage patch of essences. One only eats what the Lord has provided without worrying about to and fro. I must straighten my path and query their whereabouts to see if I know about their whereabouts. I am almost upon them.*

Springing like a board from the darkness into the light, for God is on the move, she says, "Hey, I come with a message, a message from the Lord."

These sudden appearances are nerve-racking to the demeanor of my existence; I guess it is just the call of the wild or as wild as I hope that it will get in this new dumbfounded environment. A familiar voice has seemed to enter my consciousness in my new travels, as it seems that this is only me who can hear it. It has brought a sudden comfort to the weariness of this lamb's wool.

"*Be still and listen… Out of the mouths of babes and nursing infants and even the little creatures of the forest, I, the Lord, speak. This furry friend is an instrument of proclamation of the tide of change. The donkey shall see the angel of the Lord in the way of their adversaries against him, with his three servants and companions of the forest, who will multiply in their quest. For the messenger will proclaim the way you shall go, into the field down a narrow path, and his foe shall be conquered with his head on the ground. Do not turn right or left. I shall be your guide against his two adversaries as the angels' messenger speaks forth to a donkey, a rabbit, and a meek sheep. Listen to Penny, Aly…*"

Penny cross-examines the reaction of her fellow homesteaders to see if any of them show interest in her seldom-abused attention span. Or maybe they aren't listening to the magnitude of the circumstances, and a definition needs to be acquired.

"I am the messenger, and I have a message from the Lord; are any of you listening? I know that the two of you are able to comprehend; don't act like the fools of this world…" before Penny can complete a full sentence, Mr. Ebb speaks forth with attitude.

"Aw, Penny, are you going to speak forth again? Always proclaiming the name of the Lord, saying she hears from Him, out loud, geez!" he responds in a discouraging, spirited voice.

I give him a look that could paralyze him in time, but Penny is not even phased by Mr. Ebb's remark because she calmly replies, "Mr. Ebb, why are you going to be that way?! I know the way, the truth, into His life."

(13)

With such a destructive attitude and probably going a little too far with his intrusive remark, he says, "A messenger of what? You're just a rodent of a pitter-pattering rabbit."

I choose my battles wisely, and so I reply, "She's the messenger, the one that I personally seek from the Lord, and I will receive this, so let's listen. Mr. Ebb. Let's listen to what Penny has to say."

Tickled pink, she goes on, "Well, let me tell you what. I come with a message from the Lord. Yes, Mr. Ebb. The message from the Lord said, not I, just for the record, 'I will send a plentiful rain and have confirmed all prepared, for it will be wearisome but cleansing for the congregation that is sent forth, and God shall provide in this quest for goodness and the poor in heart. Though you lie down amongst the sheepfold, you will be like the wings of a dove, grasping for a snapped twig for their young squab's nest. Three kings shall see their fate placed before them this very day. One shall rise, and two shall fall in my chosen time for each of them, and the glory of the Lord will shine upon a young man and the great nation of Israel.'"

THE MEADOWLANDS

I look in the direction of Penny with astoundment, but my verbal assault is directed toward a gullible donkey that is in the sense that one should know better than to criticize a person who is only giving the message. And I say my message to him, "There is a distinct pattern of an old mule, Mr. Ebb, and you qualify for this role. Oh, I am so sorry that I said that; it is not in me to normally say such things, but if the shoe fits… Did you even listen to what Penny had to say?!"

Now I look in his direction for some kind of remark; who knows what that will look or sound like! A donkey's tail facing in my direction, swiftly swaying at the flies gathering around as I think to myself, *Oh, looky here, I am looking at the point of entry to where all his remarks are protruding from so far in all of Mr. Ebb's conversations with me.*

But (pun intended), before I can think of another thought, Mr. Ebb replies, "Yes, I understand what the Lord has said and hmmm… what Penny has said!"

And then silence. Oh, this isn't happening, the silent treatment to enhance the tension level on the rise, waiting patiently for him to continue on, and then my explosion, "What?! You are the donkey here, Mr. Ebb, and you better translate all I have to say, mister, mister donkey, I mean, Mr. Ebb!" I sigh in a deep breath and ask him to "speak forth!"

Gathering his oats or whatever you want to call this mule's mental capacity toward others, he slowly turns in our direction, facing the two of us, and proceeds on, "Hold your knickers on here! Oh, I know what you meant, and you're right. I am an old mule; I wouldn't have it any other way. You gotta go with what you do best, my friend; that's my philosophy!" I just roll my eyes. "So, what she is saying is that David will rise to power while two others in the leadership role fall from their reign, one greater than, and one lesser than. The first king of Israel and a self-proclaimed champion. That David and his company shall prosper in their quest to help out the heartlands and become the nation that Abraham had envisioned by the Lord. Oh, yeah, and one shall lose his head, another his kingdom! Yep, that's it, yeppers, no more, no less." His monotone voice, in speaking forth these matters, almost makes them out to be common in nature, with no emotional value in it whatsoever.

"Nothing more, that's it, geez, Mr. Ebb, she's the messenger. I was called to look for her. And she will lead the way. Penny, go forth and scout out the area for which we are to take and confirm what was told by Mr. Ebb. Go now, Godspeed!"

Looking at Mr. Ebb for clarification, I ask, "You can hear the Lord talk to each of us all the time?"

"Yes, yes indeed, if the Lord wants me to hear, just saying so."

Penny's Quest
(14)

Thinking about frantic fanatic kings of one who is and one to come and losing her head over the matters of what this could all mean in one day's timing has become the mindset of this hairy beast of a hare. Don't worry; she can run with the best, with her imagination running wild in the lead, thinking to herself but at times out loud, depending. *I must be quick, for there is a great distance to cover and return for my heart is set on all the words which the Lord has given me this day and to be careful, to observe all things and my life. I call upon heaven and earth as a witness, blessing, and cursing. Therefore, I choose life so that mankind shall live. I cling to Him, for He is my life's blood flow. Boy, I think that's dramatic; enough said. Now go.* As Penny goes into the confidence of the day, as her voice of life, her all in all, the calling of the Lord vocalizes affirmations to a loyal at heart.

"Be strong and of good courage, my little one, for I shall cross over before you and lead the way you should go. I will not leave you nor forsake you as my spoken word. You are called to be my special people."

Yes, I am sent to spy out the land of the thunderous mountains of vengeance that lies between our blessing and curses in this season of ripe grapes. Let's go up at once and take possession of this quest given. Penny comes to a halt to catch her breath; she must rest now. I don't remember any narrow ways in this area that I trampled over these many years, but then again, there's so much ground to cover. Must keep on the move. And then, over the horizon, the sun blares onto the onlooking mountains standing taller than one can remember; the thunderous sound of laughter echoes on the walls of this ponderous place, setting the tone of this time. Now, a shorter distance for my heart has leaped inside of me, knowing this is the place. A familiar voice, a companion to many, and a close personal friend to me speaks...

"*Yes, the place where man has said of the angels, even angels fear to tread, but they are there surrounding the valley way at my command. This is the valley way David has recited to me many times. 'I shall fear no evil,' he says, as I go with him, sheltering him in my presence.*"

Such a little thing indeed, compared to the virtues that will be defended in the lower valley way this day. The setting of the sun will settle all matters to the closing of a day, as a ton of thoughts shelter her being in many aspects of the little significance of her mind's viewing as her thoughts continue on. The valley, yes, the valley, so she hurries to the ledge of these victorious mountains and ponders as the drop-off takes her breath away, deep into the pits. *In this fiery damnation, soldiers of the enemies surround and fill these mountain clefts in multitudes of numbers—and in the middle, a large statue of a man mocks our Lord, our God. How dare he? I have heard and seen enough. Our quest is in sight of the destination where all things shall come to pass. Must hurry back. It will be shorter for David and his comrades as they have quickened their pace before I left, thanks to Aly's plea to Mr. Ebb.*

All but dust fills the air as Penny is nothing more than a blur of forelegs and hind legs of a fury, blurry saint. And then she comes to a sudden halt, and everything stops in motion.

A Donkey's Tale

In such a short amount of time on the road, the nerves are already beginning to counteract each other. I talk to my acquaintance, for the inception of friendship is still many miles away from this point in the mileage spent together thus far to even arrive at the point of innocent conversation, which lands up onto the landmarks of rudeness spoken by even myself.

"Hurry up, Eb. The time is at hand."

Ebenezer, hearing the tone being presented, says, "I'll show you my hand or hoof if you want. Just show me where to place it. I'm pacing myself, if you don't mind!"

Where else am I to go with this if the only road being taken is one full of negativity? So I go there, "Oh, you're such a smart… oh, you get on my nerves sometimes, Mr. Ebb!"

The burrow's perimeter is strung out, oh so very deep and wide in the vibes that are meticulously in character distributed into the nature of the disturbance, to the sounds of grunts, snorts, and whatever sounds that a distressed sheep can summon up to a frantic David.

"Will you stop the racket and shush already!" David continues his pace of walking, but Ebenezer stops dead in his tracks as if something has startled him out of his very skin. In his vision (for in my mind, there are no signs of any type of danger in the area) Mr. Ebb starts muttering around as if he had taken too much wine (not to be confused with his amount of whining).

He asserts, "Something big is happening right now. He is doing something right now!"

I ask the most common question asked when something doesn't seem right, "Mr. Ebb, are you okay?"

THE MEADOWLANDS

With his jawbone dropped, he says, "Define okay. What do you think? This is not good. A vision has been brought forth. Shush. I must be still and listen!" The donkey is still pacing around back and forth, and then he stands erect, I mean straight up. "Aw, oh, this is not good."

Confusion is written all over my face, and I can feel it penetrating into my pores. "What's not good? You're not saying any words, Mr. Ebb. Here you go again, not saying anything. Translation, please."

He mutters, almost to himself, one word, "Penny!"

My heart stops beating for a second time, or who knows how many times, one could lose count. Then Mr. Ebb points a hoof at me and then to his mouth and says, "Shush, you fur ball, please. Be still and listen."

(15)

The mountains proclaim in a thunderous sound as two sides, divided and in silhouette form, appear in the valley overshadowed by the mountain's crest. The great stature of a Philistine champion. His name is known or is making his name known to all, even to an animated, loveable hare of nature watching overhead, listening to this egotistical beast of a man. His shining bronze armor and sword blind her with the sun's glare, listening in to hear his thunderous voice taunting in the wind. His taunts are many and loud.

"Am I not a Philistine, a champion of the Philistines, and you the servant of Saul? Therefore, choose a man and let him come down to me if he is able to fight" (54).

This man of stature has defied the armies of a holy God, and my anger is against him. Though Saul and his army have heard these chosen words of defiance, they do nothing, sitting on Mr. Ebb. (You can figure out what metaphor is in use.) Let's just say they're doing nothing.

"*Forty days' time passed to the present, for I have sent for David, a man after my own heart...*"

Certain words are taken to heart, but they have to be spoken into your heart first unless you are a mind reader, so here I stand once again, left in my own dark thoughts as I hear his response, "My heart is racing, Aly, to this spoken word!"

I'm doing my best to navigate this newfound body with its limitations, resorting to the sign language of a goat, bound and tied up in the moment. "What, Mr. Ebb, What?" We go back to the short conversation; it is a game that brings too many doubts to the circumstances! Ebenezer has picked up on some of my frustrations put in motion by the shaking of my head.

"Sorry, no time for chit-chat, mate. We must hurry. David is being summoned by the Lord. Also, Penny has made it there safely and has overlooked all to see, out of harm's way. This is like sending relief to our sisterhood dwelling on the mountainside of despair! We must hurry!"

Finally, for some well-needed relief of tension and direction, we need to fill David into this loop of circumstantial evidence that is being presented, but we have yet to come to our own observations. I'm thinking to myself, *But how? I can't converse with David, nothing, not even sign language,* and then Mr. Ebb makes a silly request directed to me to do an action of great courage.

On impulse, he suggests, "Nip him, Aly. You know, just a little peck on his cheek and then run. Run as fast as you can!"

However, a sheep is supposed to speak in a language understood by man with different sound effects that have great definition to them without saying a whole lotta words in doing so. I say, "Naw, I don't think so. He's my friend, and I like him, Mr. Ebb."

But no, this explanation is not good with my new counterpartner, and he boldly answers so, "Well, sometimes you must hurt the ones you love to protect and secure them. So let them know we care. Go ahead. I'll mark the spot for you!"

Picking up the seriousness in his voice, he says, "Oh, so you go on to volunteer me to do the dirty work. I don't think so!" I have already seen enough times in our short "friendship," I say this loosely, this same grin on his face of an action that will become an influential reaction of mischievousness.

"Well, all right then. Get ready to run!" Another old-time human gesture given then,

"What're you up to, Mr. Ebb?"

Slowly creeping up but still in range of his voice to give a commentary on his actions, he says, "Watch, he's bending over to pick something up. Out the way, Aly. No time to waste. Timing is everything!"

As his snout gnarls back and his mouth protrudes open, his timing couldn't have been any better than now as David is starting to upright and then nip right between the cheeks and gum. I mean literally between. I've only known David for a short time, and the expression on his face tells me Mr. Ebb's life span may be shortened. And what the heck got into Mr. Ebb? After his great entry, he starts dancing around, kicking like a stubborn mule, literally, making his far-fetched hee-hawing noises, laughing his snout off, snorting up a storm, approaching tears as raindrops fill his eyes. You know, the whole chabootabang. David's not pleased with this at all.

"Ouchy! You silly heifer, you better run. Oooh, what's gotten into you two? I'm trying to gather these things that dropped from your saddle pack. You've been acting strange and shedding gear left and right since Aly came along. Must I separate the two of you? Oh, don't you go there, Ebenezer. And you hush, Aly. It's going to take some healing, and it will be a while before I am able to sit!"

Now Mr. Ebb is snorting like a hog in hog heaven, geez.

"Get it, Aly? He said, 'Separate the two.' Get it? You know, cheeks, separate them. Woo-hoo!" Mr. Ebb just doesn't know when to stop. My annoyance meter is high up there.

"Not funny. Just keep running. He'll catch up with us, Mr. Ebb. I can't believe you!" That same silly grin; will I ever get over its sight? I doubt it.

"Oh, by the way, Aly, you don't have top teeth, so you wouldn't have gotten the same results anyway. That's all I have to say. That's that, and let's go…"

That voice of clarity enters my twisted mind to release me of the image of David's buttock glare.

(16)

The beauty of the sun rising on the fluffiness of Penny and the shadow that it casts over her back over-exceeds her actual height in stature, as it is a foreshadowing of her own enemy, the mind. A weakness for all; otherwise, why would you need all of the self-help books? Just saying!

"Yes, Penny, go! *The pace of a gazelle fleeing in distress of a lioness on the prowl to feed her cubs, just as the Philistines have no remorse in attitude. For David cannot (literally), will not sit down (giggles and grins from Mr. Ebb) 'til he comes here. Bring him here. Arise, for the time is at hand. Seek out a man who is a skillful player. One who will not be taunted, one who will stand his ground, he is the anointed one; David shall fight the champion for my glory to be known.*"

At a complete halt, I turn once again to look over the edge, as I am over the edge of these matters, but for what purpose am I to return? His taunting. Oh, I can't stand his taunting. Here, I have run the hairs off my hairy body, and he is toying around and being disgraceful. Yes, Lord. David will stand his ground. But how, Lord? I am your loyal servant. Reveal all you have of plans. I am blindsided in all that matters in the security of David, Lord.

Then, a voice of reason enters my soul, and I comprehend my return. The Lord wants to reveal something to me at my overwatch haven. For there is no other like me. I have a name, and it is Penny!

For now, she rests in herself proclaimed confidence but for how long, we shall see! She listens to a voice that whispers to overcome all of her own thoughts that race to her heartbeat.

(17)

"Blind. I am the eyes of the blind and shelter for all to feel secure, and I search out for those who make a mockery out of me. I am the light of appearance and chose the way for them to comfort those who mourn. One thing I have made known to Penny. You were blind, but now you see. By a great light, a great, great light. That you say you are blindsided and that you have been when looking over into the depths of the valley a silhouette had been cast in the shadows by a great reflection of light. This is an answer to many questions you seek. There is one smaller than you who will flow from the riverbeds of life. I have called on him to bring an object that will make a magnitude of difference in this quest. He will make himself known. Proceed, my speedy faithful one, go. For in the dark, there will always come the light of truth."

(18)

Now, we have gotten past the dark side of the moon. Poor David; that had to hurt. My goodness, the size of Mr. Ebb's cutters up front and how he was able to extend them past his gum line. Scary stuff, I do say so myself. Similar to the evil extraterrestrial from the Alien movie. Now, it will take time for that scene to get out of my head; I will not be able to look at either of them in the same light. Speaking of light, I see it written all over his snooty snout and am waiting for any kind of response so maybe I can be in the light of this conversation, "You're always keeping me in the dark, Mr. Ebb. We are way out of hearing range of David, maybe a little too far for my comfort level or the lack of?"

Stubborn as he is, he still doesn't slow his pace down as we are further away from David than when I first started wanting some answers to the mystic occurrence a while back.

"Well then, here's some light for you, okay? The army of God is fleeing from him and is dreadfully afraid!" Another long pause, one that seems longer than his snout.

"Who's him, Mr. Ebb? Do tell!" Even to myself, the sarcasm thing is getting old, but it sure triggers Ebenezer back into logical conversation.

"The champion of the Philistines, a legend to all, now is before them, taunting them to fight, coaxing with great wealth for someone to challenge him. Someone very dear to your heart and mine, Aly, he just hasn't seen it yet, but it is a matter of time; it is inevitable!"

I'm confused about some things that need to be answered, but this one is easy to answer with a single word, "David!"

Ebenezer is more energetic and faster in responding, "Yes, David! The Lord is calling us to be separated from him, for there is a great task and accomplishment that we must proceed to do…!"

Anticipation has gotten the best of me. "But wait, didn't Penny go off in the other direction? Aren't we backtracking? Or are we to turn around and speed past David?!"

Ebenezer, in all of his structure and voice, says, "We are not going to look for Penny; she is fine and is called to seek the one who has already been set in motion. The Lord has summoned a hardshell tortoise to the brook of life to retrieve the first of five stones to be brought to David. For now, there are more questions than answers and so little time to do so. You and I, Alymore, must go to the place of light that leads to an entrance down a narrow path that cannot be mistaken for another way into the depths of despair! We must have courage!"

An angered man, one called by the Lord to have steadfast patience, now has no patience at all, "Okay, you guys. Where'd you go, from one extreme to the other? Fast to slow, slow to fast. And now in and out of sight. A nice pace in the middle will do. This inconsistency is at my last toll. I am in a hurry here. We haven't even arrived at the 'still waters' before the sun reaches its destination. You two stop your clowning around and get back over here! Ebenezer, Alymore!"

Each and every question David announced out loud has had a long pause between each question asked, to the point one would think that it has taken all of his efforts to think of the next question to be asked. Or maybe an emphasis on his dwindling patience and practicing breathing techniques so that he doesn't explode! It might not be physical tension that lies heavy upon us, but it is enough to know that. "You got us into a pickle, Mr. Ebb, with no direction known, so where do we stand, Mr. Ebb?"

There's confidence on his face as if there is only one logical answer to this complex question. "We stand in faith; without faith, it is impossible to please God. And He is a rewarder of those who seek Him. For if anyone lacks wisdom, let him ask the one who gives to all freely. Ask with no doubt, for he who doubts will be like chaff scattered in the wind."

(19)

"And all of those wandering souls shall fall, and those who remain shall be scattered to every wind. For all shall fall as if by the sword of a man. For there is a way that seems right to a man, but its end is the way to his death. So do not be drawn away by your own desires or strength. Listen to my voice alone and do not be deceived, for I am the Father of lights; no shadows shall be cast upon you. Nor shall you be turned, only to be led by the words of truth. I have called on other fellow creation creatures of the forest who have yet to make themselves known. But for now, you must return to a place of reckoning by many voices of the timberland. Aly knows of the entrance of the forest path, and Ebenezer knows of the stories of the legendary way to make known to help avoid the temptations and ensembled voices of despair."

An easterly wind sweeps dust into the face of our beloved bunny, and in Penny's state of confused mind, she is a mutton of muttering madness, searching, "The Lord is talking in parables, the mysteries of this kingdom, in abundance, Lord, do not let my heart grow dull! The request for David and a multitude of hidden treasures spoken by the Lord. I still hear Gargantua's cries of defiance in the distance!"

And that's the last thing I hear other than my thick paw pads stomping this hard, cracking desert of a place floor. I must find my way to the still waters in a hurry. After the word is spoken by still waters to Penny's heart, the sounds of silence are no more. *Here comes the annoying sound of a grackle's call, intentionally draining the thoughts of the many still waters that I seek.* Only one being has that sound that penetrates like a lightning flash passing through your anatomy and quickness of breath, trying to cram a multitude of words in a single breath. "Gretchen."

Best to say "good riddance," which composes a symphony of guilt throughout my internal being. Penny, shame for shame. I'll play the too-busy card and call it a day's work. "Well, hello, Gretchen, fancy running into you. Well, gotta go. Have an urgent call to make. David's on hold with the others and need to move them along in a hurry!" *If she wasn't so noisy, I guess it wouldn't be so bad. There are probably going to be some repercussions set in a later time. Forgive me, Lord.*

The beauty of her blackish tones in her coat, with a touch of grey and silver lining in her wings as she grips tightly to the branch of an elm tree's tender leaves, brushing lightly to its comforts and rests in the arms of its provided shelter. Barely having time to breathe to an outlet of today's gab on her mind, in the rudeness of a departure performed by Penny, by the way very unconvincing if I say to myself in astonishment to the utterance of a singular meaning phrase, "Oh, okay?!" That must be the shortest sentence ever formed by Gretchen. Mind-blowing.

Penny takes her opportunity to depart Godspeed, leaving a bird called Gretchen, of intrusive behavior, on her own eavesdropping adventuring of peaks and valleys.

"Hmmm… wonder what that's all about," she says as her mind goes into motion.

The calm trickling of water achieved from the current of the brook stream caressing a broken tree limb from a great oak carried to its modest resting spot. The hard shell of a redneck turtle basks in the morning sunlight as the dew begins to evaporate, retreating in nature's cycle, once abundant water now finding itself in a peaceful crook of the brook. Alert for active duty, he waits for his call; not being a slug, but able to be at attention to the calling with all the required preparedness!

"Be still and listen.

"I am doing a great thing right now. I call upon you, my hard-shell friend, for you are of great need in the army of God. I know you observe these brooks in full detail and to which they flow. There is a great need for your service. Go into the brook of 'Life Flow Brook' near the field of green pastures on the dock in the bottom depths of an abyss. Underneath an enchanted stone vessel lies a jagged stone brought forth from the river of 'Destination's Peak' that has been etched out and jagged over the aging of time. Bring it to the surface, and I shall provide for its safety on your way to the still waters. Now go."

Who can say? Is it a strong impulse that starts in the mind and then proceeds to the passageways of the heart of this calling, but it is enough for this green-back beret to respond urgently, diving from his post on command and swimming to the shores of Galilee and landing on the beaches of Normandy's silent calling?

"Yes, sir. Reporting for duty, yes, sir! Godspeed, or as quick as I can."

Gretchen has an aerial view as she observes a lone figure, belly to the ground, wearing headgear and a soldier's helmet, crawling to stay as low as possible, avoiding artillery rounds being fired at this soldier in the army of God. Such a crazy, impulsive thought continues to travel through her mind when she decides to shake it off and return to her flight to nowhere in particular.

— Chapter Two —
History Made Clear in the Gospel of Ebenezer, the Donkey

The Lord is so pronounced in his pleas to my return to a place that has haunted my inner being. Shivers go up and down the foundation of my spine. If only I could voice my opinion on the matter, but now am I to discount this request given. I can't! Without a cause or case petition of my weakness. I look at Mr. Ebb in my dismay and express myself openly to him, "Not again, Mr. Ebb, I can't return. I know of this entrance; there is such a prominence of directional light that casts its way into the forest wall. Where wailing and a state of complete emptiness surpass any hope of joy. My strength became challenged, drawing me like water from a well, but the eagerness to see David has helped overcome my inner fears; but do I dare enter?"

The actual concern lies in the unusually apathetic response of a normally emotionless donkey. "Aw, now why do you want to go on and say something as cowardly as that? God is a God of second chances, or should I just go ahead and call you 'Jonah'? 'Cause you smell like fish to me! We are being directed by a loving God who hears and knows all things, and you just want to go on and drop the ball and fumble? I think not, Aly! You're allowing fear to overshadow the sound of footsteps on the path of your faith in Him. We must walk in faith toward our designated destination, and He will clarify our purpose and goal of reaching the harbor—translated in fisherman's terms as 'where to go.'"

A long pause of silence is broken by the sound of footsteps on the path we've taken, a soundless approach of another, broken by the voice of David. "Aw, come on now, guys, where are you? You silly little goobers. Time is of the essence!"

His domed crown bobs to and fro, up and down, glancing through briars sharp as a tack, floral greenery, overlooking a neighboring neigh and the bleating cry of a sheep in distress. Hidden from the sight of David but seen by the naked eye of the two friendly portrayers in still-life form. I glance over my shoulder to look at Mr. Ebb with his fiery, piercing grin that covers his entire face from ear to ear, showing his ivories. Discouraged, David slowly walks away down the routed pathway and out of sight.

"Aly, follow me; we will go through skirting the outside of Engarlands Way of the timberland, through the upper slopes, avoiding the open meadows where even the smallest of nature's animated beings can be sighted effortlessly. And when the silence surrounds us, we will halt our pace for the importance of you listening intently to my knowledge of this legend we seek."

"Okay, all is right for the complexity of this legend; with time at hand, I'll give it to you in a nutshell before our destination's arrival time!"

(20)

I listen to the sound of silence, and then *bam*.

"Okay, hmmm, where to start? Anyway, the legend proceeds

back to the times of my great, great ancestors. A servant of Balaam, back in the day of Balak's evil reign, where a donkey manifested his voice to a mortal, finding his voice to warn Balaam. Now Balaam, in his own strength, had been corrupted in his decisions to proceed in matters of his own voice and not the guidance of the Lord, becoming his own self-willed ways of destruction and his own archfoe of dismay and mishap almost hindering himself lifeless by an archangel's way. So, he had saddled up one of our ancient champions and conquering heroes, 'Nolan the *Burro;*' you heard me right. Who, if no other, changed the course of Balaam's destruction by allowing him to open his eyes to see the mercy of the Lord? Even though Balaam caused many afflictions to Nolan, Nolan remained faithful to the Lord and turned Balaam's curses into blessings by using understood dialogue. Through that change, he became obedient. Are you listening, Aly? Henceforth comes the saying 'stubborn as a mule.' And greatness came forth because Balaam now listened, being still, and sent forth speaking what the Lord asked of him. So, he set his face toward the wilderness in the valleys, gardens, and riversides we now walk. Don't you understand, Aly? History repeats itself; yesterday's history is today's good news!"

Confusion has set deeply into my mind; I have heard about a donkey who had spoken to a human that stopped him from being butchered by an angel of the Lord due to his disobedience and self-pride, but what?

"Come on, Ebb, you're talking in parables again; translate for me, please!"

Frustration is written all over Ebenezer's face. "Okay, you're being sheepish here, Aly, but here it goes; it's like this: if we are obedient and go in the directional path the Lord has set for our course by the strength of this wild donkey and meek sheep that you are, we will do great things, greater than one could imagine. All things are possible!"

"Also, we must understand that our foe will become very aggressive with us because we are blessed and have become a mighty weapon of warfare. We cannot do things on our own will even if great amounts of haunting spirits try corrupting our souls. The spirit of Barak's evil ways and the disobedience of Balaam, at first, are also in these woods; henceforth, the legend is birthed because the threat of greatness today is at hand. Now, back to the latter days of ole. They are three-fold: one is the coming of the Messiah, and the other is the reign from a man who has the courage to stand up for what is right!"

Then bells and whistles go off as if I won the prize, and a name comes to mind, "David, and the spiraling downfall of Saul's leadership or lack of!"

Kicking and wailing is one happy-go-lucky donkey. "Right Aly; therefore, the Forest of Desolation Souls has awakened, Aly, because of God's battle against defiance's calling! Hope, pray, and listen as the adventure begins to unfold when we access and enter this entrance of enchanted voices, trying to undermine the undivided voice of the Lord. For this is just a touch of what is to come this day for our quest, Aly; we will be instructed in the Lord's calibrated word. It is not complicated if there is focus, a centered focus of understanding Aly, that the little insignificant but miraculous event in time when a donkey spoke truth into the life of Balaam that gave all others life. There are more histories of the legends' past awakenings, spanning the period from the allocation of sorrows and their shared distributions. All was silent for these forsaken souls until the later guidance of Moses and the pivotal leadership transition marked by Joshua's passing, which heralds 'the awakening.' In the time of the corrupted judges, a captain in Deborah's army, Barak, came to the journey with the white donkeys, witnessing and saying, 'Oh, please do tell of Sisera's evil reign and especially his downfall.' This set in motion the conquering quest of Barak and Deborah's quest!" he says, as a big ole donkey grin appears on his face once again.

(21)

Done to the point of hesitation that could be filled in by saying, "Oh, just wait, there's more," he continues on in his new, talented, enchanting voice. "By the valley, near the still waters, Barak's command emerges, but not alone; it is under the leadership of Deborah who stands in front. In following this victory's venture, we acknowledge the time and place where credit is due to those who altered the sequences during the era of corrupted judges—only Othniel, Ehud, and Shamgar, whose valor put the mighty men to shame. Perhaps I've left a few out by saying so... *hmmmm*. Another turnabout has occurred to expose evil ways. With Barak's confidence rising, those who love Him, like the sun when it shines in its full strength, set men in motion alongside Deborah in full stride to conquer all who stand against them. Sisera's slippery leadership has been splintered in his temple by the tent covering of Jael."

Aly, thinking to himself but remaining silent, recalls his buttery descent into a tent and concludes that nothing good happens in tents; enough said.

"For one can ask in history's timetable, 'Why is the chariot so long to come?' In Deborah's song of Psalms, there are many hidden treasures of the white donkey's conceited riders and those of nature's servants served with them of battles victory against the army of Sisera!"

The gleeful quotes that are sometimes not quoted at all in these written scrolls of mankind...

"Oh, sing the song of Psalms tale telling of the white donkeys, who are addressed by those who attire themselves in lush robes, riding the streets of the captives, as they listen to the poor in heart reciting the ways of the Lord. Mighty warriors Deborah and Barak attend into the valley of green pastures of sheepfolds call. To the bleating bleat of the ba, ba, sheep, and the battle cries of hysteric horses half-passing and cantering in glorious motion pride, are all searching for their triumphal hearts as Sisera is no more!"

Disbelief fills my eyes, and doubt entertains my mind, "Oh, not so, Ebb, you're making it up as you speak!" Maybe not the right choice of words at the moment as he gives me an alternate look of "How dare you," a face of hurt.

"It is in mankind's holy scripts and is also foretold in the history of the oak tree logs, a whole new can of worms to open, but not now. So, there you go... *hmmmm!*"

Not always a given, but now, in these times of uncertainty, it is a mandated requirement.

"Translation, please, Ebb! In a nutshell, please!"

A donkey catches his breath, taking a huge inhale of some of my oxygen with him. "Okay, Aly, once again, history is repeating itself in intervals of forty years. Other events have occurred in this gap frame, but you know the nutshell needs to be cracked open. This means that Barak, who lacked confidence, needed Deborah to give him motivation, leadership, and execution to complete courageous tactics. As Aly, you need me, Ebb, to stand by your side to help you conquer your inner beast and fear, but only you, Aly, must figure out how to make it work under the guidance of the Lord and me. My voice shall be as one with the Lord, Him alone. The same has been done for Baalam and Barak, which shall be mine as well!

"Let me dig a hole a little bit deeper to bring it more updated. So, all being said, to this point, there are a couple of reoccurring events that have awakened these hauntings, not going into the results of the legend but the history recordings that are in the oak tree logs. So, in these repetitive seasons of awakenings, mankind does not and cannot hear the taunting of the forest. It is only nature calls heartbeat and elements of confusion and despair of a fallen shepherd and his sheep that were lured into its depths and vanished to a pack of wolves, led by a hideous overlord named 'Sabre,' for obvious reasons. Now Sabre is long gone and deceased, but through offspring from generation to generation, others in his lineage have ruled, and many other souls have collected in those woods over an exhausting timeline. Now Hunter reigns. These spirits, over these lapses of an era, are misleading for the weak at heart and help lure others into a forest of domination, depths of emptiness never to be seen again! With this legend that I have spoken into motion, I must cease for fear of pouring fuel onto the fire and igniting more condemnation and power to an already existing fire. We must quench all power given to this legend. Okay, enough said, be done with this right now! Do you understand my point given to you, Aly?"

Looking at Ebb with his concerned look on his snout, no smiles of joy to penetrate his aged lines of hardness this season, I say, "Yes, Ebb, God is calling me to do this extreme deed of courageous act not knowing until His voice is clear and you're here more so for support and diversion of the spirits in flight!"

A glare of gladness glosses the covering of his eyes as Ebb proclaims, "You hit the hammer right on the nail, Aly. Now let's pray; Lord, call upon us so that we may respond as Samuel did at a young age, 'Here I am, send me!' Okay, so are things sinking in real deep into your inner being, Aly?"

Intense nerves spike one's soul, as well as those of a donkey and a sheep, while that small whisper of a familiar voice, normally heard, is now magnified in a merciful awakening to nature's kindness.

Awakening Silence Call
(22)

"A great whirlwind shall rise up in the west as the sound of a shepherd's cry nearby, rolling about the ashes of past destruction where wailing and crying of the lost sheep and shepherd once roamed the green pastures of past times. One other must lead the flock to their safety as his

numbers have increased. For the days of slaughter are now fulfilled and cannot escape. I will take from them their voices; I am against those who lead by their lies and recklessness. Be careful not to do this great evil against yourself with a deceived word of prey. When you call upon my name through this desolated deadwood place. This too shall come to pass in the plundering of these pastures given him this man who will conquer the beast of the fields, bringing all those who enter back to their safety and peace shall roam without fear in the exuberant Tavor Oaks of the ancient burial grounds. Am I not a God who is near at hand, not a God that is far from you? Do I not fill heaven and earth? Are not My spoken words like fire and a hammer that has broken the rocks into five pieces? For these shall return to Me through my servants of a special kind with their whole hearts. I will set my eyes on them for good and bring them back from this land on eagle's wings from the bare fields, hills, and the forest. Sent to you all creatures servanthood that dwells in the land given to roam freely. I will bring them up and restore them to this place of predestined calling. Peace you will have peace when you pray to a loving God. I will listen to you and hear your pleas. You will seek Me and find Me with all your heart. Great is My power of faithfulness. Protection by my outstretched hands like the wings of the mighty eagle, to heed the words of My servants just as I made Myself known to Samuel at a young age.

"Ebb and Penny, I call upon you as prophets of the Lord, who prophesize of peace when the words spoken come to pass and will be known as the ones whom the Lord has truly sent. Speak My words faithfully.

"Be still and know that I am God. As the sound of silence falls you two are ready to lead these chosen and called to do great things by your guidance of prayers when you call My name.

"My voice is now silent.

"By the choices you make of free will.

"There will be others to the calling who will help in the wisdom and understanding in each of their lives. Each shall do their God-given part."

Sheldon

"Sheldon, our lovable, sociable turtle, takes direct orders seriously, is a friend to all, and slowly pokes his way down the outer part of a throughway-beaten road. He has yet to make himself known to our loveable bunny, who was last seen with moodiness leading into madness, head spinning faster than her hind end feet could take her back to her delightful sheep and obnoxious, stubborn mule, who is very intelligent although he doesn't show it, and David, a man with a destination of birthed greatness and the calling of the Lord. However, Sheldon is very sociable and not easily distracted, with the gift of multitasking while holding a conversation. He is always on alert for the critters above his food chain, and rightly so. That is why his post always goes and lingers on in the most active hours of the early day. Just lollygagging out loud, talking to the Lord, and, rightly so, praying. But today is different because this time, he has been summoned by the Lord of all creation of critters, big or small. He is relieved from his post again, and rightly so. His orders to find the first stone of life signify a profound shift in attitude toward life. Sheldon likes talking to himself because, well, he's slow in all aspects of his life, but when given a chance, he'll take flight at an alarming rate of gab. Not annoying or fast, just a whole lot of words. You see there is a common bond developing to this band of characters that will unite in togetherness. The Lord has given light to each in the direction of course taken for sisters and brothers of faith. Believe me, it is happening and is the best thing to talk about since creation itself; just wish I had someone to share this great day of joy, for I am Sheldon, and this is my report written in the journal of my heart. How am I able to give all these accountable facts of the events in progress? Well, first, the

Lord all in all, but second, because Penny just sped past me without pondering on me; I guess I was moving too slow or something like that. But worse of all, she has missed a great opportunity to be blessed on this day for one, meeting me in person and, two, the recovery of the first stone, which is in progress. The third is I have a very active mind and an imagination to go along with it. I am stating another fact in my log of circumstances in chronological order which I believe is an important one. One may notice that this place is not geographically correct in names, scenery, and maybe some of the creatures in this area, but one must do so to keep the Dreamline going in this fictitious delusional setting in a very rational, historically correct current of events in biblical times. Fourth, the mind is moderately to some extent hazy at first when going into the depths of waters, awakening while tossing and turning, suddenly to wit's end, and then plunging deep back into slumber's way. That's why it is best to keep a written log; henceforth, you got it. Now one, I, Sheldon, need to pay closer to the initial landmarks along the way, precisely leading me to my destination location. Now, please return to your accurate account of this life happenings of Sheldon; please, I don't want to come off as rude."

THE COMPANY OF TWO

So let's see, okay, here's Sheldon moving at a fast-paced speed, aw, heck, about as fast-paced as my thoughts right now, moving along through a patch of high thick grass close to the bend in the pathway where his destination is at hand but is quickly gifted by the annoyance of a quite visible red ant mound, so he is able to move around quickly enough to avoid any mishap when suddenly Sheldon picks up two hitchhikers who are also trying to avoid the inconvenience of the red ants that are swarming at an alarming rate as he moves more inside the road.

I can still feel my two guests; they are on top of my hard, camo shell when one of them does a spectacular backflip in front of me and then a roundhouse to the side of me, followed by a double-head spinning cartwheel back onto my back, a venture of a risky tactic, as I hear the giggle of a squeaky female voice saying, "You're so funny, Albert," which makes Albert even more so rustling and active on my what is now a stage to perform on for this courting session of two active jumping spiders. A hypnotic array of vivid colors of the rainbow, fuzzy looking, bug-eyed but cute species are holding a conversation of giggles; another audible name, Sara, is mentioned with more giggling and whispering. I am glad that I cannot comprehend. I clear my voice just in case they don't realize they have company.

"Oh," I hear the male voice of my new acquaintances.

"Excuse me, you're on my shell, and unless you can hold your breath for a long time, I suggest you may need to be moving along, although I wish I had more time to get enlightened by your company."

The quietness is sealed tightly to the point of thinking, *Did these two guests depart in their ways?* Only to be disrupted by a gentleman's voice, "And where would one be going on this lovely day? It is such a beautiful time to cruise along this once-is-enough, looked-over path. Would you like to be my chauffeur and be blessed by our sophisticated conversation?"

Moving along swiftly through the pages of my daily log, I have to emphasize by notification marks that two unexpected guests are now accounted for and are still on the premises of my shell, "I am so sorry, but I can take a raincheck for this is my entrance needed to be taken..." and then rudely interrupted I hear them in unison. The male stout voice asks a simple question that seems to want to lead into something lengthier, but this should do for bait, "What do you have in mind this day?"

"Oh, okay, so I will bite on this one, but I need to keep it governmental protocol with as much limited information as possible, 'It is of utmost importance, and I am so called to do so in the recovery of a priceless stone for I am a responsible soldier in the army...'"

Again, I am cut off this time by the name that he had given me for the record by the name of Albert, saying, "An adventure or quest, you may say?!"

A conversation is now logged to the official starting point, taking note, "Yes, one may say so, and thank you!"

My patience is evaluating this erratic atmosphere. Albert is now slightly irritated, for he has a point he would like to make; "We have others of our kind in numerous numbers if one is ever in need or take on a defense stand. Just saying. I am of a general of a mighty brigade located nearby." Another important fact taken and now is logged and accounted for, "Well, glad to make your acquaintance, General Albert, and out of all due respect to an officer at hand, my accountant will take notice of this exchange of words and associated matters of our conversation but for now with a hand or foot salute, I bid you two farewells!"

Albert salutes with rigid authority and goes back to embracing his loved one, Sara, as Sheldon scuffles into the thick grass terrain and into where the brook widens and plunges deep into a circular-shaped surrounding that is cleared out for those weary travelers to gather water for their parched souls. But all is quiet along this way for humankind because of the territorial battles up yonder way as ripples and tiny air bubbles surface toward the embankment of solitude, and Sheldon disappears into the abyss that awaits him.

INTO THE GREAT ABYSS

"Solitude's entrance into a mild current that follows the edge of the streamside, into the depths where the water is a little murky due to the absence of the current's flow. As our friendly friend Sheldon emerges, he dives deep into his thoughts, landing in an area unfamiliar with his presence. A broken vessel in past time, will it be easily spotted in an array of colors? Or camouflaged like the very shell that my mobilized home is settled as a part of my structure of strength within? My lung capacity will be challenged this day, but while the Lord will not give me more than I can handle, it still is a little nerve-wracking. Swimming around in nothingness is nothing of enjoyment, broken twigs lying on a bedded brook floor as I am approaching when a school of juvenile black speckled trout come out to investigate my approach, swimming very close to my presence trying to rattle this hardheaded shell of a guy. Can we be of some assistance to you, my young man, as they circle for the kill like a pack of wolves one time did to me? That's a whole other story there; the important thing is I survived! Oh, we can tell how we are intimidating you by the release of tiny bubbles from your backfiring backside, little one. I'm not ready to fry my fish, so I just kind of turn around slowly and thank God for my ability to swim seventy times seven faster than I can walk. I hear them laughing in the waters, saying, 'Yeah, you better go!' In a whirlpool of lost direction, I bonk my head into an object on its side that emerged in the muddling brook floor, a broken vessel with more than one entrance and a little current swirling sand in and out these two exits depending on your location of in or out anyway it is big enough for me to enter for it is just the massive body part with the handle clearly visible as if swimming against a stream I see a sharp object trapped on the underside of the vessel, I break the golden rule of command in an area of uniqueness is to scout out the perimeter before entrance or of disturbing the areas of contact, put that all aside as I come in with all newness of excitement and with my snout nose shaped mouth I dislodge the sharp flint-like stone from under the vessel, that captivated this importance of a stone, edged out over long periods of time from a rapid brook's stream and settled here, now is in my mouth. When a fog bank of miry waters and cloud dust of sand make visions clarity or lack of a directional challenge, but I recover when I see the bubbles moving up over what appears to be an open edge, and it is as I swim hard and fast until I break free from the backlash like trying to escape the nets of a human trying to collect his daily net catch of trout, and come firing like a cannon releasing a cannonball, free. And as if reaching to the skies, I start my ascension and gasp out a *pheww*... which is twofold now; one, I let out my last air pocket in my lungs, and two, the stone! Now, this character of over time etchings of the stone has created some dynamic movements, and a lighter pull of gravity's law of water and nature starts its descent in a comical fearful sight to see, for I am way past my air reserve supply, but God is strengthening out of the faithfulness that has molded the object I pursue and myself into a predestined instruments of our calling eroding the edges of fear and is shaping us into a unit of oneness. Now, because of the shape that was stated in this script of log and the distance left in dissension, it is moving in a zig-zag pattern, which allows me to swim past and under the stone just as it zigs and able to catch it on the zag and quickly to the surface using some acrobatic maneuvers that I have master I toss the stone up swim down and have it rest on my shell come to the surface, which allows me to gasp for much-needed air!"

What Now?

Collapsing just on the outer bank, Sheldon lays the stone down and in sight, then relaxes in much-needed rest, all his inner strength drained. With his five itty-bitty toes and webbed feet, he now grasps the stone, keeping it secure. Now what? As Sheldon sprawls out the appendages of his shell, including his neck, one may think of something other than him resting his weariness aside, soothing his inner thoughts out loud in prayer. So now what, Lord? You said that You would take care of the rest, so please, give me direction of some sort. And then, out of the blue skies in the same direction that Penny made her first entrance, it's Penny again, quickly approaching not so far away in the near distance, making toward the bend in the road. Sheldon slowly creeps away from the nooks' niche and heads up the small banks, inclined to the sound of thumping and a dust cloud settling like misty rain. Reaching the top, Sheldon places the stone in front of him with his toes locked around its sharp, flint-like end for the best gripping position that he can task. With his mouth open, stretching out his neck as far as he can, he grabs a long clump of crabgrass to pull himself up. Just as Sheldon looks up, admiring that his climbing skills from a survival boot camp he attended last spring have now come in handy ways, Penny makes direct eye contact, locking her gaze on this odd creature of faith. She scratches her head and flips her long floppy ears out of the way, with no success, as they enter her vision again. Penny pauses to catch a much-needed breath as both take turns inhaling the fresh, clean air. Both fumble for words of clarity, sounding gibberish exhaustion, and are in a hurry.

A recognition of a question enters Penny's mind and asks, "Do I know you from somewhere? It seems like just recently. Oh, anyways, my name is Penny. No time to catch up with things, I must run; see you later," and just before Sheldon can open his mouth to speak, she says, "Goodbye for now, gotta run." And run indeed she does. Sheldon looks in a glare of amazement, turns, and looks straight into a camera as if there were an existing one available in this day and age. He says...

(Oh, by the way, please make a footnote here that the Dreamer, in irate sleep mode, has a reoccurring scene for clarity to verify that Penny has made herself known to Sheldon, the one the Lord has set for divine acquaintance has, for the second time, missed the mark due to an overactive worrying disorder about what to do in an unusual set of circumstances. A thorn on her side, but this is recognition of a complete sentence spoken by Penny. She does not see the stone securely under Sheldon's outer foot with her eyes, missing the blessing she was to receive, as the Dreamer has changed to the flip side of the pillow.)

"Now what, Lord? I am a soldier in Your army, Sir, and ready for Your next command. The limitation of my stature is all put aside; just lead me to whomever this stone is to be placed in the hands You desire to have. It shall be in my care until You make this known, for this too shall pass."

Turning west to set the positioning of the sun, Sheldon has one understanding that all shall come to pass on this day because it has been said in a crystal-clear tone of the urgency authorized placement of this animated object. For even the stones cry out for deliverance this day in the awakening.

"Gretchen, my child, listen.

"In the awakenings of the easterly rising continues into the western skies of another day. Out of the east on eagle's wings, shelter takes to flight, and the sound of victory shall fulfill the silver lining in the clouds covering and a new day awakening comes to pass, and the past shall weep for its days of reign and are no more. A man will stand looking to the west and take a stand in the defense of a king's company and two shall multiply into a multitude of many special peoples in the hands of the Lord. The grackle's call sizzles into the temple in the undertones of defeat's outlook of despair leading the way to victory's call. Gretchen, my child, stand still."

As the screeching sounds of a grackle fill the air, in an inferior, foot stomping, dancing around in confusion of a bird in distress over exaggeration and unrealistic, imagination gone wild, thinking that one's broken limb and waiting to be the pouncing prey of a predator, but in reality, it is only the uncertainty of thoughts that whispers gently in her mind clearing out the cobwebs of all the wives' tales, and whereabouts of others and a glossary of gossip. That has become a fulfillment of false joy in her busybody life. The lifestyle of a grackle named Gretchen now cannot comprehend the Lord's spoken words of reason because of the dulling of her heart. A stony, callused heart that breaks into two hemispheres. "The eastern hemisphere stone is in motion but needs assistance and the other in the western hemisphere stone is about to enter and must stand alone, but not in silence." The crying of a grackle's heart saddens the love of her Lord, who many times has tried to comfort her from her entrapments of insecurities, has now taken her captive and is in a battlefield of the mind. Not a place anyone needs to be in, for one cannot stand alone, and that battle belongs to the Lord. Weeping out loud and nowhere to turn, Penny has abandoned her heart and is trying to hold it all together, for she is a good friend, although most of the time, she rolls her eyes at me, thinking I haven't seen her do so.

Penny understands these inner thoughts and could help me decipher these words that have entered now into conflict's possession. Gretchen's somberly spirit has quieted her innermost being, and a voice of reasoning penetrates a beating heart healing, is now able to proceed forward in her thoughts of clarity. *My only hope out of this depressed spirit is to go and find Penny and to make things right in the standing of our early days of friendship.* She speaks forth in prayer for the first time in a long time, "Lord, take away these self-pitying emotions and help me listen again to that small whispering voice that I so long want to hear clearly again, through all of this clutter. That's what I must do; Penny's fast, but when my mind is set and mouth shut, I can soar to new heights at the speed of a falcon, well, chasing things like me (not good, that's another destructive thought)."

So, our grackle of tense spirit falls wayside, and a new one takes flight to recover the miles between and apart from a friend in distance and spirit, a friend that she now sees the beauty of companionship in its truest form and trust. Soaring free above the tree line and seeing how the brook follows parallel to the path and in the distance, she sees and hears a speck in the road, knowing that it's not Penny as a small whispering voice, known in familiarity, tells her to *go down to the roadside, for someone else is calling on the Lord.* And in a song of soaring, she says, "I no longer carry the weight I placed on the wings and breast of my chest, for now, I have felt the emotions of true freedom's call."

Gretchen zeroes in on our hard-shelled friend, like a homing missile on its guided path; Sheldon now tenses at the sight of a shadow's casting lot in front of him, not left or right, puts a hard hat turtle in lockdown mode, thinking out aloud, as usual, going into procedures' protocol, appendages in, check, tailgate hatch up, check, periscope down *(I always smile at that one, when pulling my neck inside of my hatchway)*, check. Sheldon is now in shellshock as past tense fear of close calling tactics of acts many times being tossed to and fro, shaken and stirred, well this may just be one of those in the present form… he is now quavering….

Quavering from her overexertion of the speed of flight and distance, Gretchen lands on top of Sheldon, badly mistaking him for a small boulder, as a burning sensation of her wing spanned wings, finally at ease and comes to rest. When all is still, well, almost when the comfort of the stationary object begins to quiver and talk in a very loud, authoritative, thunderstruck voice.

Gretchen asks, "Is this an earthquake?" and from Sheldon's safety bunker of a shell, he proclaims, "I am only required to give you my name, rank, and serial number. Sheldon, officer in the army of God ON-773H-HO, or Oscar-November-Seven-Seven-Three-Hotel-Hotel-Oscar, is that a copy? Do you understand that I am not coming out, no matter the torture!?"

Are the fears of hearing new voices what have me shaking in my shoes, or is this stone trying to knock my block off its turf?

"Woah, where's that coming from? I didn't mean to startle you; I thought you were a rock!" she says to settle the problem between her and whatever this may be. *Lord, give me clarification!*

A two-toned boulder, now at ease, announces, "I have already given you my certification information, so go ahead and throw your rocks at me, and as hard as you want to, my shell won't budge and is very durable at that! There are many layers of bone and cartilage…" Then he gasps, realizing that he has leaked valuable information and maybe just a little bit of leakage in the lower deck where the artillery is stored…

He hears a strong giggling sound from whatever is outside of his covering as Gretchen is trying so hard to contain herself that she, too, might have leaked a little because of the laughter inside her head. She asks, "You do realize you are saying all those words out loud, right? And why?"

"Must keep a log so my officers to whom I report know of all my activity. Now stop interrogating me! Not another word from me other than name, rank…"

"Got it, or should I say at ease, Officer Sheldon, I am just a private, Private Gretchen, N3VA3H-NO-77AC in the army of God, reporting for duty, sir!"

As Sheldon slightly peeks out of the crack of his front hatch, he replies, "Oh, I see, you're trying to play mind games with me now; you can be in a disorder of impersonating a military officer, an imposter, which is more of a moral ethic; if you are who you say you are, state your mission on God's calling, without hesitation, and I'll know if you're lying or not! Speak!"

"My mission, sir, is to locate Penny, recover our friendship, and discuss God's code given to me so that I can understand what is said to me, sir!"

"Well, fire out the torpedoes," he says, as all the appendages rapidly fire out and boing; Sheldon is standing at attention. "For the record, make note Private Gretchen has been released of any verbal clarification of impersonating a military officer immediately. The point is now written in an official journal."

"Oh, okay, well, this is all starting to make a little more sense now; God has said to me that he would provide the safety for the object requested for Penny to carry back with her and that she should be able to have recognition of whom to would be the transporter of this object. But she is definitely very frantic and wrapped up in her troubled anxieties of failing, so she has overlooked my presence and did not give me the opportunity to clear her mind's intuitions of this foreknowledge and this stone."

Sheldon pushes it in the direction of Gretchen, saying, "Maybe my camo-covered shell and striped, red-neck markings intimidated her a little too much." Sheldon begins to pace back and forth, each time touching his stone of obsession, and he tells her that Penny is in dire need of this stone and is in demand of it. "That information has not been obtained by me for classification reasons, I presume, or a time issue is at hand, and that is why Penny was summoned to carry this blessed burden upon her to a chosen community on a quest of great magnitude."

Gretchen sees daylight for the first time in these so intense findings and is in good cheer to find out that others can respond to the voice she has heard as well, knowing that it is from the Lord!

"Yes, yes, Sheldon. A whisper of a voice led me in the direction of your location, telling me to go to you, for there is one praying, and I did. I was called to take Penny's place due to this slight misfortune on her account, and I understand my mind is a cluttered mess, but I believe in my whole heart that it is my calling to deliver the stone to Penny."

Sheldon's itty bitty eyes begin to gleam as he speaks forth, "For the journals' sake, let it be noted that Private Gretchen is called to deliver one flint-shaped stone to be transported by Penny at a pace far greater than I could ever accomplish through all conditions that may arise. My advice is to stay low in the shelter of the tree lines cover and to be accompanied by two or three others so that the Lord's presence will be glorified amongst His fellowship; there is strength in numbers. If all agree, say, 'aye.'"

"Aye."

"Then let the record show that we agree on all matters discussed here. Note taken!"

Gretchen can no longer contain the laughter overwhelming her heart and soul, telling Sheldon to stop, for her side is beginning to ache because of the hard laughter, which is gut-wrenching in a very good way!

"You're so cute, Sheldon," she says, as he blushes, turning a bright red blending with his markings, and is humbled in his embarrassment.

"I am not able to give you this stone until I see your party gathered before Officer Sheldon; the mission cannot and will not fail under my command, Private Gretchen. Understood, soldier?"

"Yes, sir, Officer Sheldon. I shall return in a given time of, oh, twenty minutes max time. At this precise location."

Sheldon's mind's eye is considered always a ticking engine of many concerns, referring quickly to his data of her arrival and then departure, calculating the wind dynamics and all other scenarios. With his right leg pointing upward in a gesture that could be considered redundant, he replies, "That'll get her done!"

Gretchen's Flight

A sense of accomplishment has intertwined with this attitude of servanthood or parenthood. Yet, the group being brought together has not fully embraced the living water; instead, they are misusing the grace given. But who is to judge? To do so would be hypocritical, looking outward rather than inward. Now, Gretchen, with a newfound purpose and life-changing calling, must find a way to fulfill this mission. As Sheldon wisely stated, no one can stand alone, especially when there is the risk of failing. Circling around for an aerial view of Sheldon's walking pancake profile, she locates a familiar blemish in the brook in the nook of the beating arteries way to the heartland of life. Who can beat happiness and love to its abundance? She heads in a southern spiraling rotation to where a grackle begins a crackling that can be heard from every long distance farther than one can see. A calling recognized by her weekly gatherings of chatter, or at least at their usual conclusion. She would foster a sisterly friendship at the infamous mulberry tree, where they could chat and get lost in the odd demoralization of events. Nestled in the tree, they enjoyed people-watching, feeling secure in its non-transparent embrace. She waits for the opportunity to verbally paralyze a helpless, insecure body. A bashing of a spirit of denial and misuse of God's influence. Now, Gretchen must guide the sisters and direct them in an orderly fashion of faith.

And off into the highest of highest bluffs, at a greater distance than the four eyes of our two friends' ability to see or hear, with a smirk, a baffled, bewildered red-tailed hawk crosses over the desert floor because of a great disturbance in the eastern skies. Now seeking peace, an appetite becomes a complementary escape from fear and the vociferous opposition that covers the homeland's mountains and valleys—now occupied by a taunting, egotistical combatant. Admired by the sharp claws and beak of our hawk, the two are as one in spirit—predators ready to destroy and prey on anyone who dares cross their territory in this fleeting moment. And just like the sun glares off the metal and sword of his newfound role model in the valley of death, our red-tailed hawk masks himself in the light rays of secrecy and moves swiftly into a better positioning for what looks to be an appetizing bite or, to the sound of it, more than one. Now he's quietly nestled in the broadness of one nearby oak, for there is no shame in not wanting to share in this complex food chain world of a red-tailed hawk named Destiny, although his few friends call him Destin because he is destined to the greatness of one, and a key factor to greatness is ruthlessness, patience, and timing. Without these, you are nothing, for being ruthless is the greatest trait of them all.

(23)

In the covering amongst the treelined forest, Gretchen begins to think and talk out loud; it seems as if Sheldon is rubbing off on her.

"How do I go about this task gathering my companions in a positive way? I do not want to become a clanging instrument of brass or metal, for I could speak as the angels in heavenly words, but without love, I am nothing." A joyous melody springs into the essence of life, a song of redemption and instruction to her friends in this place of recognition and common ground. "This is the appointed time when the sisters are united and become one in celebration with all our hearts together, God's redemption plan. Trusting each life will be changed into a productive tool and instrument of God's hands. Living our lives in community and leading by example with this lifestyle in servanthood. Let the only fire be the one that consumes the dross of our minds and sets ablaze into a wildfire in our hearts. Come all, and we shall set forth in a quest to find the messenger and to search out a resting place for this stone (forgive me, Lord, for I do not have the stone, but I'm using it for motivation), clutched in my independent claws. Let the flame burn with a desire to mature and be consumed into a spiritual maturity. Awaken, my friends, into this blaze of passionate fire of serving others more so than ourselves. Take this spirit that has been rested upon me as a nest of security in God's divine plan. Follow with hearts upon the wind's revolution, answering the upwind calling, my friends in faith. A long, profound pause of silence, a stillness in unwavering dedication, now crashing through the barrier that once contained these spirits in confinement and despair—now set free..."

In every direction, united in friendship, seven fiery grackles led by Gretchen now abide in faith, hope, and love, but the greatest is love.

---

(24)

From the tallest oak in the forest, Destin plunges at great speed to the roots of the tree and crouches into the shrubbery nearby, looking up to watch the flock of seven at the treetops joyously fly overhead. *Oh, such a lovely sound at being off guard, but not yet; they haven't reached the potential of their so-called calling. Yes, but soon, they will be calling whomever they say that they serve in His so-called glory. Just something to fall back on in times of despair, pitiful creature's habit, is my opinion in a nutshell of life's hard knocks. I've heard them say that God is so true and every man a liar, well they at least have the second part right, and aye, all I see is a bunch of wishy-washy so-called "we are better than them" attitude; it is my song to my own glory.*

As Destin basks in his own intellectualness of nothingness, he kinda has his own song in self-praise.

"Oh, this free gift, this free gift, oh, there's always a price to pay, I'd say! Am I trapped in this delinquent misdeed of circumstantial evidence? This is where I chose to be, in a realm of power in this neck of the woods, just to say in a figure of speech, you figure it out, for all is okay in my world. Freedom is the freedom to choose as you please, and if there are consequences, well, then pay them and be done. Who wants to be a slave to a so-called holy God? I hear them proclaiming. I'm sure they will be nagging their praises when they get me in their sights, but not now, oh, no, not until after their great exchange because I want to possess what they can never have in this stone. And what is this? Where can you seek God when there is no physical being in sight? How can this even begin to be possible? Why the hassle when they say that I am as the one in an open tomb, or that is to put one in its open tomb, for I am swift to shed blood in less than one's next heartbeat! The wage of sin is death; well, that is something that I don't recognize, this so-called sin. That is made up by mankind, so just throw that out as hogwash and be better off. Live life to its fullest at a fast pace, and soon enough, we all will reach our destinations."

Count that as your upward calling!

The seven grackles are as sporadic in their flight formation as so is their conversation with Gretchen, leading and weaving in and out of branches, when a voice is heard to the left of Gretchen, the stern voice of Harriot, speaking in a smirky tone of deliverance, "Now what about this calling? And who is this messenger? Gretchen, you make her sound at the most important and as all can see, that's me, so what does this messenger have over me? Is there a set time frame and a destination, a point of entry, or whereabouts? Are we just following blindfolded here?"

Gretchen looks to her left in disbelief, Harriot totally ignoring the briefing she gave at her beck and call to all of them. She looks to her left in acknowledgment.

She says, "Would you give me time to speak over your rudeness or go take a backseat, for there is a short time frame here? As far as blindsided goes, I know the destination, so have a little patience, please, and thank you very much! First things first, we must go to the basics to gather the stone!" *The truth must be told earlier than I wanted but later than intended to stir up this mess I am in; help me, Lord, please.*

Harriot screeches, "The what?! I thought you already had the stone,"

A stoned question is delivered from the right of Gretchen as

Amber broadcasts out loud in a demanding voice, "How can I protect something that I can't see or hold on to? And yes, who is the messenger?" Gretchen, seeing where this diverse spirit is coming from, is now hesitant, for this is not going to go over very well, in this spirit, to the answer she is about to give them. So, she flat-out yells, "Penny, okay!"

In unison, all of them repeat the name in almost disgust, "Penny!"

The six of them, in a harsh harmonical tone to the choir, are singing in soprano in an off-key vibrato tone, and they deliver their tone in disbelief. Amber continues the conversation by choice of infectious emphasis words, saying rudely she always has a message from the Lord… as she is bluntly overruled by Alette saying, "Silly, henceforth, the messenger, get it!"

"Doesn't take a whole lot to figure out; just saying," is another stone thrown from the back side and in agreement by Delora, always worried that she will be ridiculed for her remark later.

Another stone is thrown by Bellamy as she chimes in, "I thought you two despised each other, Gretchen, and now you're letting her in on our clique, really. I am always going to be your friend, but it is your decision here!" and she mutters aloud, "Penny."

"Why not throw another stone, Amber?" She vividly speaks forth, "Penny of all people? I guess we were supposed to stop on a dime."

In her anger, you can hear a low chuckle from Delora, a rarity in itself because of her known stagnant sense of humor with riddles that only she could understand. She says, "And that makes a total of eleven in the common senses department." Then she replies, "I just want to know the risk factor in this matter. Are we going to die?" Ah, now that sounds more like the Delora who is known so well for shaking and trembling.

Finally, the silent one speaks the words of truth that Gretchen so silently prayed for at the down-spiraling before the beginning of this God-calling event, as Nicole speaks words of reasoning into these off-balance ladies of faith. "Hey, shush already here; you're all missing the point. We will not accomplish one iota if we do not get organized and conquer this bickering and just fly through the motions, going nowhere in particular with our conversation; listen to yourselves! So, let's rest and settle down to regroup in all intentions. Then, when we first began this quest, we left it in an adventure of uncertainty by triumphing with God's leadership, okay?!"

"*Ooooo*, I'm up for an adventure," Aletta replies in her instinctive personality of all free-spiritedness.

Then, out of nowhere, Delora started to quicken up a conversation in anxiety. "I have heard these happenings wavering back and forth of good and evil, like a flickering as lighting speed overcoming and overtaking all things good just by changing events and the outcome, so what happens if we fail? Maybe there's a greater force than we can manage. Have you looked at our stature, have you taken this into account? I mean, what's in a stone? Can a small object such as this really change an event? And what if others want to possess this item? Such is mankind, waiting and waiting for a solution, not willing to act and paralyzed in this coming fate. Oh, I cannot bear this pressure placed upon us. And this waiting, did I mention about the waiting? The aurora in the skies above us is haunting; something like a hunter's spirit has taken over the atmosphere's air pockets, for my breathing is rapid, and I'm going to die if we wait another minute!"

"Oh, Delora, settle down your wigging on us; we have to act on faith alone, for patience is a virtue; just you wait and see, Delora. Victory shall be ours," is spoken forth by a flaming heart in Nicole, of a warriors' cry, who will lead the flock in due time, just you wait and see. "Now, let's end this on a positive note. In closing, Gretchen, will you please pray for God's plan for us?"

Gretchen begins to pour out her heart to an understanding counselor, our God.

In Waiting: A Time in Prayer
(25)

"A faithful prayer has been set in motion; please do something with our hearts. Let the beauty of the Lord our God be upon us, that we may gain a heart of wisdom. Open our eyes and let us listen to Your glorious voice, for we do not understand the significance this stone brings and the people You have chosen to serve, big or small or even your creatures of creation, for You are our creator and all things great or small that have come to pass, to serve for Your purpose alone. In Your divine will, each of us has a purpose in this short life's breath given, so let us not waste our breath on this day, and let's serve a glorious, loving God."

In unison, in a moment's time, God's chosen special people have been set into an advancement to a battlefield dominion, not in this world but a kingdom of good and evil powers, spiritual influences, and some physical disturbances. Having called upon his name out of despair and circumstances overload. The absence of a gentle whisper and a gentle breeze letting them know that Your presence is at hand is now replaced by the rasping sound of their own fears in a whirlwind of thoughts. Only to become a mask of false hope in each and everyone's life.

In the near distance, a hunter's spirit haunts all of nature's calls in the vicinity, for they know him. Destin has made his pursuit amongst them and is waiting patiently for the right moment in time, and it's coming, for he can feel it in his heart and a gut feeling of hope, he prays. Just you wait and see.

Sheldon looks toward the threatening clouds coming in from the south, moving in an eastern swirling pattern, waiting patiently for the storm to close in on him, and prays that the skies will burst through with a familiar grackle's voice and just like the rain, hoping Gretchen will be coming with a band of others, just you wait and see.

Coming to the entrance in the nook of the woods, the thickets and briars, one would think not to go through this mess without at least multiple scratches and scars covering the face and body, when all Aly can think about is that he hopes he doesn't get in briars tangled up in his wool. While the donkey is rearing in a chaotic fit, saying, "This is no good. Aly, are you sure this is the way to the entrance? I feel it in my bones, but I want to remain in this self-denial at what is to come; just you wait, just you wait and see. Now get over here, Aly, and let's pray like never before!"

Penny, frozen in her tracks, now believing that she has somehow, in her frantic spirit, terribly missed her mark due to the fact she can see the silhouette of a lone man on the outskirts of the beaten road, not singing this time but doing something else in another chord, let's just leave it at that! I have to turn back when a slight whisper tells her, "Just you wait, just you wait and see!" Please, Lord, show yourself…

Now fumigated by the two clowns that he calls friends and servants, David now calls them out by other names, let's just leave it at that, but continues faithfully along the beaten path as off in the distance, he sees a furry critter in a pause in the road and smiles once again and mutters, "Oh you two, just you wait, just you wait and see! Lead me, Lord, into this calling my father has made me responsible in deliverance…"

Jacob has returned to the homeland of Jesse with all the sheep, except the one David adores, and he explains to Jesse the mishap that he has encountered. He is in fear that Aly has wandered off into the deep woods out of chaos' calling and confusion, as Jacob has set in his heart to seek and save the lost sheep. But he mutters,

"Why? Wouldn't you just answer my beck and call as any other sheep would?" Frustrated, he mutters out loud, "Oh, just you wait, just wait and see!"

As his troops of jumping spiders gather in multitudes, each accounted for, there comes a calling—a whispering voice shouting out to them… "Arise and head west, for you are in call of the army of God."

"General Albert, all troops are gathered at the base of the oaks and are ready to report for your instructions, sir!"

"Very well, at ease. I'm on my way; I just need to gather my staff of command!" Hopping stiff-legged all eight of his legs in unison as if he is on a pogo stick, moving in at a rapid pace, now to confront his fellow spiderets of the Green Berets Squad 4TOGO, he says, "Men, we are in the waiting, so just you wait, just you wait and see. Now bow your heads, and let's each pray to be mobile and on the move, God almighty!"

Harbors' Anchoring Stone
(26)

"The Lord answering a prayer to all His special peoples."

"In the silence of endurance into the wilderness hardships, having performed all things, and showed to be faithful in each life touched, setting all fears aside for they will only interfere with perception and decisions each has to make along the way. Walk with Me. Come harbor in the secret place and abide under the shadow of the Almighty's wing, and I shall in one accord set angels amongst you in all ways chosen. Continue in the leadership to the ones appointed and do so, stand fast in accountability. Take hold, captivating the mind's eye to alertness, and maintain patience in a harbor deep enough to rest anchored in love.

"Listen and be still…

"Behold, listen, all the peoples who cherish each and every breath of *life. Things foretold by a prophet of old, leading into this present time, and foreshadowing things to come; a prophecy in My timing shall come to pass. The silver lining in the clouds is parted by the path of glory as He rides on a white horse toward redemption. Salvation will have already been established, and in the waiting, a time will come when everyone shall see Him. Each soul will one day face the consequence of their free will—choosing either the everlasting sorrow or the glorious beginning that awaits them. Oh, what a glorious day this shall be, God Almighty... And David is amongst this genealogy; this lineage cannot be broken, for his connection is of many important origins in faith's calling. And David's leadership begins with this insignificant stone, for even the stones will cry out My name. And one greater than David shall come in a time such as these and will become the cornerstone of every man's faith if one only believes."*

— Chapter Three —
THE MAGNIFICENT SEVEN

 A rushing wind comes in from the south as a mighty storm approaches into the sight by our form-fitting formations of grackles developing into the eastern horizon, now being chased by the forthcoming disturbance. With eyes glaring broadly in focus and wings descending into the soaring winds, Nicole, our loveable warrior, hollers out a battle cry like thunder as lighting aluminates the sky, outlining the formation order by our assembled feathered ruffled friends. Gretchen frantically takes the lead, settling the pace of the others, with Nicole's victory way to her right and Amber's fire to the left in the compact triangular force formation. Bellamy's beautiful friends-for-life mentality with Gretchen and following her lead in the anchor line of four, including Harriot, the caring big sister, and despairing Delora, with an obsessive mind and alertness always in the middle of all things big and small, which complements Aletta's carefree attitude in flight. With their determined souls leading the way and a serene sense of security following (well, three of them, except for Delora, although she remains keen-eyed and highly aware), they form the Magnificent Seven, new recruits in the army of God.

THE MEADOWLANDS

And into the darkest cloud lining, a sparkle of stardust enters into the atmosphere's color scheme as an image of tiny specks emerges, seven grackles in flight approaching in a lively manner, still miles and miles from the destination. The thick clouds devour them up again, only to spit them out.

The thick cloud coverage advances rapidly, absorbing the sun rays into the overcast shadows that gently chase hills and valleys up and over the tree line continuing down the slopes of the countryside, as if guiding and leading all to the entrance to a promised land, the great Exodus journey in the days of Moses. Let our hearts be set on fire in our travels in the sudden eclipse by nightfall, the darkest thoughts to the mind that send out lighting flashes on visible channels of memoirs and imagery disruptive sparks into the air as a thunderclap breaks the silence ravaging, adverse thoughts. All to the audience of one. Sheldon. That is, Officer Sheldon, ON-773H-HO, in the army of God, under attack of an unsighted enemy that has the power to rule and rampage in downpouring rain that will flood deep channels developed over the years of an overactive mind. But this principality is messing around with a foundation built on the solid rock of a true foundation of faith and the faith of others as he waits patiently for the arrival of Gretchen, Private Gretchen, N3VA3H-NO-77AC in the army of God, soon to be promoted to Transporter Specialist of the army of God. The weaponry department carries one flint stone into the hands of Penny. When delivered, it will be the dawning of a new day for Sheldon. And at the speed of sound, a triangular formation now breaks into fragments of each individual personality, descending in time's given grace into the life of Sheldon, bringing thoughts of joy and relief into this hard-shelled life of a soldier.

The storm wall has become stationary but still puts out a display of electrical beauty and crashing cymbals in the thunder's way. Sheldon waits honorably in the nook by the road where the two first got acquainted, with his neck stretched out and looking skyward to the descending order of the grackles with Gretchen's lead. She makes her way into eased relief. When Gretchen barely gets out a "Hello, good to make your acquaintance again…" and then lets the rudeness begin. Not more than seven minutes ago, Gretchen had to scorn the girls because of their childish behavior; now they are completely ignoring Gretchen and, more so, Sheldon, looking around franticly, going in a circle of dismay. Now, with Harriot taking the lead, with her head just spinning, entering a world of materialistic wants, she speaks forth in a screech of excitement, "Okay, where is it? I want to see if it will match the color of my eyes or maybe it will clash with my beautiful, shiny coat."

"Why are you always first when it comes to new pendants?" Amber's fire rages again, "Well, let me look at it at least and maybe try it on, so at least I can see how it complements my personality!"

"Here I go again, having to be the voice of logic. We can take turns and then draw straws to see who gets to admire the new attire; just call me Nicole, the quick fix!"

Delora walks straight over to Sheldon and straight out asks him, "Okay, where's the rock, the gem, the jewel, you know, the stone?" Aletta and Bellamy are huddled together, just snickering.

Gretchen steps forward into their view with a very disappointed look on her face and says, "Way to go on making a good first impression on Sheldon. Do you think that he will let us be worthy of this great responsibility that he has placed upon each of us as a group to be responsible adults here? Apologies are long overdue girls; now, get to it, now!" says Gretchen, trying to knock some common sense into their hard noggins. For the first time since their landing, they say something in unison voices.

"Forgive us, Sheldon, with all of our hearts apologies," Delora chimes in.

Sheldon just stares off into a daze of *what the*... "Oh, okay, apologies accepted."

Gretchen gives them one last hard glance and then looks over to Sheldon, "Well, wasn't that entertaining?"

"Yes, yes indeed." A stunned Sheldon takes in a deep breath to readjust his composure of assertiveness, commanding, "Okay, let's get this started," says Sheldon, pushing the stone forward toward Gretchen, ever so slightly looking side to side as if it was a heist of some great classified papers in exchange for an inside job straight from the enemy's camp. Once again, Gretchen is cut off from her response, not even getting in one word, when once again, the girls, in more boisterous voices, exclaim, "That's the stone? It's just an ordinary rock, what the—!"

"I'm not carrying that on any part of me..."

The whimsical Gretchen, who can't believe her ears, says, "Stop it right now; only I shall carry this, for it is my calling and responsibility. You're all with me for moral support! Now start supporting me and get this bickering in check!"

Now it's Sheldon's turn to go off as he declares his statement, "For the record, it is one flint-shaped stone that is a weapon of destruction with only one purpose that is unmentionable, that shall put one into his place and fall into eternal rest!"

The girls get really quiet and bewildered by the outburst. Silence is finally broken. "You're right, Gretchen; now, how are you going to carry this item? You may drop it if you just clutch onto it with your claw, sweetie." A very good question that is asked by her best friend, Bellamy.

"Good point. Any suggestions, anyone?" Gretchen is trying to settle her last nerves about the attitudes that are trying to nest and make themselves at home.

A good solution is brought forth by Aletta. "*Oooo*, I have an idea, I'm crafty, and we all had young-ins at one time; remember the nest-building days? Well, I kinda kept it up but have made it into a hobby of crafts to occupy my time in an empty nest. Anyways, I make trinkets by weaving wicker of different dyed colors to hold the items in place, and then different types of corn, string, or whatever I can find. Will that do?"

"Awesome, get to it, girl, now we're talking! Girls, any other ideas on how to make this easier to carry?" says Gretchen, starting to settle in.

"We could use briars or thorns to stick you…"

"Amber, really? I want to be able to hold water whenever I need a drink," Gretchen replies, irritated.

Sheldon is now all excited and commends the girls on their comments when he replies, "I have the solution on how to make it wearable; it's just a matter of getting his attention and his whereabouts! I'll give it my best shot. He said he was only a holler away, so here goes. General Albert, report to Officer Sheldon immediately; an urgent matter is at hand!" Silence.

Aletta steps out into the open and asks, "Did someone holler for me? I was just finishing, and voilà, here it is. I just guesstimated the stone size, but I have a pretty good sense of judgment on these matters; here you go," she says, tossing it over to Gretchen, who takes it in her claws and works the stone into the trinket, saying, "Perfect fit, you go, girl!"

And then from an overhanging low branch, as if he was walking in thin air, a fuzzy, multicolor of Jacob's robe, a jumping spider comes suspended, defying gravity, and flips around upside down directly in front of Sheldon, saying, "Messenger Collinsworth, reporting to your urgent call for General Albert who is not available currently, but I am here to assist you in all your commands, sir!"

An unsettling frown on Sheldon's face then gives in to the friendly smile of his own nature. "Very well, Messenger Collinsworth, is the general's location under classified security restrictions?"

Lickety-split is the response of Officer Collinsworth, "Yes, sir, and under the general's orders I can give you this information but not in this open area with the possibility of being overheard!"

With all ears, of course, Delora glances over to ask, "Did you call for me?"

Sheldon heads off the curiosity of Delora by just ignoring her as she leaves frustrated, and he says, "At ease, soldier, thanks for your concerns. Fine young man, how are you at such a high rank for your age, sir? Armor bearer would be your next rank?"

A humble Collinsworth says, "Correct, sir, but once again, this is not the place or time; sorry, sir," to the inspiring heart of Sheldon.

"No apologies needed, anyway Private Gretchen now has been promoted to Transporter of weaponry, and we need assistance in locking down this item onto herself for easier navigational reason and self-defense!"

Collinsworth steps up and pounces on the opportunity to serve in a time of need. "Very well, I can do so; the webbing will last for about twelve or so hours. Until then, it will be stuck to her, so let me know where to suspend it."

Sheldon looks over in the direction of Gretchen to bring her into the loop of officialness. "Sounds good. Okay Gretchen, where do you want this stone for placement?"

Taking the cue, "I want to be able to see it, I guess near my neck; I'm used to wearing necklaces and such, so yes, there, please." With front legs a-flapping and eyes a-bugging, Messenger Collinsworth crafts a tight webbing from the trinket to Gretchen's neck, leaving the front of the trinket open so that the stone can be removed from it as the fans go wild and crazy seeing the mastery of the webbing being placed in such a quick time frame. "Good to go, and I am out of here. Peace out, sir!" and just like that, Collinsworth has departed from his duty.

Gretchen, looking at the craftsmanship of both pieces to the assemblage into one, says, "Okay girls, we need to go. Let's assemble in one corresponding force and continue at low altitudes under these threatening skies. Nicole takes the lead, I will be in the middle surrounded, with Amber to my right, Harriot to my left, Delora directly behind me, Aletta to her left, and Bellamy to the right to complete the anchoring back line and the seven, in aviation formation flight!"

As the lighting strike brightens the treelined roadside, a crafty predator repositions to another outpost as another lighting strike spotlights Destin in mid-stride of his new landing location. With attentive eyesight, Delora spots Destin in her peripheral vision in her line of sight, but by the next quick glance, he disperses out of her sight like he was never there; oh, but he was, and Delora knows it, by the bangs a-clanging in her early warning system of paranoia's best! Sheldon watches the military aviation formation and salutes their departure, almost bringing tears to the eyes of this hard-to-crack, hard-headed turtle.

JESSE AND THE PRODIGAL BOYS
(27)

With a storm in his sight, the wisdom of Jesse, who has seen many disturbances race across these plains many times in past years, can tell that this is a very strange incident, a most peculiar way as thoughts by the day event creep into a chronical order at this day forth. Thinking to himself, *Maybe this is what got into those hardheaded boys don't understand what got into them this day, but it got into the three of them really good of misfortunate circumstances to sequential events. Just before the departure of David, the matter of the uneasy mind of King Saul, who has many times called upon David to tame the thoughts racing through the weary mind of the first ruler over the people. And Aly, who is always friendly to David but never as clingy as he was before he left and shows disobedience toward Jacob's friendly guidance, maybe I'm thinking into it way too much! But the boys, who*

THE MEADOWLANDS

I have called by names too other than their given names, Ace, Duke, and Rocco, done topped it all!

Who knows what goes into the minds of a very intelligent breed of the Border Collie, mystically synchronizing in motion along the plains, herding the sheep in a controlled manner? A beautiful sight to see! If only I could read into this, my heart would be at ease, but there is something in the air, and it is not good! As far as the boys go, I only know of the aftermath of that early morning event when I went to see David off, no more than a fifteen-minute task, and I came back into a house in total shambles of chaos, mud flung, and dripping off tables, chairs overturned, with hoof marks and paw prints in every which direction, leaving all types of circumstantial evidence or direct evidence who knows other than those three, with no other eyewitnesses, figures, only one can speculate of the incidents. All I know is that they were not to be seen in who knows how long when the mind is fumigating in a blinding anger only to be reprimanded by the Lord's correction, and so rightfully so. Because the boys are just amazing to a loyal pet owner like myself, they're always giving joy and affection, and sometimes I believe they understand all my outspoken thoughts of concern for all who enter and leave this humble home. I know it doesn't sound right, but sometimes, especially in these times, I get more out of the dogs than my own boys, just saying, while all of them are out fighting a battle for who's purpose. So, with the absence of all my loved ones, the heart becomes sorrowful, and forgetful to episodes of discord, forgiving. The dogs are back, and that matters a lot to me in this empty nest. There being anxious in a most peculiar way, to lead on as if they, too, feel like something just isn't right.

ALLEN W. LEAFGREEN

Here's the Rest of the Story—"Three Dog Perspective Point of View"

Forevermore, from the rising sun until sunset's closure calling in nightfall's eve, the loyalty of three intertwined lives proceeds with pride—three dogs named Ace, Duke, and Rocco (who haven't had a proper introduction to their lives until now). And just like any other day, their life's work, although one cannot call it work if you get enjoyment, satisfaction, and delight regarding compassion, a merry heart, and the desire in mind to take haste in plundering the day in the provinces of the countryside. Rocco opens to self-awareness and conversation with a different approach in attitude, as if it is a burden that remains trapped in a pig pen of life's royalties; he begins the journey within to release all life has in encouraging words at being hog-tied in a gob of slippery wet mud.

"Draw near to the fun, *oof*" is a way to express one's dismay, waddling in a day of self-pity as my friends are always with me, moving toward this rebel's delight in self-expression, hollering out loud, making sure that they hear him at this distance apart. "Ace and Duke, ole buddy and pals! Be one as of the pig or hog's life's charm in the coolness to mud-packed paws and clumped entangled coat."

Now Ace and Duke have routines to maintain and even so, manage at doing them. Headmost is being set free, commencing in the daily habit customary welcoming Jesse and David in the burrow den, but this day is contrasting and contradictory in itself. For there is no friendly conversation amongst them of the day's event to set in motion with great anticipation, somehow, I missed the mark on that one, looking toward Duke, who is stretching, yawning, and has released a silent but deadly… well let's just call it what it is: a fart, and he is proud of it too.

Ace inquires, "Where is everybody?"

"No one but you and me, not even Rocco, who about right now would be looking for the remaining food particles and sweeping up dust bunnies at the same time, a never-ending search and always craving and begging!" Ace says. "Speaking of Rocco, I hear him bellowing out back something about needing to hog-tie one of the pigs in a frantic voice; hurry, let's go see, maybe there's trouble!"

Yep, that's Ace and Duke for you; always assertive when it comes to harm's way, one to all, three of them, traits in loyalty, but sometimes not always following through, "like forgetting to dot the i's and crossing the t's," about the back door, leaving it wide open, sending out an invitation to entrance way. Oh, but it gets better; just you wait, just you wait and see!

"Look, Rocco is over there; he must have his mind in the lost and not found, taking a wrong turn from sanity's way, where his mind should be in a safe and sound gathering, not waddling in the mud, or let's give him the benefit of the doubt, maybe he is trying to wrangle up a pig, trying to round him up, for what reasoning I do not know! Heck, he might as well just be eating the pig pod's slop while he's at it!"

So slowly approaching the gate, Ace and Duke rest their paws on the lower railing, leaning in as the gate, not being latched properly, opens wide, setting the boys off balance, and both roll in as Rocco gleefully says, "No, you do that inside the mud, it's very relaxing indeed, come on!"

All you can see are Rocco's sparkling blue eyes; he has, on many occasions, received the prize of the last bite due to those baby blues. The two are just astounded how this sophisticated dog could head south for the winter by the mentality part of the conversation and are more amazed when the three hogs, who have unmentionable personalities to discuss but not here, are in a hurry to get out of harm's way of Rocco's rolling madness. As the two gander in disbelief and shock, the three sows head toward Jesse's humble home of welcoming strangers into their care on a journey's way to wherever time may lead them. And there is nothing stranger than watching three not little pigs go hog-wild inside a home that comforts all.

Maybe a heavy draft from a developing situation has occurred, leaving the pigs contained in a claustrophobic atmosphere of destruction as Rocco hollers, "I'll go get them," playing the hero, although Rocco is always the bravest of the three and is the lead dog.

"No, you silly buffoon, you're going to make things worse!" Paralyzed in their usual synchronic movements or lack of, Ace says, "This isn't good, not good at all!"

Now Rocco's obedience is starting to show as he gets the door on the way in, the two in disbelief just shake their heads and start to react. Duke frantically tells Ace, "I'll get the door open, it's not easy, but I have done it before," as he runs to the door and places his two paws on the lever hatch, pushing it down and springing in a backward motion gets the door open.

Ace, coming in with cobbs of corn in his mouth, starts to try persuading the pigs out of the devastated interior and into the wide-open yonder's way; to their amazement, it is working. Now that the pigs are outside, the three can start to do the magical powers over other four-legged creatures leading them back to their pens and closing the gate and latch. All is well, but not really!

"What's gotten into you, Rocco? Have you gone mad?!"

"Oh, we are in so much trouble; no way out of this one, boys!"

"Rocco, go wash up in the pond, go get your dignity reclaimed, and get back over here!" says Ace, now taking control of the matter, moving toward the open doorway to take a look. Duke says, "You know, Ace, if we had gone up front to notify Jesse of the perspective conditions with clean paws and led Jesse to the scene, we could have settled down with us off the hook, but now that you sent Rocco to the pond, to wash up, we're all guilty of this crime!"

"So, what are we to do? Have you seen the house, Duke? It's horrifying, and oh, the mud, how do you presume that it got up on the ceiling?"

"Come on, Ace, I was the first one in to try and get those pigs back in control. They just plowed through, pushing me to the side and making headway to wherever the hoofs may land, yes, I got a first account of the matter; that's done with, now what to do from here?" And in a sprint timing, their synchronicity kicks in, and they cry out loud so all can hear, "Run to the Northern Outlook, now, Rocco!" They startle Rocco into a side-angle cartwheel turn and past the other two in an unspoken agreement.

THE NORTHERN OUTLOOK

Never has there ever been so much beauty in the passageway to the Northern Outlook; the path intertwines with the many wildflowers that are in bloom this spring with the smell of freshly made honey to a honeybee comb of delight throughout the tamed timberlands and crisscross by a small stream and then inclines into an altitude of hollows and clefts of different lookout viewpoints at all the surrounding from miles afar, especially at the Northern Heights, a spot viewed by many on cool summer nights. A place of tranquility and to gather one's thoughts, such as what the boys have gotten themselves into.

Catching his breath from the adrenaline within, Rocco asks, "Do you think Jesse will recover from this misfortune, Duke?"

"In a matter of time, yes, but that is one of the reasons we are here, to let things cool down a little and to at least observe the…"

And then a hollering that follows up a path of tranquility hollows up into the heaven's skies. A slight roar of a familiar voice breaks the wind (not what you're thinking) and penetrates the top of the Northern Outlook!

"Just you wait, just you wait, the three of you boys!" and then silence calls.

"Well, that answers that," answers Ace, as the three bow their heads to pray, pray for a better day, such as today gets a whole lot better other than these strange events of the past time's way.

Out of nowhere, Ace steps up to the flat-shaped limestone rock that overhangs the cliff about a quarter's way out in secrecy, the shrubs and holly's growth inclosing the area, and decides to be the commentator of the upcoming events that take into motion.

Clearing his throat, he begins in a stern tone, "You better get a move on," he says in a toned voice as he proceeds to speak words of wisdom to all who will listen. "Jesse steps out front and moves his head from side to side as if looking, well, looking for the three of us. I can't see any facial expressions, but from the only vocals that we heard earlier probably hasn't changed. Oh, now things make sense why we were alone in the den this morning when we awoke. David is pretty much down the road and way past the monumental stone. Heading in an eastern steady pace with provisions and Ebb hauling them, that stubborn mule, at critical times by stress, seems to be in full operational spirits this day. Kicking up dust and swaying to his own musical theme. Well well, looks as if it is another fleeting moment of time spent catering to the boys at war and a whimsically acting king of hidden integrity or, should I say, depleting. Forty days in and out of nap times waiting for David's roiling report to this stalemate battle scene with the increased numbers of the opposition. Just waiting to see who will take a stand for the right of all right spree."

"Oh, let's see, hmmm… A man to the east surrounded in the security by an open field, the tall grasses of the meadowlands, a place where not much happens, and now the herd, our herd, the man, awwwww, we're missing the prescience of Jacob, the noble friend to David and ours, who has settled in the open meadows by our heart. The herd is grazing the tall grass; oh, what a lazy day this would have been."

Rocco blurts out, "Don't go there, Ace!"

"Just giving you the play-by-play of the day here, okay?"

"Oh, I know where you were going with that unspoken comment, that's all I'm saying," says a futile Rocco, knowing his own self-defeat without being reminded.

Ace continues his dictation, "The perimeter looks secure without us currently and Jacob is stationery looking in the opposite direction of the herd, some kind of distraction maybe. Oh, now I see Aly, walking free, alone at about fifty yards to the south, also looking easterly, looking, of course, in the direction of David's disappearing point, figures, a very close bond to a loyalty that is so seldom, has won the hearts and especially Aly's easy to drift spirit in adventures calling. Jacob is very attentive to all things in his circular vision, noticing that the mothers are gathering their ewes, circling them up, but why? I think Jacob senses it as well; he has his staff clutched in both hands as if going to battle but of an unknown enemy in his mind. Aly is showing no interest in the rising circumstances, and I am flabbergasted myself. Hurry, boys, help me search out the perimeter of their location; something isn't right in this open field of doubt. Look intensively, boys!"

Duke hollers, "Nothing on the valley floor or approaching from the forest tree line!"

"Why are the prairie dogs popping in and out of their domains, squirming?" says Ace, as he scans the new quick occurrence in the once silent meadow. "Is someone sending out a decoy of distraction?"

(28)

A two-winged shadow from the northern hills casts over the boys as they move at a quick pace. Jacob, now aware of the approaching threat, frantically tries to get Aly's attention, motioning for him to come closer. As the shadow draws nearer, Jacob turns to face the incoming predators, instinctively shifting into protective mode.

"A second shadow, which is now known as two eagles, and the first one is now in our sights, boys, enemy known!" Ace is back to his solitary unbelieving commentary, barely breathing or audible, saying, "The nightmare in this awakening transpires into a natural scene of a predator, a walking food chain, the herd, trying to single out the youngest and easiest prey to satisfy their hunger. The eagles screech to paralyze in fear in their crafty approach; it's not quite enough that the elders of past events have encountered times like these, but the skittish must, too, well, of course, like Aly!"

In unison, all three repeat his name, "Aly!" And God Almighty, being on the move, alters the directional point of the two eagles, who must be blind because they go for the middle of the pack, hoping to clutch an ewe in their grasp and all will be said and done so the rest of the herd can go on living the day out for just this day.

"Man, Ace, you are good with this commentary thing, but we can't do anything to help because the threat will be done by the time we reach them!"

"Just start praying out loud, like Gideon's takeover of the Midianites!" Ace proclaims with a new authority to these circumstances. "It's working; they missed after all three of them proclaimed this day. Let's keep it up, just louder this time, something that David would say in song. Come on, silence is our enemy at this time; speak forth, now! Many are the eagles of the skies, strong in their stature and who treat us as prey; we will not fear those fowls who surround us be like the mountains surrounding us great in stature in these open fields of our fear, for You alone are our shield to the sheep in this field, Lord, God Almighty, the God of Abraham, Jesse, and David, our comforters by faith! Salvation belongs to the Lord! Set the captives free!"

"That worked even better this time, but the enemy is back on the prowl. The tactic is twofold: the first is a decoy and a missed attempt at that, while the second eagle is swooping down to an alert

Jacob, who is now in the middle of a tightly-packed herd, swaying his staff in an upward circular pattern striking the eagle across his blindside blindness and screeches off in pain. Our friend Aly is able to duck out of sight between the sides by the hollow to the unseen beaten path, but it isn't that easy for our friend; oh no, I say he got out of sight, but what I meant to say is that he tucked and rolled with the whole dismount into the covering of the beaten path, that's our Aly!"

A low chuckle releases the tension from the others. Ace, with his heart in his throat, continues on with his visual antics, "Both eagles are now together as they are circulating around from the northwest, not quite directly over our heads. Jacob has picked up objects. No, he is getting them out of his pouch along his side and loading up his sling, just waiting, oh, just you wait, a direct hit that has stunned the first from pursuing and has drifted out of view while the other is approaching to see Jacob quickly loaded and ready to strike when the eagle back peddles in flight veering to the western skies and is heading north trying to catch up to his comrade. The eagle has landed!"

"Oh, through the excitement, I forgot about Aly; he is farther down the road and almost out of sight. He's swaying to the left and right, acting a little confused in matters. He keeps looking toward the tree line, hesitating to move forward, then taking a few steps back to repeat the procedure, making it look like he is doing the *cha-cha-cha* dance moves with his body and legs wobbling down. He's safe for now but out of the sight of Jacob's sight, but I believe not his voice because he started to head back in the direction of Jacob; they are only separated by the bend in the road and hollows, but if Aly proceeds forward about 25 yards or so he should be in Jacob's vision. Darn, he stopped, has turned back around, and now is sprinting away from Jacob and to my sight, nowhere near to the calling of David. He is out there alone, guys; our departure time is near, men, but we know that the Lord will not leave him or forsake him in this time of separation from the herd! He is out of sight now, like into a light falling fog cover of the morning dew. Jacob is approaching our direction just as a storm is forming in the foreshadowing direction of a sheepish sheep named Aly! So is the closing of this commentary, boys; we must hurry back homeland and take responsibility for all of our shortcomings and the consequences brought forward by them of this day. Let's go, Godspeed. Jacob is heading home to Jesse with one less sheep and recovery of one lost, dancing in the alleyways of his troubled mind!"

Jacob's Entrance

With a storm up into the distance horizon line, rational thoughts in strategic decisions race through the mind of Jacob, our very concerned unwavering shepherd, jogging over the plateau land, cuts in by the deep upper slopes that keep the homeland hidden when entering by this way. Just at the hilltop, he spots Jesse throwing out grain to the chicks, hens, and roosters, settled down quite a bit since that last time around. As he stands at the highest elevation, he hollers for Jesse and quickens his pace again.

"Jesse, come forth. I need you to tend to the sheep that is just a stone's throw away from me. I must go and recover Aly again!"

Now standing next to Jesse, he tells him briefly about the mishap. "Two eagles disturbed the flock, startling them; most of them gathered and circled the ewes for safety. I was able to ward them off with my sling and staff. Aly started heading east, and I lost sight of him over the slopes; I called for him and headed down a path of emptiness. The good thing is he shouldn't have gone too far. I've come back for the boys and a mount; that's if the boys have returned from who knows where. And Betsy will do; she is quick at the feet when she senses my distress!"

Jesse replies, "Yes, they're back, and it is best that they get outta sight as well now. Go, I've got the sheep!"

"Good," says Jacob, and he enters the gateway of tranquility, settling in a sudden prayer of guidance in a silent calling while calling out loud for the boys.

Now, the boys are three rambunctious Border Collies, but they are faithful in the call and respond quickly in the decisive way of a sheepdog, working strategically as a tri-team with loyalty to the end, at harm's way! At once, the boys gather by Jacob's side and are very anxious to get started, with all three circling around Jacob, going back and forth toward the exiting door.

"I know you boys must be feeding off my hardship, so let me gather Betsy's reins and bit, then we will be out of here soon. Now, come on, I have to watch you three closely. I think you understand; now, outside with it!" In much grief, the boys are emotional, but more so when they get a glance of Betsy being led out of the gates of the stalls with an enormous, not-so-friendly smile.

She walks past the boys and asks, "So, which one of you renovated the den area this morning? I would have loved directing you to the new arrangement of furniture in a modern-day fashion, not the prehistoric cave look, definitely not my choice, and Jesse didn't seem to take it so lightly!" she says, as she lets out a long smirky neigh! Yes, Betsy's another story; although she is the quickest and is at ease in stressful matters, she is spoiled, as in rotten, and lets the boys know that she is the prize in this homeland. She pounces around with her head in the clouds, full of her own thoughts, but she, too, is loyal and very much loved by all who glance at her bronze-toned markings and jet-black mane. Jacob has come prepared with a few items: a quiver of arrows, a bow strapped around his shoulders, and a sheath with a hunter's blade attached to his belt. Grabbing onto her mane and the pommel on the saddle, Jacob hoists up onto Betsy grabbing the reins to control a horse that doesn't want to be controlled but gently, which Jacob already has understood by experience in her and his younger days.

Hastening call at a competitive pace keeps the boys on the move as Jacob has set a stride not to exhaust anyone of our four amigos' stamina. Jacob's heart is racing the same to keep up with his high adrenaline rush of anxiety, care, and attention to a lost sheep. Looking ahead into the intense colors of the forest wall and nature's canvas pastel colors in the foreground and tertiary colors with a pitch-black background from an approaching storm that has energetic lighting strikes to ignite the senses to the beauty in a chaotic situation at hand. Does misfortune await, going through the hollow and around the bend where mishap and the vanishing of Aly's last sighting had taken place? Or is mayhem coming around the blindside appearance of the natural curving into annihilating destruction of lost hope in the heart at these heartlands? Lost time is hard to set the right course to reassure the mind that it is well, and it is just a matter of time before Aly appears in the sight of Jacob's calling.

Then, finally, at a greater distance than Jacob could hope for, he pulls on Betsy's reins to come to a complete halt so that his vision can focus on two small images in front of an aurora, a lighted entrance into the treelined haven that awaits Aly and Ebb?! And out of the mouth of Jacob comes a gasp of delight and amazement, asking to himself, "Did Ebb find Aly? But where is David? Maybe they're resting because Aly can't keep up or something; definitely, an explanation so much needed!" And just as quickly as that, the light encloses around them and vanishes into the grasping great, ancient sycamore tree, surrounded by the oaks of a customary place of rest for weary travelers! And now a sheepish sheep named Aly and his acquainted friend, Ebb, that stubborn ole' mule! God help us!

Meeting Mark and Lotus Bloom, Leaving Their Marks in Life
(29)

"Whirling dust and rustling feathers in flight with cargo intact surround a solo pilot, who is being escorted by six inexperienced companions, more qualified in imperfections than mission flights, as Sheldon watches them take flight until they no longer can be seen. No need to look for a second glance for I, Sheldon, being bonded in faith and free as in the carefree of a blessing, am pouring out my soul to complete the task of "Project Bathing in Water," in jargon called P.B. & J. for the search and recovery of one flint, stone, a weapon of destruction, and have placed into the hands of the transporter, Gretchen, and friends, who are now in flight with a storm approaching in from the east and heading northwest moving slowly. God's anointing sound of thunder and lightning is lighted by glory's way to the coming of a new king. Could it be a great disturbance of havoc into a most peculiar foreseen milestone by faith's calling? This whirlwind set performances into motion. Is destiny the predetermined outcome of an enemy approaching or the blessing of predestination to another? God's whispering Spirit to one officer, Sheldon, a soldier of steadfast faith! God so help them to steadfast ways, when in the opposition of the predators' ravaging attempts, to hold off opposition in flight. Surrounding the militants, transporters into the realms of heaven. Security in a stronghold of faith and into a consuming fire by deliverance completion into an open field of circumstances success. The Lord's hands be upon them. And Your will be done in the outcome of Your divine blessings upon mankind. I am oh so grateful to serve a loving God, and for the record, I will do it all over again for the glory of our God's calling!"

"New coordinates for Officer Sheldon, heading into a western direction, outside the perimeter at the landmarking campsite located north by the forest line of the day's outpost positioning. Search is in progress for the advancement of the messenger, Penny, who will be instructed by me personally in a military tutorial course on covering your tracks when in the enemy's territory discreetly! The subject's approximate maximum speed, due to the separation in tracks, was recorded at twenty-five mph in a sporadic rhythm of paw print placement on a slightly sandy surface. Apprehending more ground than I can possibly obtain in a day's journey by land or even by naval assistance that would be lacking the ability to fully observe the land dwellers' progress. Proceed on, soldier!

"When marching in an open field, there are many situations and circumstances to be concerned of. Let's review some of these tactics of warfare. Blindside attacks, when moving into an unfamiliar landmark such as these. Into the characteristics to safety measures, low-lying, ease up on quick decisions, eyes on alert, three points of contact for balance, and especially be observant at peculiar circumstances and practice slow breathing patterns by praying and meditation. Guerilla warfare on those hiding in a field of high grass blades advances in the field in a scouting operational mode. Sights of broken or snapped twigs and trampled leaves. Look for directional change in tall grass areas and a heavily wooded area for settings of ambush from an unknown source. That could lead to a tempest setting of a greater magnitude. Precautionary avoidance maneuvers are always necessary. Personal traits to avoid: never have overconfidence, do not assume, no such thing as being paranoid, avoid arrogant attitudes and out of them all, especially complacency, and always watch your back.

"Shush, only talk in low tones and only when necessary; over there, a sighting of an unidentified object in an invasive territory while in wildwood growth. Soldier, look at the three o'clock position. There's no movement, with shallow breathing, the object in sight. Sighting near a decaying tree limb in a thick patch of tall, bladed grass. Watch a camouflage specialist mimicking leaves swaying in the breeze; very crafty and effective, trying oh, so carefully to blend with the tones of the earth or surroundings. Reference report of classification: Insecta, the infamous walking stick, known as the devil's needlework due to the structure of the body. Suspended in time in close observation, aware of an enemy in striking distance in the hidden, mimic tactics oh, so very effective, but not today. An approaching arch enemy, the lifestyle of ambush specialist in guerrilla warfare. Reference report of classification: Insecta, the praying mantis. Watch moving slightly, slinking into position, keeping the body perfectly still, while moving the triangular head, rotating side to side, staying in focus, and then yep, striking the victim, the walking stick, no more! So much is the life of the food chain. Did I say there is no such thing as being paranoid? Just saying! Shake it off, soldier, there are far greater things to fear, live on and live another day of blessings, for each breath is a blessing in this moment's time.

"Now, when going into surface change, look for any chance of hidden land mines; the disturbed soil may be an indication of some kind of tampering. Stay focused for this time about intervals of three feet spacing, specializing in high-tracking paths such as these. Stop, soldier, up ahead, to the slight right, analytics data in progress of unclassified material. First observation, usually by sight, the grassy area to the side of the road is clumped and flattened, as if trampled. Second observation: the heavy tracked area, both seem freshly applied. Third observation, sometimes the portrayer has an undistinctive smell of their origin, no offense; everyone gets hot and sweaty, also along with other body functions I wish not to mention. This unclassified material has a very pronounced and pungent odor, analog to the smells of broccoli or sauerkraut. When approaching an unclassified material take small steps and be precautious by all means. Now, soldiers, in close vicinity, for closer observation, record in a journal for future reference, try to be as accurate as possible. Textural composition, slimy and heavy mucous, brownish-green tones. Under all tactics of scientific observations, I have attained a finalization conclusion. Reference confirmed: Mammalia, Bos Taurus. Common name, cow or cattle, meaning more than one, and definitely so. The matter or substance after diagnostical evaluation is a cow's daily constitution. Also known more commonly in slang as a cow patty, which is how the frisbee was invented. And more than one. Yep, and quite a steaming pile of an air freshener, pew!"

"Now that the material is identified, don't move; stay still for any chances of any trick wires. Leading into unseen places, none that can be seen, precautious, move closer, now observe in detail, without touching matter, no disturbance. Soldier, did you notice that the cow patty has already been disturbed from the center point and tracking, with a deep channeling down the middle, like the facial wrinkles embedded in the skin over a lifetime of travel, from a heavy object in motion proceeding onward, freshly tracking marks of some existing purpose calling? Proceed onward, soldier, into an open terrain where Penny's tracks are slightly visible but disturbed by the mighty hoof prints of cattle, cattle into the distance sun rays light. Small indentions move side to side of the deep channels from a struggling critter, apparently on the move at a very slow pace but nowhere in sight.

"Instincts and experience are two key factors when in search for an anonymous species obviously moving at an alarming slow rate and out of their natural habitat, for something this small in tracks normally would not be traveling into the great wide open especially since the mobility of this individual is at a snail's pace; hmmm, no, snails don't have impressionable marks as these. And for what purpose? Should I be putting my searching heart into a species at first unseen impression with little or no dignity in personal hygiene? But one must give a slight token of respect. In putting so much dedication in producing movement of such an awkward and cumbersome commodity. Life's not always fair, who am I to paint a portrait of such negativity in someone I haven't thus far encountered face to face? And cowardly, not to say it to them but behind their backs, so meanspirited. Such are not my intentions, for I have a gut feeling looking more into this and out into the window of wisdom. This is just a small piece of the puzzle by a larger scale of possibilities, for nothing is impossible with God!

"At first glance, the only object of direct confrontations of this lodestar is a rock showing the way, a particular situation in navigational skills, 'dead reckoning'; from this point forward, all tracks have dissipated, even Penny's. Maybe she did a better job in covering her tracks than I have given her credit for. Anyway, the only facts known now are that she's heading north at a dead crawl speed in the mid-morning sun, and navigational tracks are currently absent. Well, not totally true; there are still several, small indentions around the spherical object of placement. In turning my head toward the brook, I am thinking about changing my course of action and dog paddle the brook in a tugboat fashion; it will be faster, and this part of the brook runs parallel to the peaceful water's flow. One last look at what is the last evidence of my tracking skills. Then I notice, on the stone, two spiky legs slowly appearing while a tiny female voice says, 'Go check it out, honey, is he gone yet?'"

"Give me time, sweetie, it's not so easy pulling myself on top of this thing to take my stand to defend our honor and God-given object to cater to, okay?"

"Oh, I'm sorry, that wasn't meant to sound like that; I'm not upset, just a little jittery at the moment."

That was definitely a male voice, and it now has sprung up on top of the sphere in a defense standoff. "Hey, you! Are you going to try and take this stone from us? Well, think again, mister, I'll fight you until the bitter end. Do you see my spiky tusks and horns, well reach for them, and I'll gouge you with them. How's that, sweetie? Did I sound threatening?"

"Oh, honey, I like it when you're so aggressive. Did he leave yet?"

"Uh, no, now what?"

"Try talking reasoning to him, honey; that may work."

"Good suggestion. Excuse me, sir, were you talking to yourself earlier? Because it sounds as if you were talking with another very silent partner, which is okay, to be shy, just enjoying the company of others. You were very boisterous if you were trying to sneak up on us and gain ground and quite hilarious in your tactical teachings, and look who just got blindsided; not me, I heard you coming from miles away, well at least in my perspective of things! I said, reasoning not insulting, silly," she says.

"Oh, sorry, sweetie, didn't mean to come over that way."

"Apologize to the person, so you don't have to make me a widow, honey."

Okay, here goes a voice of reasoning.

"But at ease, good soldier, sad to say I am defenseless in other than what the good Lord has given me to defend my sweetie at all costs but not at the large magnitude of your acquaintance made known. We are tuckered out and just resting and then shall continue our way. God will not give us more than we can handle, and His strength is sufficient for us. Just let us live, and I promise God will bless you for your participation in God's great plan of redemption of spirit. He shall complete what God has started in us. Carry on, good soldier, carry on."

"Okay, sweetie, I have done all that I can. Come on out, we must be going. God shall provide for our safety and this stone burden we must carry."

"I am so proud of you, honey, and if we go, we shall go together serving the Lord, honey!"

"Awwwww, come on guys, you're going to make me cry. It's

THE MEADOWLANDS

not like that at all. I'm on your side, doing all things for the glory of God Almighty, the servanthood of a soldier. Called into doodie, sorry, I meant duty, the call of duty."

Both think that is hilarious and has become the ice breaker, talking the language of love for two dung beetles, classified as insects, commonly known as rainbow scarabs, or dung beetles.

"My name is Officer Sheldon. Oops, sorry, I am amongst friends; you can call me Sheldon, and I have already participated in servicing a transporter of a stone this day. Not to sound critical, just testing the spirit, are you sure God called you to move this stone?"

"Yes, He did, and we are aware of the seven grackles that are in travels, just about, oh, say, twenty minutes or so ago transporting a stone for the Lord's use," the couple proudly announces in unison. "Please let us introduce ourselves. We are the Blooms, Mark and Lotus. God has whispered to us on many nights leading into today and then some. God has placed us in a situation of knowing our strengths and weaknesses, but it wasn't until us doing our daily routine that He made known His plan for our lives in this particular stone, He just told us that He would provide and for us to be diligent with joy, so here we are at this setting of time."

"Officer Sheldon at your service, and I'm finding it a joy to make your acquaintance. How may I be of some service? I believe that God hasn't called on you to handle this burden alone. I can help you carry this stone of service and even allow transportation in doing so; my shell is wide enough for the three of you, and you two will only have to keep the stone from shifting. Let us find a docking area so that it will be easier to make placement without such a steep incline; that is of course, if you will accept my blessing to you."

"Oh, yes, that would be so awesome, and thank you, may God bless you, Sheldon, on this mission!"

The three of them begin to scout an area and notice over to the right a shallow slanting slope to where Sheldon can pull up to allow them to roll the stone onto his back, and there you go. Just as quickly as that, the three of them continue down the same beaten path that his other friend Penny has pondered on as well as others in the multitudes, and when they approach where the road and brooks start to curve around the bend out of sight of the great beyond, they joyfully chat and continue in the day's offering.

But speaking of multitudes, Sheldon begins to hear tones of a whole lot of murmuring. Like thousands upon thousands of honeybees breezing around the beauty of life. And where the scenery comes back into view and more pronounced to what lies ahead has now made its presence known of landmarks, leading to a bridge crossing over the brook. A familiar voice, a face to go with the sound, has made itself known, lost in a sea of sea sand along the seashore of a magnitude of spiders on one side and fire ants opposing them on the other side. Enough to take away your breath and head off in the other direction. But a whisper tells us to move forward, so we do so ever so, precautious, approaching my friend who is too busy in command to notice my appearance.

"Officer Sheldon, Mark, and Lotus reporting for duty, General Albert!" he says, turning around with a big grin on his face and joy in a multi-eye of reflections. "Reflections of myself looking at myself in his eyes. Wow, kinda creepy. I wouldn't want to be on the lower part of the food chain right about now, just saying!"

"Oh, and say you did, my friend Sheldon, and hopefully, by past time before the storm kicks in, we will have a settlement here!"

"What's all the commotion about; there is a lot gathered here just to settle in words. Looks more like taking action to me, sir!"

"Right again, Sheldon, my friend, we are prepared to enforce our words if action needs to be taken! The commotion is that the ant colonies have set up an embargo limiting our travels to much-needed provisions for our families. We have tried to settle things in the past without any settlements, and today, they threaten some of our adolescent family, so we are now a band of brothers. What brings the three of you here? They will not let anyone pass; that is, anyone that they can bully around."

"I am giving this couple escorting and security of another priceless stone. Go figure, how am I so fortunate to be blessed in servanthood once again, little ole Officer Sheldon," he says, grinning at General Albert. "I am honored to offer any service that I can, but it is about to get really ugly here, and it's time to bring out my whippin' stick of justice!" he says, showing it already in hand. And just as the scene darkens here, so does the quick-moving storm of whirlwinds blowing, with the smell of rain in the air ready to disperse!

Destin's Calling
(30)

In a frantic frenzy, the storm has increased in magnitude, with branches and leaves being wind-blown into the face of our ladies of faith, making visibility hard for them and one another in flight as well, keeping out of sight but in pursuance and in junctions flight, course to the others. Just slightly below the bellies of our magnificent seven and in striking distance, Destin, our red-tailed hawk, has his sighting by the one in the middle of the pack in a tight, secure flight pattern. Gretchen says words of encouragement, vocalizing the commands at the lead.

Nicole says to her, "Veer as close to the treetops as possible, for it is going to be impossible to weave through this mess; stay tight and secure, women, we can do this."

In the background, you can hear Delora cry out in a panicked voice, "Are we going to die?"

An evil voice says out loud, louder than Destin had planned, "Oh, at least one, and probably more than one, will surely die this day!"

It got real silent in the storm for some odd reason, but reason enough, for the sensitive ears of Delora, our eyes and ears in a matter such as the one in occurrence as we speak, and speaking out loud, Delora says, "I heard a male voice nearby, I mean real close so that his presence is being known now, below us, I heard him, I heard him; does anyone hear me? Lord, help us, please!"

Destin mutters to himself, "Go ahead and cry out to your God. See what I told you? Only in their distress do they call on a so-called living God; go ahead, ladies, cry out all you want. He doesn't listen to your cries, you pitiful little sight to see!"

Gretchen, with a realistic concern about Delora's logistics, "I hear you, Delora; we have to react quickly, ladies. The three-tight triangle section with Bellamy becoming the rear guard in our flight will veer down into the branches; it has quieted down enough to do so, the back three. Delora, you dead drop and collide on top of him; you have the ability of the surprise attack and will not expect it, but you only have one shot. Time it just right. You can do it, Delora. Harriott and Aletta, veer left, both of you, and knock him off course to buy some time. Nicole, Amber, Bellamy, and I will continue in a straight western over the tree line, the quickest route, until either you three or our predator makes himself known again; we will meet somewhere along the line, so on the count of three girl's breakoff at God speed! Okay, one, two, three… go!"

And the winds began to howl, with the lighting striking, illuminating the skies showing the silhouettes of all the flying fowls, and the pouring rainfall on the good and evil, as the thunderclaps quicken to startle and make our enemy that is in high pursuit hesitate, and oh, so close, too close for comfort. All in the presence of an angry God. You don't mess with God's anointed!

It's a deadfall's call as Delora takes her last breath and is at peace with herself in the last remembrance of her blessed life, as a visual of past memoirs flashes through the still-life mind by a servant's heartfelt message, straight into the predator's face, a surprise awakening at the least, followed by the pursuit attack from the left by Harriott and Aletta with eyes closed and tearing in the rains downpouring of the soul. Vanishing temporarily, Destin is out of the sight of the girls and spiraling out of control but makes a last correctional in-flight recovery. Shaken but okay, at least to say of one at the fowls, for Destin has gotten a taste of blood. Harriott and Aletta have rerouted with only ruffled feathers, while Aletta asks Harriot, "I don't think we have taken out the hawk, but we at least know who our enemy is now. But what about Delora? Did you see her hit the hawk dead on his face? That didn't look good to me; let's just pray that she is okay."

Yes, the mind is an incredible thinking machine. Let's go into the predator mind of Destin. "Recover quickly, yes indeed, Destin, blinded not only by the hard rainfall but the anger cruising my mind with the thought of revenge on all of them, no mercy required! Inward thoughts of hate controlling every aspect of my flight now. I fly so much better out of frustration, quickly to make up lagged time and to repursue them one at a time, so be it. Up ahead in the cover of the limbs, the two who blindsided me; now I'm tucking my wings into the side, diving down from this upward heavenly view to pursue the two ladies again, weaving as they weave with no other intention as I am one with the surroundings! Revenge shall be all mine! Oh, so close, can't you feel my breath? I am so close to devouring you; I have had the taste of blood. Ask your other friend. Aw, don't worry about her. Some other scavenger will eat the remains, dead or alive; it doesn't matter as long as the blood is warm because it tastes so sweet! Weep for your friend for she is no more. Watch over your other friends as I devour them in front of your tearing eyes! Arise, for your destiny will be my delight! And it will be painful, yes, very painful, while your attention is on me as I ravage your flesh, feeding it to my young, which will become God's will being done, oh and He can watch too, makes no difference at all!"

Tree limbs sway when the ladies sway; just enough time for Destin to clear. A branch falls, letting all three free from the darkness of uncertainty. Risks are getting closer to a disastrous conclusion to someone or to all, it is in the Lord's hands. Destin's fall will happen and at his own expense in the decisions that must be made daily. Free-willed choice for all; the proud can change their course, some do, but most just continue a flight of disastrous callings. The wicked rest shall be in the Lord's anger. Another warning for repentance calls from a cold stone heart, overlooked as a lightning flash strikes a nearby tree, splits the tree in two, and the thunder crashes, setting our one in flight off balance, swaying to the fear that has suddenly entered into the depths of his soul, not because of nature's call. The Lord is not the thunder or lightning, but the judgment call of a day in reckoning is the fear each one will face without the peace of God deeply embedded in their eternal soul. That is the fear that has now given birth to our red-tailed hawk named Destin! The lightning strikes twice, causing an eternal flame to ignite mental suffering; pain, but it is not mentally inclined, for reality has come, between the separation of the tree of two destinations by choice, torment, and peace. Destin and Delora's calling.

ARISE LAZARUS

A plan of ingenious behavior or a miracle needs to happen now, and suddenly, it does. Out of inspiration, with no spoken words required, Harriott veers right off the lightning strike. Out of intuition in truth's reasoning, Aletta veers left at the sound of thunder and, through fear and frustration's call, blinds the decision of our hawk friend, as the oak tree, in all of its massive and ancient age, splits in two. The predestined flight between two widening wedges of the trunk suddenly shifts course. Out of nowhere comes Delora, with her angels in flight watching over her, who has been pursuing—whether as tracker or hunter, you decide. She quickens her pace, bouncing off the head of justice served, veering sharply right at lightning speed. It's her second close call today, but this time, Destin isn't so lucky. He swerves just enough to avoid the fallen oak, only to find himself in the middle of an angry squirrel's home. Now stuck and at the mercy of his favorite meal—a red-tailed squirrel—he's seeing red, and it's best to leave it at that. Once again, the storm has quieted down for Delora, who is at peace, for all is well with her soul; rest becomes the heart of Delora, no longer beating nor her lungs filled with air, now replaced by serenity, and she has reached her eternal home.

Harriot and Aletta, after some incredible navigational maneuvers, are now gathered as one in flight, hidden in the tangled tree limbs, a magnificent maze. *Are we alone? Or are we still being pursued? What about Delora?* The thoughts race through the two minds in a synchronized outcome of fear, letting it get the best of them. They are constantly looking over their shoulder as tree limbs ricochet against their bodies because of close flight. They look at each other, with no words spoken, just a saddened spirit arising in their hearts for the uncertainty but the likeliness of a soldier down is an inevitable outcome of Delora's destination at hand. Neurotic disorders captivate and intervene with unnerving principles of a mindful life as the two pursue soundness and stability, wondering where the location of their enemy within has materialized into reality, but where? And to what dispute?

THE BRIDGE BY THE BROOK

Now the dispute that is holding ground near the brook is a winding road with the placement of a natural stone-made bridge that crosses over the brook and runs parallel to the right angle but then continues perpendicular and out of sight into the heavy marshland area. The only field without trees or brushes. The marshland algae have invaded the area with a spongy peat moss overgrowth and are oversaturated with moisture along the open road. Over a period of time, this has allowed it to slither its way toward and consume the bridge. This is the area that is sought because of the nutrient-holding capabilities that the peat moss can provide in obtaining moisture to plant life for an eco-friendly environment and for the growth of natural healing herbs in the area. The affray has been the center focus of the two combative parties for over six cycles of time and now is in its third generation of feuding and colliding into a conclusive ending in this present time. In terms of the cycle of a bug.

General Albert approaches Sheldon and steps up on him, onto his hard shell that is being used as a make-shift platform for convenience's sake, and opens with a personal greeting to his guest, praying that it could be better circumstances, then goes right into wartime protocol, and gives a speech of encouragement.

"Men, my men of many rights, standing up for moral values, serve with all integrity in servanthood to the Lord our God. In providing for our families, loved ones, and all in all, our communities, for the commonwealth to every man and woman, and to all who take in the breath of life. The freedom of entrepreneurs is being threatened by limiting supplies, and they are now under the regulations of another force, setting unmanageable restrictions. Not allowing travelers by our kind to cross the bridge by the brook— this must come to an end, this day! We do not fight over material world items, but who is to hinder the calling of our God? For it is not flesh and blood we rage war for, but for the purpose of each one's calling, must not be hindered. Our guest is set forth on a conquest realm and is to deliver this christened stone of dedication, to place judgment on the one who mocks our living God, not by the laws of men but by the living word. Do not treat the confrontation in the eastern valley battle as a rumor of a man who causes fear to all those in his presence, dishonoring the army of our God. Our confrontation must come to pass and shall; to advance, we must conclude this dispute of the bridge by the brook. So doing this, in victory's calling, allows the passage to the western terrain and for this quest to carry on. This determines the Battle in the Valley's outcome in guiding this stone to one man who is in search of the heart of God. So, my question to all is, are you in search of the heart of God? Every man must answer that question for himself. It is a free gift to all and will determine your attitudes and set its course through the passages of your mind, leading to your soul. We all need to be driven by a purpose! Men, watch over your neighbors, become your brother's keeper, bear arms, and reign on in battle! There is a storm on the rise into the horizon of the eastern atmosphere; lightning will strike, thunder will clap, and the redemption of rain will fall this day! Fear not, my men, for today is the day of our Lord, and He shall guide us in this battle's rage! Men, take a knee and let us pray that the Lord will shine His grace upon us! We shall gather in thirty! Make peace with your neighbor and God."

— Chapter Four —
THE FLIGHT OF THE BUMBLEBEE

The bubbly, joyful hum of a bumblebee, with no alternative but to stay busy as a bee, impelled and content, buzzing along so freely. Drawn by the fate of a blossoming flower, it is inspired and motivated, intertwining with the honorable men of faith, listening in to a humbled presence...

This day has come,
Past the visible horizon and into the vision.
To unite the stillness
of men in prayer.
Their hearts begin to harmonize,
into an object of one's affections
and the taste of sweet surrender,
to carry the weight,
life force set free.
As a heart burns with passion,
built strong in the promises of His Word,

THE MEADOWLANDS

expressed in strong approval, Amen.
The Psalm song of hope takes flight!
And onto the battlefield!

General Abbot approaches Sheldon shortly after prayer, saying, "This could get ugly, kid; there are rough seas ahead. My men will escort you through this turbulence in a surrounding formation, with stronger forces up front in a wedge that will keep the enemy away from your perimeter. With all that being said, you will need to excuse your guests; this is no place for a couple, with all due respect. The Lord is not done with you two yet, but for now, you are dismissed, good soldiers of faith!" The General salutes them. "We will have you two escorted out into a safer environment."

Sheldon approaches the Blooms, thanking them for their grateful company and saying it has been an honor for him to carry this burden for the sake of the kingdom of God. Our company climbs on a hammock of webbing and are swept off their feet by the prancing and juking of the ever so quickly jumping spiders, to the safety of the road heading east, to where the Blooms regain their foothold, as they waddle away to find and search out where the fragrance of their delicacy awaits them in the backwoods of nature's calling.

"Now for you, Sheldon, we are going to intertwine the stone tightly, with webbing, to your torso so that my men will be able to see your backside without any hindrance in movement. All right then, let's gather up the men in double V-formation with flanks to the right and left, double standard, and stronghold on the back side. I'll be in the heart of the matter with Sheldon. Send out the squadrons before in five divisions of faith's calling, double time followed by the escorting formation. Be prepared to follow up with squadrons proceeding around us once we penetrate their line! Okay, men, we have a battle to win; may the heart of God follow you into this battle and the peace that passes all understanding! With no fear, men! Arise! Let's go!"

As the troops move in a forward formation, so does the eastern sky, for the rain is quickly approaching and not a gentle pitter-patter but a gutter-washing, downright visibility-reducing kind of storm.

"The general and Sheldon, we are devoured into the mouth of a raging beast of jumping spiders casting numbers, moving ever so slowly, marching on, getting closer to the assault of the fiery red ants' hostile environment. As the ants' antennas start to twitch frantically, keeping up in pace with their movement, the red ants engage in a language of their own and break into formations of ginormous numbers, like acrobats on a gymnasium floor. Countering the approaching jumping spiders, letting them advance with no struggle, just letting them enter, as if by invitation. *Hip hop, bippity boop*, as the ants start crawling all over the place, weaving in and out, up and down, over each other without the "excuse me," just being rude and liking it! Interlocking, fastening, coupling, and interlacing, yes, all these procedures, leading to the formation of moveable bridges, trying to hurl over the jumping spiders' front wedge."

"Sorry to interrupt you, Officer Sheldon; you do realize you're talking out loud? I am seeing the same tactical maneuvers as you are!" A slightly irritated General speaks forth a command to the front line, "Use your webbing to form a blockade, quickly!"

"No offense, General Albert, I'm just speaking out loud so that the records will stand clear for historical documentation of this battle call, sir!"

"Oh, okay, well, then, carry on, Officer Sheldon. Call in the backup squadrons to march double time around wedge and advance toward the front to incircle the penetrating red ants!" a concerned General says frantically.

The webbing of the spiders has slowed down the first wave of attack as the ants swim trapped in their own movements. The second wave of agitated ants counters and starts to build onto their struggling mates to increase the size of the ladder, toppling over the webbing, helping it to give them support as a multitude of ants breach the wall! "The wall is breached, men; second squadron follow in from behind and enclose the wall to fight in hand-to-hand combat to regain stability!" The cup runs over as it is a mangled mess of fury's edge, venom a biting and stingers stinging, standing in a stalemate of erupted movement like two sumo wrestlers in a deadlock of massive weight! "Fall back, men, and regroup, bring up both flanks and circle around the fray in a single melee round in our favor! Bring up the back squadrons five deep, allowing Sheldon and I to collapse into your embracing plunge to the front line in a struggling push! Two steps forward, several steps back, until the lines relax and start to backpedal when the attacking troops stop inward penetration!"

They gain ground only for it to be stolen back by the enemy, who have also taken time to see the casualties of twisted deceased bodies banded and clustered in a heap of neutral territory.

"Rest, men, and take a knee; this is harder than I anticipated. We need to pray once again, magnifying our Lord in His battle, not ours. We are just His instruments!"

(31)
Help us to cast down our pride and merit efforts,
that silently strangle our spirit's roar.
As the seasons change, so must the attitudes of our heart,
Let Your colors of life magnify Your glorious name.
To a new awakening, helping us from going under.
Nourish and plant a seed of future and hope.
Our enemy has become organized and has strengthened in numbers,
disarming all our defense.
We wait on You, Lord, to renew our strength.
Mount us on the wings of the mighty eagle! So be it! Amen!

Thirty minutes time, with the absence of guiding light and into the darkness of uncertainty, begins fate's calling, for this bumblebee calls men of flight to take up arms and join in this air strike with the pouring of arsenals rain. Into the flowers, fields, and along the brook, the bumble bee soars to address each destination with the battle cry of urgency. The burrowing yellow jackets and the fluttering hypnotic sound of the dragonflies hovering over the ponds. The solitude of the praying mantis, the smell of the leaf beetles. The humming of the hummingbirds' wings just flap in the breeze; they have a sweet and savory appetite and a sociable delight as the bumbling bumblebee always works without hesitation to call off the hindrance way between those at the bridge by the brook. To the healing herbs and the many wonders of the peat moss, providing for our families in the time of past droughts.

"Come, all, to the living waters as we gather at the brook. Our ground troops are many, with the jumping spiders in abundance, yet by odds' end, the red ants are favored by sheer sight alone, intimidating in their numbers. But most importantly, we stand at this critical point, serving the Lord and His army. For He has appointed a time to cross the crossroads, break the stronghold of obstruction, and lead us over the hindrance of faith."

"Who dares to stand in the way of God's anointed! Carrying the rock, the cornerstone of destiny's call!"

A black cloud from miles end has developed in the western skies, but not one that is filled with moisture or debris but with nature's calling. A swarming of feathers from all kinds of things with wings, singing their enchanted song.

> *Who is like our God, God almighty!*
> *Flying under the shelter of His wing.*
> *With our God almighty,*
> *in all His security, our hope, and dreams.*
> *Take flight and be excited in serving our God almighty!*
> *Hello to the King of Kings,*
> *Lord of Lords, our true ruling king.*

THE MEADOWLANDS

Do not place your trust in the numbers that you,
have set in your heart, count them taken out
one at a time.
Look around, where does our enemy stand now,
In the hands of our God, almighty!
Rage on in this battle cry,
In the hands of our God, almighty!

Following the brook paths' winding stream, its once flowing crystal-clear water is now murky due to the eastern disturbance in the water flow, removing all rocks and pebbles like purifying the dross from silver and gold. Eroding and crumbly the banks of security edge and carrying fear and doubt away like rubbish. A massive black wall of faint-heartedness overshadows the land. Our astronomical air pursuit takes flight, and now flying overhead in the lead is our loveable bumble bee in his flight of the bumblebee!

Our commander, General Albert, announces, "Well, looky here, our air strike force has arrived!" The jumping spiders gaze up at the approaching mass and are astounded by sounds such as these, similar to thousands upon thousands of locusts chirping away in the setting of dusk hidden in a forest of green, now departed from their forestry haven, to follow close behind our bumble bee for an intimidating fear factor in as much as our enemy in sight and hearing the terror in the skies.

A scent of fresh peppermint and lavender from the many fresh herbs that have grown along the beaten path is enhanced by the rising aroma of the incoming rain. Now, this too shall pass, and sunshine is just a smile away, but for now, it is a time of war, and the arrival of the new militants has boosted the morale of the many ground troops. General Albert summons one of the hummingbirds by the color of his flank.

"We will have time for acquaintance and social grace in a more forgiving atmosphere, so excuse myself beforehand on the names of each who have arrived. For now, the hummingbird with the metallic bronze flank, please come forward and let me climb onto your neck area so that I may address the new soldiers from an aerial perspective.

"Listen up, men, here are the divisions that will go out in this order, with jumping spiders as the pilots, three to each squadron.

"First Division: dragonflies with jumping spiders in cargo will hover over areas, flying as low as possible so that my men can execute web discharge amongst the ants, entrapping them. Doing intervals of three passings in groupings of twenty, the rest of the jumping spiders and dragonflies, other than Sheldon's eight squadrons, shall be on standby.

"Second Division: yellowjackets with jumping spiders in cargo, stationery for ground attacks, and quick escapes.

"Third Division: Hummingbirds hovering in flight technique of low aerial attacks for stationery assault.

"Fourth Division: dragonflies parachute jumping spiders in the multitude of ground warfare after yellow jackets thin out the area.

"Fifth Division: leaf beetles only, if necessary, the use of intimidating warfare of psychological effects in them. Abilities in chemical warfare.

"God is the God of second chances, and we can stand on the promises of His Word. Cutting through and severing bone to the morrow, exposing all our thoughts and intentions of the heart. We can cleanse the outer cup, washing away all impurities, but our souls can be filled with devious thoughts of defilement. The red ants have crossed the line in serving their own craving demands through the idols of their selfless offerings to an unknown god. With a fulfillment of a longstanding, deep-rooted lack of empathy toward others. Self-seeking confidence has embedded them with invincibility, false hope rising, and prideful attitudes, thinking of being unstoppable, grumbling, relentless, and bustling energy flow. Now they are distracted by the dispiriting sound of the soldiery locusts and the humongous combative cloud in flight."

Round Two

"Sheldon, you are now commander of our ground troops. I will be stationary by an aerial command on my new friend, Clytie, the sunflower-colored hummingbird. We will hover over the battlefield and holler out commands at appointed times. Okay, men, we have a battle to win! Arise! Send out the whirlybirds of the First Division, dragonflies, fluttering over the nearest of the reds and web-sling them really well until they are saturated in a motionless convoy!"

"This is Commander Sheldon reporting for duty; I will document all battle procedures from a ground's point of view of aerial attacks and positioning of ground troops on advancement in stages due to the progress made by the terror in the air. General Abbot is riding on the wings of beauty in motion, a hypnotic sound of flapping wings, staying stationary, then moving up and down periodically for a closer and better view, on a hummingbird called Clytie, our sunshine bringing light into the darkness. The whirlybirds come flying in a jerky motion, then stopping, allowing the spiders to drench the reds in ribbons of sticky threads, turning matters around for our good. Troops, listen up, we are advancing ground, and we must show no mercy to those who fight against us. Most of the reds will be entangled in webs; ignore their pleas and let them be unless they are able to break ground, then exert your energy upon them. But wait and go on my command; let's allow the three rounds of flight by our hovering friends on the front-line enemies.

The second wave of reds, avoiding their trapped comrades, start to use their bodies as bridges so the third wave can climb over them in a new pursuit attempt to gain their ground back, flooding the area once again.

"Not yet, men; let's not be anxious about hitting the ground running. General Abbot is summoning the Second Division. All right, let's bring in the yellowjackets in intervals of five units, who will start the first ground attack amongst the reds!" There must be fifty to eighty black and yellow jerseys that make up a single unit of yellow jackets, now with wings a-fanning in an angry defense motion. The jerseys have landed and are face to face with the reds that extended along the coast of the enemy, who are riding the waves on the boards of the securities and backs of the laid-out compadres of reds. Like the conflict of an offense line versus a defense line in the game of football, the two lines encounter what true pain is all about; with the exchanging of stinging and dismemberment of body parts, the two teams lock up, and the odds definitely have turned to our favor in advancement. The reds are starting to crash down really hard into their own waves of self-doubt! As the wasps continue their ground assault, they turn to their navigational skills back into the air and reposition themselves into the depths of the enemy's heartbeat flow that is pulsating rapidly, sending out cross messages amongst their antennas' communication line! The sweaters gather all bunched in the middle, clogging the artery of the reds, four chambers and the jerseys start to spread out to form a blood clot in each of the reds, hearts chambers!

"Clytie's chaotic movement is communicated to General Abbot to encourage him to disperse the navigational skills of the hummingbirds' aerial tactics, who had been anticipating this moment of flight."

"Okay, men, this is it, our final assault; the clouds above us are about to burst with moisture as the lightning strikes and thunderclaps are closer and louder, so let's move in quickly! Sheldon, start the ground attack moving in and allow whatever reds to retreat as you advance. I am sending in the Third Division of hummingbirds, with the wasps working inside out and hovering over areas that demand attention to keep your ground troops safe. Also, the Fourth Division will be brought in by the squadron of dragonflies to parachute in troops of jumping spiders. The Fifth Division will march in slowly with ground troops covering them for ambush attacks against them, although it's highly unlikely because of the leaf beetles' abilities. Let's be thankful that they are our allies in this war!"

Sheldon is in command mode.

"That's our call, men; we are heading out in a slow trot to wait on the arrival of our hummers of the hummingbirds. They are now center-focused with the jerseys to thin out the perimeter and are going about it nicely! The choppers, our dragonfly buddies, have taken off with flies from the sky and will disperse the spiders-in-arms about a hundred yards or so, depending on current wind conditions! And there they are, floating down with webbing-made parachutes settling like dust amongst a whirlwind of dirt, cycling to and fro amongst the deadly assault of the ground commotion. We will split up into eight squadrons, four on four, front and rear, protecting our chemical warfare against the leaf beetles. Okay, you guys, no friendly fire from you walking elm tree leaves; you are an act of intimidation only. The remaining squadrons will advance in forward momentum with Commander Sheldon, that's me, for cleanup and join in with our friends from the sky. Now onward, Christian soldiers of faith, before all the skies break free into a blanket of drenching rain!

"The rain starts off on a slow pace of heavy dew droplets, a single drop at a time keeping with the steps of our rhythmic rising. The hummers in the swift sweeping of the battleground floors, pecking away the screaming reds at their last breaths taken, now continue to lessen the field's play, falling back and then starting the routine repeatedly! The parachuting-in spiders have tumbled and rolled into the battle scene and are now jigging and jagging, looking for the closest incoming red with fangs spread open wide, waiting for the first assault bite or kiss of death, many that will fall, all in the name of love? We are now in striking distance and the battle becomes a new prospective fighter's view of the scene in progress; as the cliché goes, it is so thick in here you could cut it with a knife! Many enemies and a band of spiders lay on the battle floor only to be replaced with a fifty-to-one living among the deceased ratio, an odd that I thought by now would have reduced, but here we are in the compact quarters. The eight squadrons behind us have separated from the group as all the squadrons are doing what needs to happen but at a slower pace than the speed of the falling rain as it picks up its pace as if setting a new pace of the battle within! Now, a downpour of buckets of rain quench the battlefield when I hear the cries of the General from above, saying, 'Call in for the standby squadrons; we are now in a rescue mission, red alert to all who fly, time to gather up all the troops by the transportation of you amongst us and our stringy web friends web flinging blankets of rescue chutes of as many as your air transporter can handle, now go! Sheldon, I am sending a tricycle of hummingbirds with spiders to collect you safely airborne, so be sure to hold on tight!'

"The Lord has sent the redemption cleansing rain by endearments calling for the recovery to our men, each man heading under the cover to the whirlybirds are the hummers of the sky, with the fierce flight by the jetting jackets of the wasps' calling frenzy. With the arms reaching to the upper skies pleading, 'Help me or take me with you!' the prideful red ants are now paying the consequences, two-fold in matters, one in lagging around in the first assault when they could have ended the battle's call and the second of overconfidence that they could handle their own affairs without the call of aerial assistance! All the living in the field of friends is escorted out into the shelter's safety of the woodlands as chaos has broken loose in a sheet-covering, gutter-washing down pouring rain, removing all the dross and washing it away into the brook, flooding out the marshlands and becoming one with the brook."

The Shoreline

"We wait until the settling elements quiet down to a gentle whispering wind that seems so surreal after all the chaotic sounds of soldiers in action and then the storm front that has moved through, annihilating all that surrounded us at one time or another. Hovering from the hummer support system that has me safely secured by the twine of our loveable jumping spiders, we have a birdlike view over the mass destruction of everything from trees uprooted to the lightning-cracked splitting of a grown oak over the decades now divided into two sections down two-thirds of the massive tree. To the more settling removal of the life's flow interaction by the red ant mounds located near the pathway near the brook. The peat moss has now become the transportation and permanent homes for the red ant soldiers, entangling them in a blanketed by weeping and gritting of teeth! Cleansing the land as a view enters my mind's clarity of landmarks that no longer exist because of nature's clearing! As the flooding waters kick in, a calmness has subsided the storms rage, and the peace of the passing all understanding takes over the calamity of the land! Brings tears to the eyes of those who lost their lives this day in a battle that belonged to the Lord; we are just His instruments of justice served!

"The importance is the lives saved and bringing this stone into heaven's heights as we wait for contact by the ground underneath our feet. Looking at miles end, witnessing the struggling ants entrapped in the enormous mounds to be gathered peat moss, becoming bait for the perch and trout feasting on the heart-wrenching reds' last breath of life to render their lungs' capacity. The brook is totally animated in this kind of life, having determined while watching a gathering of red ants playing leapfrog with the drawn-out tongue of the bullfrog. Anyway, back to the stone. This stone; why this stone? Is it because of the geological features or of the personalities who have either found them or transported them? One may guess that I am the answer to both of those questions put into operation; is it due to the fact of faithfulness and determination to do what God has sent each of us to do? Should you just walk away from this calling and forget about the one who has called upon you to do this great service? Aren't there easier ways to go about finding a stone than the lives lost? There is a purpose for all of God's placement in our lives, but are we patient enough to wait to see all the pieces of the puzzle coming simultaneously together in God's timing? Such great of a loss with what seems to be so little to gain from this stone in particular. And what is becoming of the other stone in flight, only God knows, until it is revealed to each of us involved? Are you willing to make the sacrifice? Now, don't get me wrong, not all of God's callings are dramatic, but these are questions we ponder on in crisis that we hold onto as ours to own alone when we are never meant to be alone."

Then silence is broken by the General saying, "Man, that is some deep subject matter to be said aloud. Sheldon, give your mind a rest, soldier, and fall into God's grace. We can only be faithful to what God has placed into each of our hearts and serve Him wholeheartedly, and that is how we keep our minds stable in times such as these, my good man! We are crossing the brook near the bridge and leaving this mess behind. The area on the northwestern side is not in flood waters, so we should be fine with setting ground yonder way."

Sheldon thinks to himself without speaking out loud and keeps his thoughts to himself. *Yonder way, a new destination to hope, sounds refreshing; when troubled waters' interference hinders us, there is always a blessing to come. Just overlook the circumstances, not in denial, but*

THE MEADOWLANDS

keeping our Lord God almighty as our center focus!

As my vision of hope starts to focus in on reality, my heart melts when noticing drifting in the brook near the bank between two broken tree limbs, nestled in a nest of peat moss, a feathered body lays to rest in the comforting arms of a loving God. And a gentle whisper, one that is known dearly to my heart, hears the hurt felt inside of a voice, presenting to my eyes the loss of one loved by Him dearly, saying, "Go, for I have called Delora to her eternal home. All you shall see is the shell of a warm, loving spirit that is now resting in My arms in peace and serenity's keep. Call upon her loved ones and give honor due to her name for the bravery and sacrifice to others in servanthood greatest sacrifice, love. For love never fails and endures all things, and it was embedded deep into Delora's heart. Sometimes the taunting of her insecurities immobilized her true intentions, but when what mattered most became involved, she conquered the fear that paralyzed her tranquility. The ladies are safe and still in flight, safely securing the stone. Harriot and Aletta have been separated from the pack but now are in flight to embrace the others and join as one. There will come a time for you to comfort them with all that is on your heart about Delora, for she is well admired by the ladies. Only Gretchen, Amber, and Nicole will continue with Penny, and the others will return to their homelands. Even her closest friend will have a change of heart from following Gretchen's lead and will go on to do far greater things than these. Now go and give Delora a proper burial of her body, for I have her soul."

"Gather around, men. We need to transfer this loved one a little way back east on this side of the brook where we witnessed the oak tree split by the lightning strike and ricochet into the earth, leaving a deep crevice in it. We'll clear out the debris in the area. General, can you have men prepare the hearse and casket for the travels? Slowly approach the nestled body in the nest that will become her casket; my melancholy eyes look upon the resting soul of Delora, and being humble, and at a personal level, I have only known from meeting Gretchen and the others, knowing that I could invest my trust upon them. Out of anticipation, in seeing the seven ladies at their finest hour and blessings, celebrating the stone being transported safely to its destination point, with the serving of the fermented wine of the vineyards and all the fresh fruit with the essence of fresh mint bruised to break fragrance now will apply to the mourning a dear friend to those she loved. Instead, the preparations of an obituary and burial for a friend, to the heart-wrenching of seven ladies, heartbreaking for all the 'what ifs' and 'if only' in a life that has passed. In all honors given, the primary blessings are the awarding of medals, not the saddening announcement of a casualty of an officer."

The men do a beautiful job with staining in a rich lavender tinting to their silk webbing. The sticky substance is to help give support to all the herbs and fresh flowers, that they have handpicked from the marshlands. The jumping spiders cascade down the sides of Delora's casket, intertwining in constant marching, each soldier holding onto a white lily that represents a comrade who had lost their life in battle. They are now being transported by dragonflies. Each one of the men has made mint bow ties and cummerbund around their waist made from the magnolia blossoms that had fallen. The bubbly bumble bee is leading the funeral cortege to where the memorial service will be held, with hundreds of locusts with a soft buzzing sound that is magnified by the masses. Clytie and the General are following in front of Delora, who has an open casket with her resting on her side, holding onto an olive branch and braided grapevines draped around her neck and weaving through both wings, nestled in a nest of fresh mint and lavender. A colorful apparel of the humming hummingbirds escorts along each side of the casket in a single file formation, while seven yellow jackets are flying overhead in a V-formation representing the seven women of faith, as one now breaks from the pack, veering right and has landed on the top of the casket mirroring the passing of Delora and the fallen soldiers.

"The split oak has now come into sight and sticks out like a sore thumb. The damage is immense and just amazing to look at; the bloodline of the sap looks like blood bursting from a vein, with the fragrance of sweet essences assembling in the air. The dragonflies are now hovering over the grave site, which is lined with wildflowers from the area and rose petals of a deep burgundy bud, almost of the color ebony, to offset the white lilies. The prickly thorns of the rosette stems line the base of the casket and represent the beauty and loss of a life. They gradually lower the casket, being guided into place by the militant ground squadron that was led into battle by Officer Sheldon, now assembled in prestige and dignified in all their handsomeness attire. The dignity of silence saturates the air as the hummingbirds settle and blend with the multi-colored wildflowers and now stand erect in ten-hut.

"The memorial service has attracted others of the forest to give honor and, out of respect, are bowing their heads. Some are talking in low tones to those who witnessed the incident that brought Delora to her resting destination. They are marveling at how teeny and tiny she is and that she could take down a hawk. One of the ladybugs looks my way, with a puzzled look on her face asking me, 'Who are you talking to, sir, and are you a soldier in this unit?'"

"Oh, sorry, ma'am, my apologies; with all due respect, these are conversations I'm documenting in annotations for the record of all events in history being made this day, and yes, Commander Sheldon at your service, ma'am, commander of the ground troops and part of this caravan, coordinating this service from the get-go. Oh, General Albert has dismounted Clytie and is approaching, walking pridefully like a man with great aspirations."

General Albert steps up on the shelled, slate platform and states, "At ease, men. There comes a time in everyone's life, such as these, to pay tribute to the passing of loved ones as we gather here to honor the men and Delora who have laid down their lives to serve others and to God, who has created all things and not of the works of men but by a compassionate God, to whom we give are all in all. Throughout our short life cycle, we have fought and provided many times for the advancement of our colonies, our colonies alone. But God's sovereign grace has blessed us with these opportunities provided to benefit mankind. We lost many fine armed forces this day, to a greater purpose, in the calling of our Lord, each of us sacrificing our lives on the firing line. But as soldiers, this is what we do; we fight because of the commonwealth our country provides with the freedom of choice to protect and uphold the common defense of humanity. A common stone anointed with great weight that can only be carried by those who are called while others are chosen to protect. Each of us has a purpose; may it be your hands, may it be your feet, or may it be your wings! Carried with hope at faith's door opened by many prayers and perseverance to follow from beginning to end, for what is the cost? It breaks my heart and drains my spirit to see fine men and women lose their lives on the battlefield of life. Praise God for people such as these, who are dedicated to serving. I thank you for a thankful heart, Lord, for the heart of Delora, a citizen of society and the placement of commitment…"

THE INTERRUPTION

"Aletta, we have made a commitment many years past that we would always be together in the thick of all tribulating circumstances, but here we are leaving one we love behind, and on top of that, not knowing what her wellbeing is, in this state of mind that we are in now. Come on, Aletta, we must snap out of this and get ourselves together again! We can return cautiously, and don't you think by now our pursuer would have already devoured one of us by now? Come on, think! We need to make it back to the landmark of the oak tree that split in two when lightning struck to recover our senses into proper perspective!"

"Okay, Harriot, no need for going down guilt-struck avenue, already, by golly and gee willikers! Look over there to your right, where the sounds of locusts are guiding us into the light. There is the live oak, straight ahead, I hear humming and light whispering of many, but no audible voices or anyone in sight."

The two more cautiously tiptoe and scuttle along the neighboring elm tree to gander onto the scene, cutting away one of the bothersome twigs that makes a faint crackling sound, gets the attention of our hard-shelled friend, who is now on alert mode but plays it off as late arrivals to the service. But he is always alert! The two grackles look on in disbelief as they have joined into the memorial service of someone that they recognize at a moment's glance back in times spent at the mulberry tree, an image of Delora's favorite place to be with the gals. Now resting in her eternal bed and being honored by a hoard of walking, flying, creeping, crawling things of nature. The audible voice of the General is now heard clearly, "…and there is no greater honor than laying down your life for others!"

"Oh, she is so beautiful, laying at ease, taking a nap with all that racket, and look at the corsage cuddled around her, just plain gorgeous!"

"Aletta, wake up. She has passed on!"

"No, this can't be, I won't let it! This isn't happening!" Aletta says. She swoops down as if she was in hot pursuit of a majestic butterfly in an unsettling flight pattern. Harriot follows her lead, and both are amongst the many gathered. "Please, Lord, you can't have her; she's my friend. Don't you understand? How are we going to be together at the mulberry bush and exchange our daily delights? You are an awesome God who is more than capable of breathing life back into her soul! I beg of You; let me feel the living breath crinkle my feathers. I know we are like the grass that withers away and is no more. My heart is broken into many pieces, Lord. Can You mend this broken heart? Please don't tell me 'over time,' I don't want to hear that. How is it that my heart skips a beat when I gaze at her restful face? This is more than I can handle, Lord, comfort me like You have done so many times, but nothing as I need You now! Refresh my spirit and let me know that You still care for an old fool such as myself! Please, restore the peace that passes all understanding, and let me give this over to You!"

A rushing wind comes over Aletta's fragile frame, not by the comfort of her nearby friend but by the warmth of a gentle embrace from a compassionate God.

Penny's Return in Her Mind

Meanwhile, back on the valley grounds of the foretold battle at Sochoh in the Valley of Elah, the Lord has blessed our fury friend with a glimpse of what is to happen and the taunting of Goliath from Gath. Well, one cannot call it a battle at this point in time. Let us call it for what it is at this juncture, the great forty-day standoff. Penny is at a crossroads of confusion, for she has missed her mark of running into the provider of the first stone and the talk of four more yet to be found, and if that is not enough for her plate to hold, the Lord has given her a thorn in the side by allowing her to hear the haunting laughter of Goliath in her mind's eye and ears. Not a pleasant place for her to reopen her mind.

So, back to the unknown gridlock, where nothing is happening as the taunting of a Philistine, or it might as well be any other enemy that Israel has faced in its past faith's history, as we know those outcomes of the Lord's many battles that have belonged to Him and the instrumental symphony of each inspired instrument playing in those battles for mankind to be blessed; yes, other men have been called, and Goliath knows of each one from war stories told by his other brothers that has brought fear to them all but Goliath. This so-called champion enjoys the fables of a god who helps puny humans out of their circumstantial situations of despair and His people who serve Him, even to the point of their whole hearts and minds and souls; that is, if Goliath has one, which he does, but this one thing he does not understand, he will soon find out.

This is what is going through the mind of our perplexed bunny as a thunderous voice of Goliath speaks forth of weaponry of the tongues and poison darts to impair the minds of Saul's men. "This is the people that the Lord has brought great honor too, are they all cowards. This humanity calling has brought so much fear to my homeland that they have summoned the great Goliath of Gath to settle this humdrum battle of a God who has provided exciting mythologies to my mind. And to think God could do so much for his chosen, only to see them fail Him. Or better yet," he says, as laughter and awryness enter his spirit, "that God has failed them. Someone come look at me straight in the eyes and beg to differ from me if your God has your back as I kick the holy scruff off of your faces!

"I have heard the legend of Moses splitting the Red Sea off the great Exodus, and now your god has brought forth this tremendous rainstorm to drench these battlegrounds that have soaked my armor but not my retributions to kill and put an end to this nonsense. Am I so fearful of this act of nature's calling? Or of your so-called deity that you call God, a god? I am a bystander here today, so why does your god lie in silence, calling after such a wicked downfall of moisture? The only other moisture you shall see today is the moisture coming forth from your eyes!

"Or maybe to bring back a little confidence to your spineless backs, stories of your mighty men of valor, then my favorite, the one who took over the leadership of Moses, God also split the Red Sea once again for Joshua's generation to witness the crashing walls of Jericho; for the men who taunted and laughed in Israel's men's faces, of the promised lands, things must crumble down, am I right? Moses watched Joshua being led into the promised land because of his faithfulness, so my question to all of you is, where does your faithfulness stand on this day? Crumbling like the walls of Jericho to my sight?! Or didn't Jacob wrestle with God for His blessing in such a great effort that he pulled his hip out of the socket and forever after walked with a limp, while you all stand around and put up with my callings? Am I not doing the same intuitions as those past enemies of God, and why are these mountains not crumbling before me in my sight right now?! Is it because of your lack of faith, the men who call themselves followers of a living God? Or maybe God is shaking in fear Himself. Do I dare proclaim, where is your comeback?! Someone step up! God is challenging my patience, which one of your brave men will face such a challenge to defend a God who is defenseless? Choose, or I will make my choice; bring to me your king Saul! Is he not the responsible and one of your people? Choose now!"

Penny is perplexed and stands paralyzed on a path of despair. "Why, Lord? Why are You allowing me to hear all of this? I am doing my best. Forgive me for missing the mark; am I not your servant? Tell me so."

Another voice hollers out loud; a very familiar voice indeed, but with anger and not the gentle voice she has heard over the years of her lifespan. It breaks her out of her stupor circumstances.

"Ebenezer and Alymore, listen up, mister and mister; you two need to get over here quickly; oh, just you wait and see, you're not going to see it coming!"

The wrath of God coming from this angry shepherd boy!

"My God, forgive me, Lord; I am going on to do all that both of my fathers of earth and heaven have called me to do so, with or without you, provisions or no provisions. Do not mock me,

Ebenezer, you wild *burro*! So, God, help the both of you without the protection I provided!"

"Listen, Penny, and be still. I have placed in your heart the value of these stones that must be obtained for reasons that will make sense in all due time. David's heart is very tender and is constantly seeking my face, I need his loyalty and faithfulness to be placed for this standoff in the valley. His courage has been tested in many affairs of the small things of the sheepfolds, staying faithful to the lives of those who depend on him for comfort and security. Many times, he has faced wolves and the men in sheep's clothing, trying to devour the helpless in the herd's community of life. Neither of you has missed the mark. You are in my timing and hands! You both are peaks of joy and anticipation with a humble outlook on life's calling. Both of you shall go in my direction, so let's turn this thing around and go into the direction of disposition's exchange! Move forward!"

THE TRIANGLES' FLIGHT

Penny has determination but flaws, as does everyone who stands or flies on this planet named Earth, a big rock or stone we call home, with a God who has all in His hands, and some still ridicule Him to this very day. Nothing really ever changes other than time passing. Just look back into history, and it shall tell you the stories of today. David follows in and out of the shadowy covering of the elms and oaks by their canvas, and Penny is just ahead but out of David's sight, her confidence recovering for the presence of another, although off at a distance but close enough for security's realm. History changes, but God remains the same. Today, yesterday, and tomorrow his statutes remain. Let your yes be yes, and your no be no, and amen to all. Just build your life upon the rock, our cornerstone for a true foundation.

Penny is on the move and rocking her world, in song and melody, happy as a lark, in an adventure in her mind, now in serenity, as the taunts have ceased since the arrival of David. He has a calming effect on all. But she has a watchful eye, and just as she turns around to see if she is still in the sights of David, the unexplained happens, as from out of the tree tops coverage, four ladies of faith dive bomb our clingy hare, rolling her into a ball. In the snowball effect of perpetual movement, where ears become eyes and hands become feet, in a tangle of feathery wings and fur balls in flight, she finally comes to a halt into the wings of Gretchen and three of her friends, who, at this point, are not recognizable because of the tail feathers in Penny's snout, as she coughs up a fur ball like a feline would!

Penny, shaking off the tail feathers, says, "Gretchen, have you gone mad and held our last encounter personal enough that you need others to help take me out of this world? You better have a good explanation for the invasive attack on my serenity before the storm!"

As the three other ladies shake off the dust and straighten out their civvies to recover back their dignity, Gretchen, recovering from the fumbling and, in her high-pitched voice, running sentences all together, says, "No, Penny, it's nothing like that at all. But let me tell you what went down this day, a demon child of a critter, out of the threatening skies, pursuing us, to an all-out, right into a frenzy, intruded space, and we had to separate, starting off as seven and now we are four, in this circulation of chaos, oh, Penny it is so good to hold onto you and just to see your lovely face!"

Penny tries to catch her breath to answer Gretchen, "You're not making any sense; this better not be any gossip about someone's neurotic child's tantrums toward one of the moms. Time is essential; we must keep a steady pace. So, we are out of the view of David for a good spell, so everything is cool and I'm listening now, so go ahead!"

Gretchen looks doubtful. "Oh, okay, no, it's not like that and will not be ever again. I'm a new creation in Christ; I've stepped back into the house of the Lord. All who have gathered at the mulberry bush, well, you know, can you forgive us wholeheartedly? Sister to sister in Christ. I have something of great importance to show you," she says as she grabs onto her chest to expose the stone.

Penny replies, "Geez, Gretchen, I don't want to see your breast. Come on, give me a break…"

Gretchen blushes with a little giggling. "Oh, no, it's nothing like that, silly, keep your knockers on, oh darn, you know what I mean. No, look at this." Keeping the webbing securely intact around the stone, Gretchen reveals a gem of a stone, like a diamond in the rough, as Penny's eyes almost come out of her sockets.

Penny responds, stuttering, "Bu—but how, and whe—where…" You know, all the five questions that a journalist asks. "I was to collect that from an individual alongside the road but hurried along too quickly trying to get away from… ah… aaah!"

With an understanding look on her face and then a shrug of agreement, Gretchen says, "I know me!"

Penny realizes that Gretchen is being open and honest as Gretchen continues on with the conversation, "Yes, let's keep walking, for it is a long story of how this got into the hands of the seven grackles, crackling birds and a stone of many characteristics too crazy to fathom and significant importance to God's perfect plans and purpose. Anyways, your deliverer of the stone's name is Sheldon, that is, Officer Sheldon, who is always talking his thoughts out loud for all to hear and says it is all for the purpose of keeping historical documentation of all events taking place as we speak; crazy, but such a loveable guy!"

With Gretchen and Penny in the lead, the others sway in the background listening in, continuing down the road as all circumstances and the acquaintance of the other ladies are discussed in detail, too many to place in this part of the story because it would fill the pages for eternity; for those with the gift of gab, believe me!

The sound of silent awkwardness is loudly interrupted by the storm that is quickly approaching from the east and has started to settle for a moment time. The cloud coverage has broken up; so has Nicole, for her recovery hasn't gone so well, "This is the stormfront that we started to fly through, but we weren't as fortunate then as it is now."

Amber opens the conversation by asking, "So what happens now that this stone is recovered and in the hands of the carrier intended? Are we just going to walk? Let's start something to liven things up!" Amber has a heart that is truly filled with spunk's fire and has been burned multiple times due to this fact alone.

The ladies start to walk in the debris left by a storm of great magnitude when Bellemy mentions to the others, "Look at the ancient oak tree that has been split into two sections; Now that was some kind of lightning storm, I do say so myself. Who would have thought anything of it with such a tranquil feeling in the air? Listen to the humming sounds and locusts in flight. They must be *en route* to their homes to see if they still have homes to go to!"

An uncontrollable sob is heard echoing above the treetops as a familiar voice keeps breaking up with mourning that fills the breath of life's flow. To the uncertainty of recollection reasoning by voices in the vicinity and now someone else joining in as the comforter. "I can identify the comforter's voices, no one other than Harriot, and Alleta is the one who is sobbing, but Delora and her have the same voice tones, especially in sorrow, so I cannot tell!"

Gretchen expresses herself halfway in flight in the direction of the tree as the other three take flight, "This isn't good, ladies; I can feel it deep down in my soul!" She leaves Penny to cut through the woods to search out the voices with her keen, long ears.

And with this, the memorial service concludes, with flowers of all kinds covering the burial site and gathered around, comforting those to be comforted and military soldiers saluting in a hypnotic stare, looking to the skies as the yellowjackets take flight and depart as when they first arrived. Harriot is in the middle comforting Aletta, who grasps onto the white lilies and rose petals clutching them underneath her wings. Both are in tears and in disbelief, as you can tell that their focus is on the cemetery. Penny has made her arrival coming out through an opening of the shrubs that places them in seclusion and separation before reaching the pathway and joining the four sisters walking slowly over to Alleta with feathered wings opened wide to embrace Alleta and her misery-stricken heart. No words can be spoken without taking turns in being the comforter. Sheldon makes his way over to the remaining six and goes directly over to Gretchen to console a friend in need, to just embrace and soothe her mind.

Harriot comes over to Sheldon and says to Penny, "This is Officer Sheldon, the conqueror and adventurer of the first stone. Gretchen tells me that you had an eye-opening acquaintance, very briefly and she couldn't remember the face, so now you two are enlightened of each other's presence, officially. Just wish under better circumstances, I'll let you two share each other's company."

Gretchen goes back over to Aletta, an officer in grief over the loss of a comrade, which has hit Sheldon hard.

"Well, Penny, it looks as if you have received the first stone; I see that it is still secure with Gretchen. If I had known of all this mess, I could have kept it in my presence and waited for another opportunity, but I felt the urgency to do so and called to look for you."

Penny starts to tear up in swells and states, "Hindsight is 20/20, and if I wasn't in such a hurry, I would have had the stone safely in my hands without the girl's involvement, so there's no time in this pity party. Let's mourn the passing of a friend.

Sheldon, in a firm stance in posture and in voice, says, "There is another light in this darkness that is trying to smother a positive factor. I am the carrier of the second stone that is webbed on my hind quarters to bring this stone to you as well. And I am now at your service to carry this stone and all the weight that comes with it!"

Penny develops a smile on her face and says, "This is getting very interesting."

Bellamy, who has been very silent in all these heart matters and has approached Gretchen in slow progress with puffy eyes of devotion, clears her throat as a blockage of words clutters the air.

Gretchen, so desperately trying to contain her emotions, says, "Just breathe, Bellamy, and take your time. I know that you have something heavy on your heart, and you can open up the passageways to put your mind at rest, my good friend."

Bellamy gains her composure while wiping her eyes with the tip of her wings, saying, "Yes, Gretchen, indeed, you have always been there for all my essential situations in life. Harriot and I, well, we decided that we are going to escort Alleta home in this grieving period and stay to comfort her in all her sorrowfulness. Will the three of you be all right with our departure?"

Gretchen comforts her under her wings, saying, "Aw, Bellamy, such a caring heart that you have; yes, we will be just fine with the additional ground crew to guide us high and low as a well-balanced unit. Plus, I have recently discovered that we have as much as another stone in our possession! Now, let's all gather so that we can cover everything in prayer. I need to discuss a few matters with Sheldon before we get started on the open road!"

The clearing of the clouds and the new-felt penetration of the sun's rays upon their faces lighten the affairs of these characters of compassion as Sheldon approaches the shelled, slated platform and clears his throat to gain the attention of all.

"There is important undetermined material up for discussions, but first, let us open in prayer. Our heavenly Father, God of Samuel, Moses, and all the prophets of old; through these, You have performed many miracles and blessings to comfort them in their travels to the promised land that You were guiding them to. You were fire by night and clouds in the day to comfort them and to let them know that You were always in their presence. We come before You to ask for mercy in the travels and divine protection for the ladies who have chosen to comfort Aletta in her sorrows and to take her back to their homelands. Also, our travels in proceedings leading to the recovery of the other stones yet to be found and to the stones that we have amongst us! Amen!

"Okay, first on the agenda: the departure of Aletta, Bellamy, and Harriot to provide security and comfort to Aletta, and rightfully so; we thank you for your dedication and the risks taken in this flight of the first stone to its recovery and delivery. Your service has not been a lost cause; we cannot justify things by errors made along the way, only that we have a great God who is with us in all the mistakes we make to get things back on track. We can only do the things God has placed on our hearts to our best abilities. Second: the chosen path has led us back to full circle because of altered circumstances, but we have a second stone recovered, a blessing that may not have happened under certain situations, so do not count it as lost time. Third: Nicole, Amber, and Gretchen will join Penny and myself, Officer Sheldon, along with these two stones, to follow the directional plans of the Lord our God. May God help us all!"

In the conclusive ending, the remaining party is greeted and embraced in one last settling moment by those who shall depart from this adventurous group, tearing up, not knowing what will happen next. Our humble bumblebee guides the inquirers' quest with a song of prophecies calling. It will all come to pass; just you wait and see!

There is no greater loss
than in the ones we love,

ALLEN W. LEAFGREEN

with the comforts of many words spoken.
To relieve your eternal sorrows.
From the depths and into the brook.
Such a cost for one stone.

The aroma of unpleasantries,
covered in a bed of false rosiness fragrance arising.
When hope comes calling to each of us who will remain
Dedicated to challenge the loss,
In the burden and weight of the second stone.

In these Oak Tree Scrolls,
The Lord is a mighty fountain of living water and of things to come.
To the dryness of the land.
Parched souls last in the trees,
of life's forgotten quest to tiresome travels.
Ancient lives unfold
In released souls to each
And the third stone.

To those who have a generous offering,
bartered in another's delight.
A sacrifice to one, something worn on the heart's sleeve,
compassion and meek, who shall inherit the calling
will be a blessing to another,
of this fourth stone.

While lying in the desert sands,
As in the times of Moses' retreat.
Hidden for forty years of fear's trappings,
captured finally by his own kind.
We bring this fifth stone to light.

THE MEADOWLANDS

*And when gathering of these five stone's births,
by gatherers and carriers, one for each of them,
to a destination known.
By the Valley's Brook edge, it lies asleep and ready to be awakened.
One stone will be chosen,
Into their final battle's quest!*

David slowly walks by the prophecies in flight, way over his head in this moment of time, not yet birthed in his spirit but already deeply embedded in his heart. A man after God's own heart and a poet to share with each and every one who has the courage to listen. Yes, although not fully awakened, the stone shall be placed in his hands, not alone but guided by a loving God. In an unconditional circumstance, this responsibility should be in the hands of the ruling king, King Saul! Well, suddenly, all are in full perspective in this battle scene, that this battle is in place by the Lord's hands!

One true God!
One man.
And one stone!

— Chapter Five —
ALONG THE ROADSIDE

"Penny and Sheldon, walking side by side, or as fast as one's feet can handle, as Penny is stuttering and stepping terribly, are dismayed in an apprehension that brings this group all together in the evaporation of the standing puddles, as the moisture is being released in a fine mist into the atmosphere's core. Amber and Nicole take flight, circulating in the eastern skies, just in reach of the two land dwellers. Just a hop, skip, and a crawl away to a beaten path that is known to all but leading into a directional path of the unknown calamity's silent waiting, maybe? Only the path taken will be known by the Lord for His plans for each of us! Looking both ways before crossing…!"

A brief interruption by Penny is excused, and she exclaims, "*Awww*, Sheldon, you are so adorable. General Abbott has told me so many things about your audibles out loud, of course, for historical documentation. That is so cute of you, Sheldon; please carry on. I'm a good listener. Carry on, good soldier!"

"Oh, okay, I shall."

Penny acclaims with miles on miles of smiles on her furry face!

"Oh yes, where were we, yes, before entering the roadside! En-

THE MEADOWLANDS

ter with precaution, creeping through the shrubbery, and to my left, I spy with my little eye... David's back! And he is singing, well listen, but first let's go back into the cover of the shrubs."

Penny, with deep concern, says, "Just wait a minute, Sheldon, and stop your nipping at my heels, you hardheaded goon; sorry, that was rude, forgive me. I need to see if Ebb and Aly have joined him yet. Nope, not yet; I figured Ebb could have the two on a wild goose chase and stirring his oats! Oh, you haven't met them yet, oh, but you will; long story short, they are a hoot, that pair, and an important part of the plot, I think?! Well, I know the direction we're heading in, my good friend. We're going to have to leave the security of David and head into the wildfires of life. So, Sheldon, do you like to fly?"

"Sure, not a problem; whatcha have in mind?"

"Well, Gretchen will be your aerial transporter, while Amber and Nicole will follow David for a status report in due time."

"Cool, I will become the eye in the sky!"

(32)

"Listen, David, as I implant these seeds embedded deep inside your heart and mind's eye. Do not pay attention to the sudden rise of your enemies. I know each and every one of them through the morning light and will make them visible to you. Just stand and continue forward on the path below your feet, which will become the placement of your enemies and will become your foothold to your honor. They shall walk in shame while you stride in My glory, with your household being anointed forever."

(33)

David proceeds to his destination, slowly leaving his youth out of view and in his past, for this day he shall become a man of greatness in the sight of all, with the empowerment of the Lord. But for now, he shall be an adolescent, teenaged boy, with joy overflowing amongst the wildflowers, rose petals, and white lilies scattered along the roadside, leading into the forestry, where there stands a mighty oak that has been split into two broken sections or two individual kingdoms, although that is so much further down the road. A young mind is being refined through the developing world of creativity, lost in words directed in a psalm and reaching to the realm of the heavens in admiration of his loving Father, God, taking a stronghold on the Lord's spoken word! Singing to an audience of One and all creation of all kinds of loveable, flying domain, creepy crawling and all the earth's froth, stirred by the storm. The movement of a floating leaf contains the sight, if you look really hard, of our stern General Abbot, who ever so cleverly clutches onto David's ankle and web slings past his arms in motion, for David is a very animated being, and onto the visible beige collar near his neck. Now the general can whisper sweet nothings into David's ear. And, of course, it will amount to nothing, understandably, but it will provide company to our general, as a gentle breeze surrenders to the sounds of a charitable tune.

> *My love for You, Lord, will be the strength provided, as of the rocks,*
> *along this roadside, that is, if there were any to be found.*
> *God is stronger than these timbers from the timberlands*
> *my deliverer from the storm, that has settled the dust of this pathway,*
> *trusting is in the Lord. My hope is in the Lord alone.*
> *By the strength of Your hands, my stronghold, and the*
> *shield of the sun rays.*
> *May my voice always sing the song of salvation's calling*
> *from the depths of the unknown glare of the enemy's eyes.*
> *You alone are worthy to be praised: continue to watch over*
> *this weary soul,*
> *Along this beaten path, to destinations calling! Amen!*

The weeping of the weeping willows along the brook's edge and the blubbering bumblebee know about the giants. David will encounter all in God's due timing! The bridge by the brook is only a cartwheel or two and a backflip away, for David is a very flexible being. Well, also because he has nothing but the clothes on his back, seeming that Ebenezer has all his provisions. Even his loveable, walking sweater friend in Alymore. Both are in a whole lotta trouble. Oh, just you wait, just you wait and see!

The road winds, twists, and turns with not a soul in sight as the scenery starts to blend as one over the miles in the flight of Gretchen with Sheldon with a laptop of information flowing from the movement of his lips and the sound of his voice from his mouth as Sheldon stays alert on to all circumstances arising. Penny has slowed down her pace so that she can hear Sheldon and the rustling sounds in the woods. She hopes paranoia hasn't kicked in but is mainly listening for any indication of the two who have gone AWOL.

"How far east do you think Ebb and Aly have gone, Penny?" A very good question asked by Gretchen.

"Well, the last time I came across David, it must have been at least a hop, a skip, and miles between this tree and that bend in the road. I passed him before my return, I think. Then, another sprint through the woods, keeping an eye out for lurkers more than focusing on the location, hopping to and fro over potholes in the area. I'm probably just a stone's throw away from Jesse, somewhere in between!"

These are the disadvantages of having acquired so much speed in motion for Penny, who is faster than a lightning strike. Sheldon just shakes his head in disbelief, saying," Gotcha, this is going to look strange on paper. Well, it is what it is. And for the record, this continues for miles and miles of the same ole. This is Sheldon signing off until further notice, 10–4!"

By the Sycamore Tree

The storm clouds have broken up and are drifting beyond the entranceway, where Ebenezer and Alymore are the surnames that protrude when David is not so pleased with his four-legged friends. Both are captivated in a hypnotic trance, motionless as if sculptures placed in front of the patio setting in the backyard, waiting to be admitted upon a guest's arrival. Alymore, with his mind partly cloudy and hypertension streaming through his veins, looks over to Ebenezer in an act of desperation, saying, "This is it, the place where all pandemonium breaks loose just before I lose it, the very narrow path that leads inward to the wailing voices; but where are they, in this silence?"

And then, as quick as a wink, the body language becomes very spirited and full of life, while the front leg of Ebenezer starts to pace and the neck begins to snap, and he now speaks forth, "Listen up, Aly, this is very important information. When we transit into the passage of the sycamore tree, surrounded by the Tavor Oaks, you can't go in the way you are acting now, like a sheepish sheep. You have to be sure that there is not a single bit of negativity entertaining your mind. Not one iota. Do you know any biblical scriptures that you have memorized and can concentrate on? Even if you repeat the same one over and over again until you're blue in the face! Like I have said earlier, the forest will be awakened by your fear. Let me do the talking to set the atmosphere to an inspirational setting, and you will be just fine! So let me hear your chosen scripture, Aly; what could it be? Come on, you can do it; no pressure here."

Alymore (that name sounds very sophisticated, like a man full of wisdom), Aly thinks to himself, *Strain the brain but don't get hurt, Aly, come on, oh, okay.* He says, out loud this time, "Jesus wept!"

Ebenezer, just because I like the way the name rolls off the tongue, looks at Aly with amazement and says, "Works for me. Let's go!"

Going into the underbrush away from the pathway and leaving Alymore's security, the two slither, snake-like, onto the matted and knotted ground cover and enter the fading light of the opportunity to turn around and just go home attitude. Tempered lighting from the shadows covers their sight and out of earshot's way to anyone who adventures by.

Ebenezer opens the doors of his mind's sight, going into legends past times to a once tranquil escape from the heat and weariness of the day. "Aly, the wailing voices are silent, but they're here, trust me on that; we have not entered the bloodlines flow into the forest's core. The Tavor Oaks were planted many years beforehand and surrounded the sycamore, and over time, the tree started to hollow from the inside out, leaving a gaping passage through the foundation of the trunk and becoming a temporary resting place for many of God's creatures. As you see, there are hitching posts and troughs that are in different locations next to the Tavor Oaks, with plenty of room for livestock to gather and rest, while the travelers explore deeper into the forest trails. A stone masonry well is concealed by honeysuckle and morning glory vines that are intertwined on a trellis and lattice paneling that tame the vines to a symmetrical posting, while a cobblestone ground cover encircles the well, and inclined maple wood benches set a nice place to relax. Lantern posts are throughout the trails radiating light and are maintained on a regular basis; of course, this goes way back before this place had become barren. The ancient burial grounds are a lonesome outlook deep into the back forestry represented by wooden crosses in an orderly field.

"So, I hope that I painted you a picture that you can envision, for when we enter through the sycamore, reality will conclude that imagery, and you will witness the entangled atmosphere of restless souls, and you will become breathless, gasping for air. Do not speak of the area being barren or any word that even comes close. We are entering at our own risk, but God will be with us, and the prayers will flow through this vessel of mine. We must enter slowly, and we must be awarded entrance!"

The two settle in their hearts and clear their minds as the coolness of the forest chills the bones of our two innocent, ecstatic beings. An eerie feeling of anticipation floods their minds gates into overdrive, and a slight whispering circulates in the wind, caressing them, as the hairs on Ebenezer's back spine begin to tingle and Alymore's natural curls tighten with tension.

Ebenezer, with bugged eyes, confesses, "We are being watched, but do not be concerned, let alone anxious; we must start our entry through the sycamore. Let's go, Aly, now, and memorize your scripture, life's defensive mechanism!"

(34)

The hollowness is wide enough for the unscheduled visitor to walk in broad-shouldered and side by side as the tainted smell of wood shavings fills the stagnant air. Entering the other side, a thrusting firm wind barrier halts forward motion, but only enough for them to wobble off balance.

A resounding voice echoes off the Tavor Oaks and into the minds of these foreigners' reality. "What is the word that the Lord has spoken to you? We know who you are, Ebenezer, and your ancestral roots! What brings you forth into our presence? Do you dare show your face to us on this day? And you speak knowledge of our comforting quarters offered to all who entered for rest! Please do not taunt us in your pleasantries of our past! Are you speaking in the tones of a deceitful tongue deep down flowing through your veins? We will know even that if you are speaking lies or half-truths, ingenuity disguises with more dignity, for where are my manners, my mule of wisdom?! Speak clearly and from the heart, tell the truth of our past; what has the Lord placed upon your hearts this day?"

With an attitude of respect, Ebenezer bows, showing the same respect to his loyal friend David (well, that is, on a good day), and expands his chest and breathes deeply. He responds with facial expressions as if one is eating a gobbling goo of peanut butter from the spoon straight out of the jar, but his words are spoken clearly and not muffled.

(35)

"I shall do accordingly to what is in my heart and in my mind and not let any of my words fall to the earth as it happened with your ancestors. There is no longer any widespread revelation. What happened to the voices of inspirational hymns that circulated with the gentle breeze that made you tingle with joy? Before the lamp of God went out of all the lantern posts throughout the trails. The seasons of all your descendants have abandoned these immense woodlands and passed in the flourish of their age. This has consumed your eyes and now has placed sorrow in all who remain; they are haunted with emotions. The awakening shall come to pass this day! There will be an anointing that the Engarlands Way has not seen in this parched soil. Healing of great significance with perplexity will occur in these quarters, no more, no less! Lord, I call upon Your great name. Set forth Your light as I breathe in the air of Your blessings!"

Listen to my prayer!
You restless souls of the sycamore tree,
are your leaves tender enough to the waters from the well?
Enhanced with wild fresh herbs into a healing tea,
Or have you become so bitter that even the sap from your trunk,
are no longer enriched with sweetness that once produced,
for all those who have traveled,

and graced your presence?
Did not your boroughs of the sycamore and the Tavor Oaks,
bring comfort and provide shade to foreigners
and their livestock?
Nestled near your mighty root system,
and refuge from the storm?
Remember how your figs satisfied the hunger of all
who picked your fruit!
Return to your Ancient ways!
Have not the Lord, our God, provided for such a beautiful tree,
to the ancient prophets in the heat of the summer!
Lord, how beautiful is Your name alone.
Show Your love and kind spirit to those who have given cover
and to these troubled timberlands of Engarlands Way of
the enclosed Tavor Oaks.
The mystical filtering light of the orient, "Komorebi,"
and the beauty brought
within the highlights, in the oak leaves, staining glow.
Let Your healing light once again shine upon the Sycamore.
Test my heart, where my feet stand fast on the path
of righteousness, and that my heart has not
staggered away from Your blessing.
To those who take cover in You, Lord.
As for me, I shall see Your face
in this troubled land!

Out of the humble heart of the sycamore tree and the graciousness of the Tavor Oaks in a place called Engarlands Way, the response is a simple plea from the leaves of a sycamore tree, "You have told everything and hid nothing from us! It is the Lord; let Him do what seems good, for none of your words Ebenezer, the wise donkey, in Engarlands, will fall to the ground!"

— Chapter Six —
HUNTER'S MARK

A wolfpack is very peculiar in the social world of animals, with a whole lot of uniqueness. Where to begin is the issue of explaining the beauty of these beasts. Make no mistake, they are very structured in their lifestyle. They have a strong desire to defend their territory, walk amongst the shadows cast, and are not fearful of any being, for the strength is in numbers. They need each other and work in different organizational skills to keep their pack active, and are not above themselves, unless, of course, the boss, such as Hunter! A mid-rank wolf takes on different roles and is loyal to the pack's alpha and betas; the question is amongst themselves. They struggle with who they are and who they want to become. Henceforth, where the ground needs to be guarded, they send in the terrible threesome. The wolf scouts Stalker, Smoke, and Jasper have taken advantage of all the briars and thistle that have captured many wandering inhabitants of the woods, making them easy prey to feast on without sharing it with the rest of the pack; what they don't know won't kill them. Not so lucky if you're the one trapped! Mobility for them is just another daily occurrence of a daily dose of discomfort, hoping that it will pay off. Time has passed for many travelers who continue on their journey, leaving the way to a wolf-pack's haven that runs rampant in these backtimbers. Not so this day as the three crouch down into the briars with the enjoyment of pain surfacing while their adrenaline circulates through their wicked shell of a body. Within earshot distance from the entranceway was the crunching of two, a lost donkey and a startled sheep, with no shepherd in sight. Quickness is a must. In their silence, they move rapidly deep into the walls trunk to the backcountry, missing out on some important tactics our fellow friends are in the process of gathering procedures, but this can wait a few more minutes. Our evil dose of villains must rush to give a status report to the one who has control of this tight pack, Hunter, and yes, he has a bad reputation to uphold and is not afraid to take it out on his fellow pack just to keep all in their proper perspective. He has a long line of supremacy in the rulership ancestry tree.

Gathering Provisions

Ebenezer looks from side to side to get a quick diagnostic of materials in the here and now, all of them with miraculous importance, and already has a hunch for all materials on his mental listings. Listening to his facial mutterings, Alymore is wondering what in tarnation is going on with this obsessed mule.

Ebenezer breaks the silence to his gibberish and starts to speak in guidance intervals of steps to be taken. "Aly, we must be quick; I know we have been scouted out and stalked by something not of the trees. First, I need you to locate the empty satchel bag on my saddle bags. Second, empty one of the water flasks onto the ground as a final offering to the sycamore tree out of gratitude only, not as to an idol, then hand it over to me, and I will pour the sap into the flask for later use. Third, start gathering loose sycamore bark and the freshest leaves that you can gather in the empty satchel.

We will need to gather spearmint and lavender along the way. I don't see any at this time, but I know the herbal fragrance grows rapidly here at one time. Hopefully, they've remained as sturdy as their reputation suggests, much like perennials that stand the test of time. And last but not least, we need to find the cones of the wild cypress tree for the final enhancement."

Aly, with a confused look on his face, replies, "You're sounding like you're going to MacGyver something or another." Ebenezer gives him a look, and Aly says, "Oh, never mind, you wouldn't know him!"

Ebenezer stutters but regains his confidence in knowing that he must remain strong in the Lord. "Lord, my spirit is overwhelmed, for there is a hindrance in the air that has entered my lungs. I am consumed and drowning, for I am being hunted by a stalker in these woods. Lift my spirit, Lord, along Your pathway so that my footstep may not be kicked from under my feet! Their intentions are to surround us in every direction so that hope will turn into despair. They will growl, kick, and tear apart this tender heart to obstruct us from doing the purpose for the trees; we are at peace with them. Have You allowed our entrance only to be devoured in Your sight?! My responsibility in returning Alymore back safely to David's side; would You also hinder that calling You placed in his heart as well? The two of us have put our trust into You alone, and to be under the shadow of Your wings, my everlasting hope is in You, Lord!"

Following down a path of hardship, Alymore is actually the one leading and being a guiding light of inspiration that has taken Ebenezer by a delightful surprise. One would think that maybe they both found a little catnip along the way. Several low branches become a drawback and allow them to redirect themselves slightly into the thicket of scattered leaves, elevated into a pile by the nook. The sun is able to penetrate in an inspirational beam of light, and a gentle breeze releases an aromatic balm of the spearmint leaves that are breaking free from the captivity of the smothering leaves. Aly recognizes the fragrances and says, "Over here, Ebb, I found them, the spearmint leaves and lavender in abundance; oh, they remind me of relaxing and watching the sunset with my favorite brew of tea with mint. How refreshing is that thought!"

"Awesome, Aly. Now, eat a good handful. They will help us relax during these tense times and memories, so you can learn some meaty scriptures to recite! There is a small stream that has flowed in past time but has depleted; that is where the cypress trees once thrived in the moisture of the channel's watercourse."

DAVID'S QUEST
(36)

The stillness of the day has arrived and survived the shadows cast in the darkest setting possible for them. Who would have thought that a battlefield full of cries where many have died and so many souls have been taken is this same field that bears the footsteps of our beloved David? The air is filled with the departing locusts, homeward bound to their forestry homes. For now, we are called to be at ease with ourselves, the first and foremost peace in our lives. The guiding buzzing sounds of a bubbly bumble bee in flight and the agitation of the brook's vivid flow drown the sorrows of many red ants and jumping spiders. Senses flow spontaneously for David as his secret companionship roams the area unnoticed by the eyes of David. Amber, with her heart of gold, stands alongside the two glittering gemstones basking in the rising sun. Nicole proclaims victory with the fiery decree of her heroic vocals.

Our teeny, tiny general has made a webbing hammock strapped from ear to ear on the back of the shepherd's boy neck, like a flea in action, swaying back in forth with each movement; so refreshing. But not as spiritual blessings, rather as a friendship awakening in the sight of our Lord, to witness and hear the sounds of praise in the prayerful voice of David.

> *Lord, how awesome of a God,*
> *that even disciplines the storms rise and approach.*
> *Confronted in my distress.*
> *I call upon Your great name,*
> *many of Your hidden treasures and*
> *gratitude in serving a living God*
> *has protected me from the storm's raging anger,*
> *coming in from the eastern skies, moving in a*
> *Western fashion.*
> *You have placed my feet upon an outstretched land.*
> *Your word guides and goes before my entrance*
> *And deliver me because You have delighted in me.*
> *As the storm dissolved in my sight,*
> *And no longer fear the bitterness within.*
> *In the announcing sun's glare of*
> *The morning dwindling away to the*
> *chirping of the grackles in flight.*
> *The cobwebs entanglement of the*
> *jumping, jumbled thoughts, networking*
> *through my mind, tingling the back of my head.*
> *Soaring with past indecision as the bridge by the brook*
> *Becomes the great deliverance*
> *Showing mercy and the blessings poured upon his heir.*
> *For I am a young man upcoming and a Child of God. Amen!*

The anointed name of David shall be his inheritance for now and forevermore. So be it!

The Lord has a strong calling for him to answer. For David shall respond from the desire of his heart to follow wherever the Lord shall lead into the depths of Israel's blessed king-to-be!

Taken to the Pack

Now, the fortunes of this pack have been limited and about as dry as the land, but in paid dues' patience, food had been gathered in a far and wide search to the unlucky prey's misfortunate timing. Patience is key, well, most of the time, but misfortunately our three scouts broke a pack rule of three against at least one of the two; it should not have been a problem, especially with the presence of a defenseless sheep, that is if God's providence and protection of the two hadn't kicked in for our walking TV dinners! This probably won't end well for the three of them! Perseverance rules in the household of this pack; it shows strength and endurance, but our three have neither and have one thing in mind: who will get there first to Hunter to tell him of the good news?

This caused a lot of nipping and wrestling around in a childish pup kind of way, which would put them in another negative statistic of the pack of probably being demoted to the lower rankings; just you wait and see! The positive thing is that it gives Aly and Ebenezer enough time to find the cypress cones near the desolate waters of a puny stream, but, most importantly, the arrival of Jacob and the boys! Another strike on the jokers of the pack due to, right, you guessed it, patience. Let's listen in as Smoke is the first to enter the pack to rush or, let's say, intrude onto Hunter during nap time. He even rushes by the beta, Josephine, which is not any better. Smoke, like the lack of discipline, has all the characteristics of his name because he is about to blow smoke out of his ears. Proceed on, Smoke; this is your cue, you goober!

"Important urgency, my great one of the pack, Hunter; you are not going to believe this. The two, a granted entrance even, stagnated in place and are still talking smack to his comrade and…!"

"Sounds to me as if you are the only one talking smack this very moment. Next, you're dismissed, Smoke. Out of my sight, and learn how to approach a supreme ruler. Now go!"

And as Smoke leaves with his tail between his legs, whimpering, he knows this is not good for him in his ranking.

Jacob, "What Did I Miss?"
(37)

Of course, you know Betsy is always taking advantage of a situation when no one is watching her do her mischievous outtakes in life's practical mishaps as she grazes on some of the meadowlands, waiting for Jacob's return to the saddle. The boys are panting hard, trying to catch their breath, and are laid out next to Betsy, watching, looking out for Ebb, Aly, and anything else that may wander in or hide outside of their watchful perimeter. Rocco is sitting nearest to Betsy, searching for a flea who has made a home for himself somewhere between here and the tail. All Rocco knows is that it is driving him crazy! Taking advantage, Betsy knows that she is in tail's reach of Rocco's big head and swishes her tail back and forth, blipping him and then bopping him again unnecessarily, in unison strokes of her hindmost treacherous shag.

"Hey, will you cut it out, you inexplicable twit? Cut out the...!"

Jacob breaks the attitude of the two by speaking forth. "Very strange. The smell of rain is still in the air but has dissipated and broken up, so suddenly, it is gone. Lighting flashes, thunderclaps, and all, hmmm!" And just like the whirlwind has vanished, so have Ebb and Aly into the forest walls. Jacob is surprised by the sudden disappearance and bravery of the two to wander possibly into harm's way.

"I know of the location, but why there? It is so barren and avoided David wouldn't even entertain the thought of letting them enter. Quickly, guys, on your feet, we must ride fast to the sycamore tree in the distance. Ebb, that stubborn ole' mule! God help us!"

Betsy is running at a pace that even to her, her vision is a blur of the roadside's textures and fixtures of a beaten pathway, as Jacob, who is usually tender with the feet, digs in and stings her sides with the spurs! The boys catch up to the expeditious pair who have prompted them with a rapid returning pace of saliva in streams and sweating of the nose dripping with moisture, but all is good, and they wait for Jacob's instruction out of loyalty to their friend. "Betsy can just wait here," is Rocco's attitude toward the matter. Jacob places a plan in motion, taking an extra quiver of arrows for this neck of the woods.

"Okay, Betsy, we are going to tie you loosely to the hitching post just inside the tree line in case you need to break free, but you are to remain here. Got that? Good!"

A lone dog, Rocco, howls in agreement with Jacob's wise decision.

"Boys, stay close to me; no weekend warriors on duty here. We must stay together in our limited numbers disadvantage!" The circulation of air begins to twirl in a duct-spinning motion, and cloud coverage suddenly takes flight above the four and all who are amongst the Engarlands Way. For their eyes only, darkness overwhelms the area on Jacob and the boys' entrance, knowing this journey will swallow them up into the depths of the forest, where nothing good ever happens!

The thundering of the thunderous voice overwhelms the canines as Jacob takes the lead and sightly separates from them to check on Betsy with the confidence that the safety of the approaching unknown will keep the unknown dangers in check. Betsy, on the other hand, is not at all comfortable in thunderstorms, especially in the great wide yonder, but does pretty good under the shelter provided; if her mane stays dry, she'll be just fine. The boys enter into the cavity of the sycamore tree and bow in respect, barking in tones that Jacob is not familiar with. He will never witness the conversation between the tree and the dogs. No one can, other than Balak, who had heard with his own ears the tale of a donkey named Nolan. The rest of the conversation that Jacob neglects to listen in on is disturbed by the trembling of the earth's gravest foundation due to the thunder of the heavens, as the earth bows down to the glorious sound and yields to the deepest, darkest coverings of the collapsing skies. The hard rain begins to fall upon the surface, startling the soul's pouring. It is felt by the barometer's atmospheric pressure and by a change in the attitude of the three boys' hearts and minds, drowning out the boys' conversation with the sycamore.

Approaching with all due respect, the boys bow down to the ancient one, the sycamore tree, of great cultural significance. Consider that the legend spreads rapidly over the years amongst all divine dog breeds by virtue of the dogs having many connections.

Men disregard this natural act by turning their heads and whistling while a four-legged friend relieves the acts of nature amongst them as they hike their legs.

The response of Duke breaks the ice. "Why else would a bear doo-doo in the woods, and yes, he does?!"

The sycamore barks a command out of the aging bark asking, "Do you bow down before me as if I am a god from so-called intelligent men? For if so, we will conclude this conversation before we even start, and I shall open up our branches to watch you drown in the depths of water thrust upon you!"

Duke stands and steps forward to open up in pleading, "Is this not the entrance of your great forestry greenery so much heard of in the ancient of days past?" he says, as he whines a saying directly from his heart, his tail just a-wagging, "The Lord has heard our supplications and His blessings are upon us right now!"

Rocco steps in check to elaborate, "Oh, great one, on the wings of the wind, a true offering of respect I release as a fragrance breeze, for a fart in all of its glory is an offering of the highest amongst a dog's life; it enters into this overlooked secret place of beauty in the sycamore tree. I beg you for entrance due to the absence of two whom we love dearly. One is of a wise mule and his cotton ball friend of meekness, the sheep. Please, listen to my request for the protection of your entangled limbs of great power to shelter us from the raging storm!"

A hollow voice speaks in return with a humbled spirit. The mentioning of the two allies has healed the heart of this sycamore into a spirit of giving, and he opens up to the conversation. "We can protect you with coverings from the rain, but for those things that remain rampant in our forestry, we are powerless. May God provide those accommodations in prayer for all of you with hearts of purified gold. Quickly, you may enter!"

Jacob returns from Betsy with a puzzled look on his face and pleads with the dogs, "Did I miss something? I thought I heard two voices talking. Oh, what a day this is becoming!"

THE FLOOD WITHIN

The oak, elms, and firs sway back and forth in a vertical axis vortex of energy's force. Gapping perforated openings allows rainfall to be deposited into the backlands. Causing a runoff down the soil-packed trails, swimming by the forgotten past landmarks and into the streams. Flooding the roots of the cypress trees, as flotation of the cones, bobbing around like fishing bobbers cast into a stream. Waiting for the lightning to strike within. Who could ever withstand so much effort of strength in these woodland areas of parched topsoil? The trails have turned into a life's flow to the heart of the heartland's abandoned commodity. Drenched coats of the two wanderers deep within nature's tapestry of rainfall, being weighed down by the element on a scale of truth in the matter and able to keep a positive attitude balanced as the thunder penetrates through the sound barrier walls of the eternal pines of the timbers. It is the location of our storm searchers, who have lost their way in the blind-sighted mass. With their bag of clippings, twigs, bark, and now the cones, dragging behind Aly and the weight of his wool, by the way, is capable of keeping him warm but will take days to dry. Ebenezer begins to feel the weight of the provisions provided for the king's delight. The weight of the day starts to take a toll, but unfortunately, they are only getting started! Being lost in the whereabouts of time and found in the wetness of life has given Aly and Ebb one major advantage over their unknown, life-threatening wolf pack. Hunter, the alpha, has made a lone decision expressed to the beta, Josephine, that the pack will not adventure out in this mess until fate can place things back into the hands of their control; the belief in his destiny's call of the wild has brought a whispering concern and rumor amongst the pack into the vision of Smoke, the scout's mid-range wolf, who has a pride issue to resolve.

Smoke has made known to all of the pack, in whispers, the valuable information being held back from the eternal knowledge of the pack of the discovery of today's guest entrance granted by the sycamore of ancient times and that Hunter is using the raging floods within as an excuse because of the weakness that has begun to develop in his leadership skills. Such an appropriate timing to tickle the ears, having begun as a murmur by our instigator's voice of reason to his closest friend Stalker, saying, "Hunter has had several missed opportunities and doesn't really care, for there is always someone to take the blame for his depleting discretion, and Josephine ever so much knows this believing she can make better decisions concerning the favor of the pack. Life as a top dog, Stalker! Now, if Josephine plays her hand correctly, it could benefit the advancement of the whole pack, including ourselves; the ladder steps keep climbing upwards! We can deal the cards, watching from the inside, and she can play the cards to her favor from the outside! This will start a struggle within the pack so that it will fall to the wayside! You in, Stalker?"

There's a long hesitation as Smoke waits for an answer. Stalker's simple response to a complex plan is, "Sure," as the pieces start to fall into place, colliding into each other one at a time!

The lightning strikes as parallel lines branching, very much related to the fingers on a hand; it has yet to find a destination to strike its energy flow, still pondering in illuminating the sky's ambiance character. Such is the life of Smoke, always looking for an opportunity to make a connection, putting on a display of perspective that usually strikes against his disposition. The risk of playing with the power of the source can be life-threatening when you try to get your hands wet in society's self-proclaimed praise!

Slowly and patiently for a change, he lets fear and desperation become his driving vehicle, planting a seed of defiance in the beta herself, Josephine. The storm is still fierce and is multiplying in intensity, and so is the atmosphere in the vicinity of the two. There is an advantage point in Smoke's knowledge of Josephine, knowing that she holds a grudge against Hunter already. The pack had lost a beta. Her name was Delilah; she was very delicate and brought out the best of Hunter in his prospering ways, and she was the love of Hunter's life. She left in a bizarre, unexplained passing in the season of the winter blues, leaving him a widower and father of three litters; in togetherness, he watched them grow from pups to purpose-driven alphas in the leadership in other packs. But the pack suffered the passing of Delilah's contributions in organizational skills and mannerisms enforced to the laws of the brood. Josephine, out of a pure heart's cry, mourned and tried to heal Hunter during the sorrowful period and adjustments with no personal desires other than to be a friend in her well-balanced beta responsibilities until the time Hunter started to shun her away and lay around in his new companion, misery, which would not allow him any comfort. Turning Josephine into the birth of a queen bee, that is, in a behavioral trait of life.

The thunderous clashing of the clouds has become another advantage to Smoke as all conditions are granted in his plans to further his defiance with all this racket. His approach to Josephine is hidden by the shrubbery view of the desolated haven that is on an incline and can overlook the family quarters of the pack's lifestyles. Hunter, who has found a new companion in hiding his secret pain, now awaits the quietness of the storm with the boys. The thunderclaps keep the conversation discreet. Smoke approaches the outer chambers of the retreat, where guests are able to lounge amongst the coolness of the circular cobblestone patio area, and opens up the memorized dialogue at the first insinuation with, "Oh, I thought you were Hunter. Just wanted to see if he wanted to view the lightning show through the covering of the oaks, such a spectacular view, I'd say. Oh, by the way, since you are here, do you have a moment? I have something of personal interest and could be of utmost importance to you, seeing that Hunter has shown no interest, and for your advantage! A rumor to set deep into your favor; just saying, Your Highness!"

Josephine squints her eyes, knowing the reputation he clings to. "Go on, Smoke, I'm listening; this better be good, or your execution will be at hand, so don't mess with my emotional distresses!" Smoke crouches in surrender to let her know of her domination and proceeds to light the fire in the eye of the storm.

"Hunter has passed an opportunity at these two easy preys due to the magnitude of the storm. Who has heard about a pack being afraid of getting soaked? Hunter is failing us," he says, as Josephine's left eyebrow raises in agreement, "and will be the end for us all! And as such an easy game by these two being a donkey and a sheep without the guidance of man. May it be from laziness or just being apathetic to the pack, who knows, but not to listen to those who are promoted to be the eyes and ears of the pack for such a time as these. An important burden that brings enjoyment to my flesh. I already had Stalker and Jasper on my side when he witnessed my final shunning from Hunter. That leaves Scar, Rolette, and the four omegas of the pack, Rusty, Zion, Shadow, and Bob, to make up the inner core of the pack. Maybe others that we can probably convince with the numbers who are in! So, are you in on this mutiny that is at your command, your heiress?" He is now crouching in fear, having pushed a little too hard by turning the tables over onto Hunter. The first wave of the storm starts to settle, leaving the boys in fright and in a howling frenzy! Smoke has said all that he dares to say and turns to walk away, but not before seeing Josephine's reaction.

"Well, that's my calling, Josephine. I am being summoned by the others and will not miss out on this opportunity!" Josephine lets Smoke see her smile of approval! Walking toward the altar by the cistern barren reservoir, leaving the place vacant and all to herself, thinking about the advantage of being in a pack amongst men!

Penny Picked a Pepper, or Did She?

The rain is coming down so hard that a blanket of darkness has been cast down to the ground at a distance while Sheldon's shell is in shell shock by the indignation of the storm as he addresses the whole group loudly so proper documentation of all that is said will be recorded properly.

"Listen, everyone, ten-hut! We need to come to a complete halt. For the storm has revitalized its momentum in the western hemisphere by our destination. Let us put the situation at hand into perspective. Ebb and Aly will, at one point or another, make their presence known if we remain on the roadside. More than likely, they are or have already sought shelter from the storm. So, let's take this time on reflection of our weary, spiritual attributions in these matters. At ease, ladies! All is going well, and the inscriber never has time for rest unless waiting for autocorrect to catch up on the misspelled errors along the sentence way. Not to worry; all conversations will be at most accurate when all is said and done!"

Penny has found a dry spot resting herself in an unseen alcove near the open meadows and sprawls out. Gretchen is doing the more comfortable route of resting on a tree branch to keep an eye on things, and of course, Sheldon always has the capability to seek shelter in a millisecond in time. A calmness fills the air, and even Penny begins to drift into a sea of unconscious sentiments. Penny's ears spring up, being noticed over the patch of grass on the incline part by the nook, absorbing information from an unknown tangible. She pokes her head up and answers, "Yes, Lord, over here," she says to the one who knows all things of all beings. "I am the messenger, and I am to serve You; have Your way in me!" And in the silence, she can hear the whispering voice say…

(38)

"Listen,

"The fourth stone is the complexity of emotions; a strong desire to allure in charismatic nature of possession, to esteem higher than the love greater than loving the Lord, first utmost, who has created all things for the love of mankind. They bow down and bring forth, deliver, grow, beg, borrow, and depart with, only if the return is far greater than. Somewhere along this forestry road will be in the hands of the fourth stone. Deep in the herb garden, the freshest fruits are grown, and nourishing vegetables are plentiful in the rich embedded soil of time. She searches for every green thing. Although her labor once took precedence over her desire for the words of truth that had entangled her mind in misdirection, she has now been forgiven, and her crown has been cast aside at My feet. For now, she greets the weary and invites them to rest in comfort and is a guardian, a most kindhearted host to nature's small creatures. You will understand

THE MEADOWLANDS

the continuity of her heartstrings. Clarity will be observed in the one who cares for the estate by these lands, and a sweet spot in her heart shall release her object of affection.

"Yes, your paws in the valley have tasted her fruits and vegetables and will try to compromise the one's false integrity. The answer will come from afar, but to the one you all love dearly, it will be her last true desire! Penny, wait until the storms end so that there will be no hindrances in this message at request. The time at hand is time for praying. Time is needed; when time is spent foolishly, time is always available, but time cannot be taken for granted. Penny, I have spoken of a place dear to your heart and a loved one where a resting place and time is sufficient."

Gretchen flies over, shrugging her shoulders and stating forward, "Penny, are you all right? Why are your legs in motion on the ground and thumping as if you are pacing yourself? Are you running in your dreams?" A connection of friendship is now developing for the first time between the two, as Gretchen shows love out of concern and not for gossiping purposes. Penny looks as if she has just woken up from a lullaby and a good night's dream.

"No, no, I'm okay, just lost in concentration in progressive thoughts from the Lord on the motivation required of a fourth stone!"

All of Sheldon's digits explode from his interior shell, "Statement for the record. Did I hear you mention the possibility of a fourth stone?! Sheldon has made ground contact and has recovered in his sea-like legs. Still startled by Penny's announcement. Let's calculate here; we know that two stones are in place and in our care, and the fifth one needs to be found. Then, that means the third stone is in progress and is still hidden wherever for whomever to find, but who?"

Then, in unison, all three of them announce out loud, *"Ebb and Aly,* of course! Now this equation is starting to make a lot more sense. This is the reason David is alone! May God help them all!"

ALLEN W. LEAFGREEN

Just a Boy

The bumble bee is just a-whizzing by the head of David in circular motions, weaving in and out, up and down, and side to side. The joyful flight of our bumble bee has attracted the attention of the girls, wondering how his flight is being so sporadic and for what reasons, at that? So, our little friend has gained an audience in motion. Following the flow of David's stride and keeping the tone and tempo of the beat of David's pounding feet, sounding like he is a beat bopper at his best, believe you me! The journeys continue, and then a nearby bridge by the brook becomes a sudden reality, and the wetlands of the marshes settle back into time's shell. The frogs return to their lily pads, which have moved to a new location with new acquaintances, bringing in the bass sound of a deep tone to the additional tune of the bumble bee. The dragonflies skim the water's top to cool off, touching the surface three times (for the third time's a charm) or maybe dancing to the new rhythmic section of the land. With lyrics already acquired and the rhythmic section kicking in a tune, a song starts to settle in the atmosphere's amphitheater, while the general breaks in a tune with the voice harp!

(39)
Settled in the peace of the day and into the restful night's decline.
Take the wings of the morning when the darkness falls
upon the distant, horizon sky.
Astounding are Your works in me for being a gracious bumble bee.
In my sorrowful Song, the heart of David, for he is just a boy.
This word has been placed in my heart, burning while hidden
for quite some time.
Do you see the letters flow from my life and into yours,
my beloved shepherd boy.

THE MEADOWLANDS

*As scriptures overflow, be free. There's no set inscription or script
of whom and which we are; talents overflow when released.
Understanding my thoughts, You comprehend my pathways
when You laid Your hand upon me.
Do not claim your youth, it too shall fade away, like the grass,
that withers from the fields.
You are in the Potter's house, for David is a vessel made of
clay and placed in the Potter's hand.
Do not walk in the ways of motion's plea, move forward
in the whispers I bring.
A stone's throw away from an open field. David, you are in
my life. Even for this bumble bee,
And the purpose for your heart, I have seen, will come
to pass. These that have been hidden,
In my life blood's flow, for quite some time,
for he is just a boy.*

THE PRESTIGE CYPRESS TREE OFFERING
(40)

The trees of the forest have been awakened from their isolation and sorrow with the cleansing of the rain. The warmth in their hearts is a comforting welcome as the two inspirational souls that have been praying without ceasing cast into the skyline of faith, raining encouragement and healing into the hearts of the woodlands. Their lost souls are in search of the intangible consuming light brought forward by the faithful to each annihilating and conquering darkness and utmost fear. A spiritual battle within the wolves' layer has been secretly invaded in the daylight and right before their snarling snouts, all in due timing of the Lord, for He reigns over the evil and the good! The wild beasts are known by the Engarlands Way and have angered their spirits in a protective way. How dare the wolves seek out God's anointed!? They are in fierce activity, burrowing within the prowling wolves, searching the crevasses of the concealed underground, seeking on a whim those which they shall devour. They are being observed closely by the prestige cypress pines.

Ebenezer had been foretold a legend in the hierarchy that reigned in these woods and has heard stories about those who were fortunate enough to survive the sudden attack of these same wolves that are pursuing them now. But the fierce storm has given the two ample departures for the tingling sensation of being watched has resided in his spirit. So has the awakening affection by the two followers being led in faith's intuitions and the joy of the Lord inside tense moments of time like these. Searching for the Lord, breathing and exhaling, being overtaken in their minds and soul enriched in the living spoken word, deeply enclosed in their heartbeat. Insightful intuitions that they are being stalked by a beast in a cage of hostility. Now is not the time to remind Alymore of the pack beneath Hunter's ruling. Under the mercy of the cypress trees, enlightenment is brought to the drenched coats, sheltering them from more than just the elements. Entering the promised land's tranquility of an essence quest for the cypress cones. The veiled buds are highly esteemed, a necessity, and a blessing for concluding relevance. Released into the flowing stream running water, entangled near the edge. Each of our little lamb's open sachets releases a fragrance of completion to an agenda of the forest offerings, soon to be a blessing to all who adore all of God's beauty.

Moved by the wind that whistles a glorious tune from the ends of the earth as the almond blossoms ascend from the glistening dew, a voice proclaims in the ruffling sounds of the evergreens, "You will not walk alone in the midst of these woodlands and the threatening that is within. For the heart of your friend are amongst us, enclosed by our coverings, where the shade protects those from the heat of the day and the pouring rain from the storm. Standing on the road by the entryway, a man with a quiver of sharp arrows and a knife made of flint! So, strap the laces of your sandals, and he shall come to carry you away safely. He will come swiftly and shall not rest in the restoration. The land is accessible above measure, and your feet shall not stumble, which is the way of the righteous. Your enemies shall be known, who is for the Lord and who is against because the land will be as of briars and thorns to the soles of their paws."

The low-lying branches shudder in agreement with the mighty cypress. "Continue forward in following the guiding ways of the cypress trees in the complexity of the landscape for viewing. Lost in a time of forgetfulness, if you listen closely, you will hear the voices of strangers gathering from those who walked along the stone pathway. Broadening outward in the exterior of the holly shrubs, lining the inner layer, to a stairwell. The steps flow in a casual incline, narrowing to the security of the entrance gate. For the convenience of others, it has been left open, but it has a latch to lock just before the sun sets. This access will be enclosed on both sides by trellis and lattice wiring to withstand the weight of the inner morning glories and honeysuckle. A pergola with several arches is the cover and will lead into the main sanctuary area. Hurry and close the gate within. You shall be secure, for the thicket, thorns, and briars of the holly shrubs go deep. You will hear the voices of your enemy snarling and nipping each other's heels, but they cannot reach you. Prepare yourself for the exit that leads to the cobblestone patio area of the sanctuary once they are able to enter from around to other entrances! Now go quickly!"

Jacob's Prayer
(41)

Under the feet of the rain's coverage, with the darkness now lifted and the land purified, tracking is as almost impossible as finding a bug in the rug. Removed and without a trace, Jacob calls for the team of dogs to enter the scene. Ace looks around in awe of the massive sycamore and is lost in a trance, which is in itself very unusual for him because he has always been the informative one of the three. Rocco is the first responder in this critical situation, followed by Duke, the keen one in matters such as these. He is already investigating the surroundings; a limited number of clues, but they are visible. A broken twig here and traces of lint entanglement of a wooly substance, flapping in the breeze similar to wind blowing through a windsock, let Duke know there is a gentle breeze blowing in a northwestern movement, meaning their scent should be a more noticeable factor.

The sound of Jacob's voice, in a directing tone, says, "We are what seems worlds apart from our conjuring travelers of the meek kind, and it is tearing me apart. What else could bring these savage beasts on the prowl, the smell of innocent blood, adventuring in this avenue in anguish? Okay, boys, the many miles apart need to be shortened, and we are wasting precious time. Go, boys, find Alymore and Ebenezer quickly. Stay together and close to whatever trails are visible!"

Finally, Ace snaps out of whatever he was in earlier and is beside the matter of Duke, knowing that he is the man, and asks, "Duke, come on already, are you picking anything up yet? You know, we're only looking at a distance about as close as the wagging of a tail in comparison, if they're moving at a gradual pace!"

Rocco, playing with the mud, watching the mass squish through his paws, chimes in like a bell tone, "Oh, and you're the creative one here, so get creative already; my patience is being tested!"

Duke, in an annoyed voice, answers, "Will you give me a minute? I'm trying to get past the smell of dirty, wet clothes in a hamper smell, which is probably them, but it is a dominant smell and very strong for a group of two!"

Ace, in backlash, gripes out of tune, "Well, we have to lead Jacob in some direction other than forward and at a better stride. I can even hear Betsy complaining that she can still hear us and is wondering what is up, Duke?!"

"Okay, okay, let me buy some time here, my snout is tingling in the wind, but we can pick up the pace, so let's fake it till we make it. I need something other than this awful smell to go by, for it covers the whole forest floor!" A very disturbed ole Duke boy is confused for the first time in a while. A dog lover may not be able to understand all the howling and low-tone barking that the boys are up to; he just knows that they are sensing anguish in the deadened silence. And, of course, you can only be so prepared, going in blind and knowing trouble awaits each footstep taken.

From the wings of the wind, separating the clouds canopy around them, brightness now leads them into the secret place, like coals of fire, lighting up the foundation of the wild world in vanquished silence, a howling call no one ever heard before. The blast of their breath penetrates the dogs' ears and Jacob's alertness. The wolves in the rustling and trampling have made their location known, although they are at a distance far greater than the echoes, giving false directions. As the pumping motion swells, the glands and main arteries in all cylinders fire, hoping that a piston doesn't come exploding due to an overload of circuitry from the mind's senses. Ace and Rocco, in unison, say, "Well, there you go, Duke; that should be sufficient enough for ya, my good man!"

Ace, making the whelping sounds of a young puppy shivering,

says, "How many did you hear, Duke? The howling is definitely apparent, with angered voices making mockery, right, Duke?!"

Duke is throwing a fit with paws going every which way. "You think? Now sssssssh, I'm trying to pinpoint them, silly; let's go!"

Jacob begins speaking forth to a friend and companion who is always there, and we're not talking about the boys. Call upon His name, the Lord, God Almighty.

> *We have lost our way, Lord,*
> *to seek those in their wanderings about this forestry sanctuary.*
> *The boastful howls of our enemy known has become my greatest fear,*
> *for life is endangered and at high risk, by this separation.*
> *With the fangs of the pursuers, cannot my ears discern their battle cry?*
> *Being on the prowl in pursuit of their victims.*
> *Lord, You will light the torch posts with a devouring fire,*
> *ignited by the weeping of those being hounded and of lost heart.*
> *You are a shield to all who trust in you.*
> *It is God who arms me with strength,*
> *to pull the bow strings and guide my arrows,*
> *deep within their ravishing soul.*
> *May my knife be true to the jugular vein, to their raging voices.*
> *And the natural guidance of the dog's instincts.*
> *You make my way perfect to bring the defenseless back,*
> *into the safety of Your loving arms.*

A dog's instincts are amazing on the nose, bewildering in following, and are dependent on our commands. The comfort of them on guard all the time attitude of listening to every little sound in detail. Diligent to seek their reward of a kibble, down to the smallest gestures. The boys are a team brought on by the initiative of one. Usually, Duke is the corporate there, while Rocco likes to instigate and harass whoever it might be, as the two converse with each other.

"Hey, Duke, this is your playing field, and your ballgame is on the line here! So where and how many of what kind of backbiter are we looking at?!" says Rocco, looking directly into the snout of Duke. So, where is the voice of reasoning located? How about crouching behind Jacob as Ace mentally visualizes the ferocious gnashing of teeth? Dogs can use facial expressions to get their message across to their fellow companions; Duke gives Rocco a staredown and glances over to Ace to show him that everything is going to be all right. One last look at Rocco, and the routine begins.

Duke puts his ear to the ground, tilting his head from side to side and then looking up into the heavens. He licks both of his paws, lays his head completely on the ground, chin resting on the ground floor, tail just a-wagging away, and his tongue tied and released in a slithering in-and-out between his canine teeth. He taps and counts the number of taps in session, stands up, and goes in motion in a circular pattern with a third-time's-a-charm attitude.

Then, he starts the breakdown of his analytic conclusion. Duke's response is very detailed. "The howling is from ten wolves, being led by three in a haunting hunt. They're moving in an in-and-out pattern, grinding their teeth as they brag about how they are going to manipulate their victims in a very descriptive setting. The three in the back are closely bonded together and show respect to the leader as they circle each area and come to a halt for thorough inspection. The remaining four are indecisive in their whereabouts and follow between here and there. The brood is heading north in a westerly flow, stumbling over each other's enthusiasm in a notorious characteristic way. 'Not on your life' is the motivational statement that leads them into a frenzy encouraged by those in the back lines. Yep, that's about it!"

"No way, Duke!" is the response from an astounded Ace.

"How do you come up with something as farfetched as that? We must pick up our tempo!" says Rocco in one of his best replies.

Jacob wonders what the heck has gotten into Duke with his low murmuring, barking, and whimpering without a single breath in between them. He speaks a command forth. "Not so fast, guys. We need to find a defensive positioning so that the wolves will lead into their own harm's way so that I can have an accurate account with time to release several arrows. An upper ground perspective of a hundred-yard radius viewpoint. Slow in movement as if we are the hunter and not the hunted. We pray that our two comrades will return to this direction. We need to be patient and see what the Lord may bring, so let's stand guard and watch!"

(42)

— Chapter Seven —
A RECIPE FOR DISASTER

The culinary delight of cooking is that you can be very creative, adding a little pizzazz and artistry to an entrée to make it your own creation, a spinoff of the original concoction, using the finest of ingredients based on freshness and the love for cooking. Presentation is just as important, for we visualize the dish before we even take our first bite and smell the aroma of fresh herbs that have been added to the clarity of a consommé. The important thing is that each step is to be registered so that three weeks down the line, you will come up with the same productive dish that influences and is complimented by guests. A recipe to avoid any disastrous results.

That being said, the same principles can be applied to a pack of wolves in the pursuit of their prey. The only thing about Hunter's pack is the strong influence of pride, for you can use all kinds of high-spirited alcohol to enhance flavoring, but once in the cook's hand, who starts consuming more for his delight and a little too much of his product, well, things can get blurry, and the recipe misread; you get the point. That is the representation of our front three pursuers. Smoke, Stalker, and Jasper, the cooks added mirepoix of celery, onions, and carrots. Their souls are not in line with the loyalty of the most important ingredient, Hunter. Let's listen in as Smoke leads the pack with his own integrity himself.

"The nerve of Hunter, holding the pack back due to the conditions of the weather. Maybe we should invest our hunt in finding a pair of galoshes and a raincoat for him. Who knows how far from us are the pair? The pack is with us, Stalker, and the sky's the limit; there is no stopping the forceful three that we are! And to think of all the times Hunter was the man in his glory days. He let Delilah get into his head and spirit, and then everything went south! Well, not in your life; that will not happen here ever again!"

The rest of the conversation is not worth listening in on; the important thing about using alcohol in your sauce or whatever is that you have to let the alcohol burn off and not get burned by the consuming fire of the vapors igniting into this beautiful array of color with the aroma as the vegetables compliment in the flavoring united when done properly. If not, then alcohol will be the only thing tasted in bitterness.

Then there are the hidden ingredients of a dish that bring further enhancements to the dish that, unless you tell your secret, remain unknown. They come in with herbs and spices to round out this fabulous stock but are added to the dish in all due time. These are the four wolves pursuing in the middle of the pack, always within hearing distance of the front three. Rusty, Zion, Shadow, and what about Bob; the rosemary, basil, thyme, and other secret seasonings, doing their own enhancing in stirring the pot, as Shadow opens up a carton of heavy cream and starts talking about the nasty substance cremini mushrooms sprout before being picked, if you know what I mean. They prepare for the things to come, but for now, they just need to be rinsed off really well and then sliced.

Shadow continues on in his preparation and rage. "There is definitely evil here living amongst the pack. I am not sure in which way the wind should blow, but all I know is to stay clear of the flame, or you will become part of the chaff. It is a pity that this will end up in bloodshed for the pack! It goes deeper than just the clash of pride and war of leadership, for the sword blades in this pack are dull and rusted. Give praise to our stone-carved image, for even the stones surrounding it cry out in anguish at its presence and call it an abomination!"

Rusty glances over his shoulder, smirking in a *what the...* attitude. "Have you been hitting the bottle, Shadow? Because you are talking smack that isn't making sense at all to me; next thing you know, the trumpet will be blowing, and then you will be calling in the name of the Lord and all that...!"

Shadow bites back," Don't disrespect the things you do not understand because His presence is here this day and will make himself known, I feel it in my paws and to the tip of my tailbone, and we will totally be annihilated, you and me; I am making my peace with God this very day! They say that faith alone is the way we should live, and that is where I stand firm on this day, a stone that cannot be shattered, not some man-made stone pillar!"

So, at this point in preparation, it is best to keep a watchful eye on your Merlot wine reduction so that it doesn't become a wasted reduction of time. This is the mindset of Zion as he slyly ponders off to the back of the pack where loyalty runs deep in these three amigos, for blood is thicker than a blood sausage; I know, disgusting, but so is the situation at hand. Time to gather up all those secret spices that should be on hand as part of your mirepoix but definitely not to be used until your sauce is completed and needs to be added by measurements. "For this too shall come to pass" is Zion's philosophy spoken forth to Hunter and the loyal two Scar and Rolette.

"Just to let you three know, there is a mutiny in the form of a brewing sauce in the making, and it's not pleasant in the aroma I smell amongst the other pack, for some spices are not compatible with others, just speaking in terms of this metaphor, Hunter!"

Hunter gives him an acknowledging nod of understanding and

opens up a smidge of Dijon mustard. "Oh, I am so much aware of the circumstances, and the way I see it, it will be two parts oil to two parts flour if you are in, Zion, and I hope you so much are to complete this roux mixture to tighten up the pot of the matter?! The others will either disperse or join in the stronger side; we will see!" Even the thickener of the roux has to be cooked under a low flame for now so that the impure taste of the starch can be cooked out. When added to the stock, in due time, all will be united, with a sheen of predestinated quality, for the guest's arrival.

But none of this is possible for what they are fighting to obtain; it does not come down to leadership just yet, but a starving hunger of just being famished since it has been a long time between a wholesome meal of about three weeks or so. The stock is the most important component in the matter and requires a lot of preparation in proper distribution to complete the flavors competing for a savory dish such as lamb. They know of the prey but have yet to bring it into the storehouse to break down the textures of nothing going to waste. The bones roasted with a mirepoix of vegetables with a smidge of tomato paste and then, after completion a splash more of a red wine. Then add to a pot and cover with clear stream water. That, like the wolf's appetite, needs to simmer for hours at a time filling the kitchen with the rich aroma, bringing a thick crusting of saliva to their canine choppers for cutting the meaty substance. Now you can add the reduction to the matter, and it all comes together with the oily, flour-binding action of the roux. And patiently wait, Hunter, for the opportunity; for now, you just need the tender meat so that the sauce can complement the savory lamb chops. The heavy cream, Dijon mustard, whole butter, and the cremini mushrooms will be added later after the liquid is strained through a chinois. But other work needs to be done in the waiting, patiently in the simmering mode, cleanup of things needs to be handled before the guest of three dogs and a man arrive, life's secret ingredient unknown by the wolves and the prey, only God knows of the final outcome, just you wait and see.

Speaking of our cuisine choice for the main entrée for the menu being set for our wolves, they are known by the guests and the prey, and neither one is happy about the selection. Ebenezer and Alymore have now arrived at the banquet hall's overflowing patio area, near the stone stairwell area, where many weddings and other events have taken place due to the entryway from the main sanctuary and the beautiful blooms of the spring that take place in an extravagant presentation. Jacob and the dogs haven't arrived but are in the process of determining the location of his other four-legged friends, but first, the dirty work needs to be handled in taking out the garbage that is overflowing in the back areas of the woods. Just waiting for another outburst of response from anyone, anywhere?

Ebb clears his throat due to the raspy voice from the cold, damp climate and says, "Hurry, Aly, up the stairwell to the security of the gate's latching and entrapment of the beauty within. I can hear the wolves approaching and vague body movement in the shrubs!"

The wolves have picked up the scent of their prey and go into a spastic frenzy, running into one another, seeking out the dominance of the front pursuers. What they need to be doing is watching their backs! For they are no longer servants to guests arriving at a dinner gathering, no sir, let's call them for who they are to become; carnivores, beasts, predators, or just as simple as meat-eating wolves that they are! And will not let anyone get in their way, not even certain members inside of their own wolf pack, things need to be settled now, amongst the pack and to whomever!

A terrifying growling from Hunter is like a clap of thunder in the air. *"Enough!"*

Enough is the rightful statement being taken by both parties, but more importantly, Jacob and the boys, who have now defined the location of the growl just before the thunderclap takes place in a sky so blue, wondering where the sound came from. But there is no need for that as the downpouring of the rain has started building into intensity, as do the circumstances of all the partiers based on their locations. Aly and Ebb are secured with the latching of the enclosed gate and are all the way into the walkway that leads into the main sanctuary. And now stand face to face with the pack's idol, located by the well of purification that is bone dry. Josephine, who is closer to the inner sanctuary, circles around and heads out toward Hunter, taking a direct pathway that weaves past the cemetery entrance and proceeds on into a shrubbery overflow. Lightning strikes and flashes with the deafening sound of thunders slashing into the air, removing breath from your lungs as time revolves at a slow pace. Jacob finds positioning just at the exit area of the cemetery and has the destructive hounds in view. Just in time to see the lunging of two beasts going at it in the shadows of the shrubs.

"Enough, it is time to turn this around, Smoke; just you and me, to settle this once and for all. You are poison to this pack with your negative outlook on the pack's private issues!"

The warriors enter the room and circle each other in hate and a fire is ignited deep inside. Zion, Scar, and Rolette keep watch, making sure the others keep out of this fight to keep it as fair as possible. Stalker, Jasper, and Rusty try breaking into a tight circle and commence into battle's rage. Bob and Rusty scamper off and become the first and second taken out by Jacob's archery skills and the discreet silence of an assassin in action. He stays hidden in the cover of the yew trees, telling the boys to take heed, and now they know to be still on Jacob's command.

Henceforth we are back in the make-shift coliseum of wolves in a battleground arena with the blood-howling of Hunter. "Not so easy using physical strength, is it, Smoke? Always using your words as the weapons of your artillery. I know exactly where your blood flows, and you even try to get the loyalty of the beta, Josephine. You're such a fool at heart, and how fast words travel within the pack. Do you think that your shyness goes unaware and how sounds travel in these hollows of your evil schemes? I shall have your neck before this day has commenced. I shall cast you out of this pack, but you are not going to walk away from this rage bounded by hate, Smoke. In the power of disaster, you have separated the pack, trying to bring it in your favor!"

The canine fangs penetrate deeply into Smoke's jugular, dropping him under Hunter's feet! Like heavy cream being poured into the sauce of life, with the butter being whisked in a defeating venture. And folding in the mushrooms, garnished with earthly flavor, let's leave out the Dijon mustard, because the cut is already deep enough to put Smoke to eternal rest! The perfected culinary sauce is complete and can be placed in a container in a hot water bath to hold at a proper temperature, for things are definitely getting hot in this kitchen. It is not a cool atmosphere when the staff is at each other's necks, especially when the guest can hear the commotion and, worse of all, Jacob can witness the whole action in progress, and one is illuminated by the equation of the problem at hand.

The rain once again pours down the passages like a river stream, cleansing the blood seeping slowly from the gash penetrating from Smoke, and Shadow is the next to take an arrow through his neck, striking death instantly and now getting the attention of the others since Shadow's strike was so close to home base this time around! The odds are not quite in Jacob's favor, but he is going through the due process. Josephine clearly witnesses the arrow's strike and release as she quietly approaches from behind. The dogs are infringed in the excitement of bloodshed, for they are tamed wolves at heart, but the smell of blood is just a back burner away, and so is their awareness, being caught off guard. Jacob is nocking the next arrow for its destructive aviation and is able to get his last shot off, hitting Jasper in his side, leading him, as a sniper would do so, for an accurate flight. In a leap of faith, Josephine strikes Jacob from behind, but the momentum sends her head over heels in a spiral catapulting action, landing in front of the boys. Jacob recovers with only a significant scratch below the cheekbone, blood trickling down his cheek area, bringing a shriek sound out of the mouth of Josephine due to the distinct smell of human blood in the air.

Jacob reaches for his knife and exclaims aloud, "Lord, You have taught me in battle's cry and are my protection from the secret blow of my enemy, help me to strike swiftly, for others have heard the wolves' cry and, in my vision, I see them splitting into groups as only five of the six remaining access this assault."

A weakness in one man's aggression is devastating to see, as this sight brings new life into Jacob and goes at Josephine's massive body strength one-on-one. Her energy's force once again hammers another nail of her bite into the opposite wrist area of the concealed weapon hidden between his hand and forearm, keeping the blade outward to avoid self-infliction, grasping onto Josephine's fur and riding her freestyle to the ground with a fatal severing of her neck's jugular vein. Jacob makes contact with a yew tree trunk, knocking him unconscious. At the same time Hunter makes the decision once again on his own, for his selfish desires that taunt him so dearly! The scent of lamb amongst the flowery bouquet before the great entranceway!

So now the pot has simmered over its time window in the cooking world, and all flavors are incorporated in the holding temperature of life's calling. See what happens when there are too many wannabe chefs amongst the cooks, all may have gone in a different direction, but of course, hindsight is twenty-twenty. Hunter has the capability to keep everything in an orderly, professional manner, but anger and having an empty stomach can become deceiving. The staff has to be cooperative, but as you can see, part of the staff has called in, with one out with a severe arrow in his side that Jasper will not recover from, and the doctor of circumstances of the unfortunate kind has notified Hunter to take him off of the workforce, while the heartless chef in Hunter wants to correspond with his guest to get better acquainted, that's if this were a proper sociable setting without the claws and fangs at hand. Knives should always stay in the kitchen, and the only knives in the guest area should be the steak knives to cut the savory lamb being served, but not yet!

(43)

There is still hope in the kitchen to pull off this great event where there is so much going wrong, for there is a strong supporting staff; now, whatever their title may have been, they must work as one to complete the tasks of the missing culinary positions vacant of the now inner circle remaining in Stalker. Yikes! Who would have thought him to be such a weak character at heart? One who only does no more, no less, depending on the complexity of things, but has no choice in these matters, well in less passing on, which is more likely to happen to the weakest link. Blending amongst the remaining are Scar, Rolette, and Zion (who is the salt and pepper) of these lose-fitting characters, always working overtime to keep the pack strong and loyal to Hunter. So goes the saying that only the strong survive? There is a certain feeling of gratification when there is a "smooth flow" of culinary professionals in their working habitat, their skills in action when they are at their best, but when it comes to social graces and stepping into the outer limits amongst the guests... Well, let's take Josephine, for example; she didn't do so well. But now, the remaining staff, with time on their paws, want to interact with the guest, taking advantage of Jacob's recovering time from Josephine's dismay.

"Wait, isn't that Josephine? What is she doing lying at that man's feet? Get up and show some dignity?!" is the response from, guess who, yep, Stalker. Well, what do you expect, Stalker, from such a rude entrance amongst guests? On top of that, look, Josephine is at the bottom of the totem pole, her fate final. So now the boys are aware, taking action, and are accounted for in Rocco, Duke, and

Ace, and their shepherd whom you have wounded. We properly, in good manners, introduce ourselves, and now that the pleasantries are done, we now wait for the oncoming predators in a defensive stance, ready to take the impact of the ravishing wolves that they shall become; I kid you not!

Zion is the first to appear to take a stand. Oh, Zion, you could have been so much more if only you could tame your inner beast, the special seasoning that influences greatness in others, showing concern for the pack, wanting it to become more than what it already has become, a failing unit! A strong leader's weakness is not knowing when to give in and call it a truce, to walk away and live another day, like Hunter, right, an act of cowardness at best, but there is a difference. That's a totally different story; sorry, getting ahead of myself here! Zion is joined by Scar and Rolette, who are two wolves away from joining. Then there is Stalker, who is a questionable matter at that and wants to flee this developing circumstance. But fear has a way of stopping you dead in your tracks, indecisive ways to where you just lock up, as so much he has done! So, all in all, it is a fair fight, as Zion starts to circle the three boys, seeking whom he may devour, as now so has Scar and Rolette. The boys know to stay tight in a group setting to keep the odds balanced and wait for a mishap to take place before mayhem sets in. Just as opportunity comes knocking on Rocco's front door, luring Zion and Scar into a defensive setting and a huge risk factor, for Rocco is being carried by someone other than himself, trusting the Lord that he has listened closely to what the Lord is directing him in his darkest, terrifying event.

"So is it worth it you are fighting for the others, taking your misdirection into our hands, you foolish pup? You seem to be wiser in your old age. Come on, Scar, let's finish him; he appears to be the stronger of the three!" Zion says in front while Scar approaches from the blindside of Rocco, so it seems.

Silence is key, and not to have a conversation with your opponent; oh, it looks good and cool, but it opens up the door of lost concentration as it has for Zion, and Scar is way too slow in his reaction time. While Zion leaps into his mighty signature move, the thunderous "lunge of ludicrousness" and then the "lacerations from his teeth, transferring pain" amongst his victim, or supposedly the way the move is intended to go down. Rocco may be old in his maturity and age, but one thing is he ain't is slow. In the middle of the lunge, well, let's say that Zion left his bits vulnerable, just enough for Rocco, in his speed of the matter, to shift onto his backside and see what seems to be a nice pair of dice on the stomach side of Zion. Rocco crunches down on the painful area and continues to keep fighting the good fight before Scar can say, "What the flying fish sticks is going on here?" Like I said, silence is golden when you're in a competition, for it always seems the gullible pay the price to the piper; *ooops,* probably not a proper sentence at this time, but it is what it is, oh, so close, I'll leave it at that for descriptive writing! Rocco then jumps back to his feet and springs onto the neck of Zion, not letting up as Ace comes; better late than never. Help is on the way to finish off Zion's painful last breath to send him to his destination of eternity, into the blinding reign of brimstone, and it's not the blinding rain that is down pouring on God's earth's vessel. Scar is trying his best to pull Ace off of Zion by gripping onto his tale; that is, his bite was attending to lock onto Ace's hind quarter, but because he is as slow as a sloth in a dead heat race, well, there you go, and from there on is a lost cause. The two boys make quick work of Scar, not out of disrespect, for God's creation is beautiful and so delicate. It is how we utilize our talents and for what purposes, all for the glory of God through our confession of Jesus Christ, our Lord and Savior, with our helper in the Holy Spirit, which we received at our water baptism. Neither of the trinity has ever been proclaimed or placed on Scar's hard-scarred tissue.

Jacob is beginning to come around out of a daze, but things are still a little fuzzy. But first things first, before any other action is required, he must remove the weight of Josephine off of his pulsating wounded wrist area of about a hundred-odd pounds and then inspect the two hindering wounds. Not such an easy task when your energy is seeping out of you like your blood.

"Okay, on the count of three… one, two, and three. With God's strength, I can move a mountain!" and rightfully, Jacob does so. The face wound below the cheek is an easy fix as he gets a big gob of gooey mud and packs his cut with the substance. The wrist area is a different story, and by the sight of the ground, it is a more serious matter and will require a tourniquet to help stop the bleeding until the wound can be taken care of properly. He begins to tear at the sleeve on which the wound is so there will be no irritating material to aggravate the wound before he can bandage the area. When he starts to evaluate the powerhouse in effect and around him, eye contact is made with a lonesome wolf: Stalker. They say to make eye contact when facing a predator and to broaden your chest to appear more dominant. This is true under normal circumstances, like a casual walk in the woods. But imagine—oh, by the way—here's a wolf to take care of your peaceful morning stroll. That would be shocking enough! Stalker now has a purpose in his life; to take advantage of a man when he is down, for Stalker has picked up the scent of human blood spilled in a good enough abundance to realize that he is hurting really bad. Now, seeking revenge and thrills, he has become a true stalker, not in just the name alone!

The gladiators are performing for an audience of One, the Lord, God Almighty, well, two when you count Jacob, who watches on from the cover of the yew trees. Stalker has seen a new purpose in his special gift, a blessing from and an offering from his sacred god of choice. And Duke, from the corner of his eye, sees the open battlefield of warriors lost in their combative groupings of blood and gore. Who is getting the best of whom is the unknown soldiers battle cries on in a spiraling whirlwind, thunderstruck and lighting strikes like those of arrows and spears into the pitch-black early afternoon, nightfall. One could easily get lost or turned around in this bloody mess, with no direction known. Duke so much wants to help out and participate however he can, but you have to help yourself before you can help those you dearly love! The circling of the prey begins with Rolette constantly looking for a weakness in his opponent, expanding his chest to intimidate Duke, hoping that this will commence him in fleeing so that his backside will be unprotected by the jagged teeth of Rolette. But Duke has been in many fights with predators around the sheep, with David or Jacob in the range, giving him that extra boost of confidence. All of those companions are around him, but no one can come to his call. *So he wants to be a boxer, huh? Okay,* Duke thinks as he plans how to counter-react to Rolette's tactics. Duke, on many occasions, has seen Ebenezer standing up on his hind legs, so he gives it a try and succeeds. Standing on his hindquarters, with his front paws out in arm's reach, he starts to jab and uppercut in the wind like a boxer. Dancing, dodging, and juking in a rhythmic behavior, hoping to buy time for Rocco and Ace to join in. Not out of fear but out of awareness and intelligence that Rolette may become a challenge. Duke's heart opens his personal battle cry to the Lord out loud for all to hear.

"Searching for my peace and rest, knowing I need something greater than myself. When I am with You, I am free, trapped in this loneliness, for I cannot stand my ground. My only defense is in You, Lord. For I am humbled in this anger! Lord, the all-powerful God of Israel, light for all the people of the world. Feel my soul in this homeward-bound cry as I place my trust in You!"

Rocco, licking his wounds in the rain, hears the reigning voice of Duke's cry; a close companion is the making of these two, who have grown up very close, stitched at the seams. He follows the way of his cry, stepping through the blood red water puddles of death. Ace, being a rescue pup and the youngest given to David as a gift from Jacob many years ago, now redirects himself in the direction of his cry, seeing Stalker in his predator's pursuit! Rocco joins up with Duke as Rolette pays no mind to the situation, for he believes that he is invincible and has listened to the teachings of Shadow about their god, who has shut down the heaven's rain and has parched their lands of impurities, giving the wolves to the land, for many broods passing and that their god will provide for all of their needs. (Of course, this is before his secret interest in a loving God; later on, in time, he will study the holy manuscripts, but he will never convert from the faith of his puny god.)

The Well of Living Waters
(44)

The rain has continued in its uproaring terror and has consumed the cobblestone flooring of any type of forest debris of twigs and broken limbs that sound like fingernails scraping along the stone-made passageway, breathing new life into the midst of a long-time forsaken area of worship. Ebenezer and Alymore enter gingerly into the main sanctuary with hesitation, hearing the high-pitched screeching of Josephine and the howling of the battlefields as all are in despair. The view from inside the sanctuary, looking into the botanical gardens and the yew trees of the burial grounds in the springtime, is beautiful if it is well kept; now, it is spilled with the blood of Josephine and many others. Soaring on the winds of anguish are the sounds of broken hearts as many have fallen this day. The two are completely unaware of the mishaps between the boys and Jacob, for their main focus is the well, and its placement is front and center. The whispering and haunted sounds surround the circular cistern with anguish, as water from the rain channel around the marble stone's cracks and crevices, gurgling and hissing from the quenching of its thirst.

Emotionally, Ebenezer approaches the well and says, "Many would congregate around this very well to share and partake from this clear mineral of the living water. Fellow travelers along the roadway would gather, settling in to hear the word of God being praised amongst them. The sound of joy filled the air of tranquility as people sat around the well's edge, passing the cup as if it were quality wine. Their livestock toward the entrance of the sycamore tree was attended with fresh hay and water. Now only the echoes of a dry well exist; oh, how times can change the stone-hearts of men, wanting to physically see the presence of God instead of the comfort of His Spirit. Before us stands this stone-layered pillar, dedicated to our God, once intended as a landmark of holiness. Yet, it became so much more—a symbol of meaningless chatter from which a legend was birthed. What was once an altar of praise and affection, held together by mortar and dry clay, reflected the very state of their souls: bound by hardship. Drawn to this altar, their prayers rose to the elements of the night, taunting you, Aly, even today. But it must come to an end now, in this very hour!

"There is a plan and purpose for all things Aly; what God has blessed, man has taken away from themselves, as they go on believing in their hearts that this altar will listen to them, bringing all things before this stone image. Taking the place of a holy God, while they should be surrendering with both hands lifted and on their knees. Seeing the evil, an angel of the Lord desiccated the well dry as a bone, and the lands became parched, keeping anyone from seeking what had been lost. A shepherd and his flock came seeking these timberlands for the comfort of the lands and were consumed by the wolves, never to be seen again. Then the wolves came in, believing that it was their god who parched the well and lands. After many generations of dominance in the Tavor Oaks, where the timbers became bitter and brittle, over time, the unsettled voices of the shepherd darkened the lands of any sheep who would wander into these woods, even if they approached the outer edges of the sycamore tree. As time passed, a prophecy was circulated amongst the wolves in the reign of the overlord, Sabre. That there would be a reckoning in the time period of the people's first king of Israel! And that a prophet with his lamb would appear to those in this dry land, in search of an insignificant stone monument to heal the waters of the well and the total annihilation of the wolves."

Ebenezer turns and gives him one of his serious looks, stares him down, and asks, "Are you beginning to see the picture I'm painting here, Mr. Alymore?"

Aly, with a questioning look that turns into a wide-eyed, fearful look, responds, "Hey, Ebb, I know plenty of God's word. Am I going to become the sacrificial lamb here for the atonement of sins brought on by man's shortcomings to heal these waters, or maybe the offering for Abraham instead of Isaac incident, or maybe for the Passover meal? I might as well just go out there and feed myself to the wolves. Should I bring a fork to them so they can stick a fork into me because I'm done here, Mister Ebb?! So, when were you going to tell me all of this great news?!"

Ebenezer looks at Aly in disbelief at his sacrilegious statement of the truth that has yet to come but will; just you wait and see! "Aly, there's nothing great about this at all; look over your shoulder into the terrain, where reality is in progress right before our very eyes!"

The Back Burners

A lot of things go on in the back of the kitchen, and don't listen to all the rumors that are told about sanitation and questionable products in use. Those kinds of things can't be hidden in the quality of great food. The taste is in the pudding, sort of speaking. Mainly you just have to deal with certain emotions and where they're coming from in their personal life. That is one thing that can get put on the back burner; well, you see what happens when two conflicting personalities collide. For example, the Smoke and Hunter incident. That is an excellent example of letting too much fire on the burner at high heat. Then there is Hunter himself, so why would this pack leader put his brood on the back burner, seeing how some of his friends have become extinct right in front of him?

Let's enter the mind of Hunter to see how his thought processes work to define his cowardly reaction. *Well, one thing is for sure: each generation that is placed into leadership understands the gossip that hinders the very air that is breathed, which can bring fresh insight into a legendary fate. I've kept this occurrence on a low flame so over time to check and make sure that the thought remains fresh in my mind, that I've done all through my reign. Listening to the astonishing teachings of Shadow that contradict his great, great grandfather's teachings during his reign of the altar and the pack's ritual to their god. And tried to compare this to a so-called almighty God who has come and saved the souls of each who believes. And that a predestinated lineage of heroic people of this faith who have been tested in trials, and of many miracles. Am I to believe such fable tales as these? That this God has brought them into a promised land? And then the prophecies of old, telling of those things to come. I find it a little ironic that a shepherd and his flock vanquished and then never seen again started the conquering reign of our god. But what about this foretold myth that a prophet and a sheep would appear to heal the land, and annihilate the altar, all of the wolves, and purify the well? Could this apocalypse be happening right this moment? Has not our god provided for us in time's setting? Is this not the belief of Stalker and others of the pack? My concerns became a reality when, right before my very eyes, a great celebration of the people in the anointing of a king named Saul, the first king. Is this the beginning of our downfall? These two anointed creatures must be dealt with before they can do whatever their God has set in their feeble minds! I must protect all that remains of this uproar and the legacy of my founding forefathers of time! Just to think of this mighty God who can conceive such an outrageous, extraordinary story of a man who shall become a Savior, the rock, and a cornerstone, in God's timing. Well, just maybe our god has called upon me to become a savior of the wolves and the sanctuary of the Engarlands Way!*

So, there you go. Many times, a low-burning flame on the back burner has become complacent, and before you know it, the reduction has scorched and ruined the work involved. I think such is the mind of Hunter, just because of his last false vision.

But then again, good things do come to those who wait, and the use of high heat can produce divine dishes of the Orient. The three furry friends are dancing around, shuffling in a wok of stir-fried vegetables, moving so swiftly, waiting for the garlic and ginger sauce that has been so settled on the back burner to be added to the cuisine, for Ace is indecisive in whom he should go and help next until he notices Stalker slowly approaching Jacob. So Ace scuffles in the direction of Jacob. Rocco has joined Duke and is paired together in a bowl of steamed rice, anticipating the approach of the villain himself, Rolette. The tumbling two are on the move to stay out of the way of the sharp ivories as they lunge out of Rolette's snarling snout. Complimented by two springing rolls, Duke and Rocco use many of their fundamental abilities in rounding up stray sheep, well, of course, without the threat of jagged teeth.

The stove top is a very important asset when you have all the front burners occupied in working preparation entrées, and to be blessed with six burners leaves the back three burners available for use. On the right back burner, Duke, Rocco, and Rolette are tussling near the shrubs and rose bushes leading up to the Sanctuary, the very direction Josephine had come from earlier—now, she's passed on. The middle back burner is occupied by Stalker, heading toward Jacob and near the stone-paved stairwell leading to the sanctuary's secured gate, which is the way Hunter intended to make his exit from the battle scene. He has been removed from the flame on his own behalf. The left burner is Jacob, near the cemetery exit lined with the yew trees, who has his wounds tended to. Ace is a little in between and on the edge of his last nerves and heading in the way of Jacob. So, let's crank up the heat to the back right burner to get things moving. Oh, wait a minute, something important to know, sometimes you have to switch burners with something for timing purposes; well, just watch and learn.

Duke has countered and is on the right side of Rolette, while Rocco counteracts the left side, en route in the direction of Duke's tail, trying to circle around the beast to confuse his action and play the aggressor. Rolette just crouches on all fours and is ready to spring like a mountain lion. Jacob has been watching closely trying to do the timing in their matter, to see if there is any routine in his beloved. There is a key element that has to be accomplished in kitchen etiquette, using keywords and knowing where the station ends and begins. "Behind" lets the cook know that he is approaching your blindside. "Hot stuff coming through" (doesn't mean you're the bomb for the opposite sex to be attracted to you) or "coming around" means you are approaching from the side with intentions of going on the other side of you. A white towel on a pot handle lets you know that it is hot if no one is around to tell you. So, Jacob sees more into the matter than what Rolette sees, which is a God-thing in the matter of being faithful in all things, even routines; it could just save a life or two! The boys are just doing their basic round-up of sheep until Jacob is able to approach them, tag them, brand them, you name it. A lot of the time, there is no communication at all, and you watch each other's actions, trying to get inside the head of your partner and counteracting; such is the movement of the two right now so that the intruder is totally in the dark for lack of words spoken.

Jacob now has knowledge of the two and slowly gets up so that there is no frantic movement to startle the quiet or stunned fixture that Rolette has become. Completely on his feet, Jacob draws his attention to the others in the area. Another thing that happens to the back burners is that sometimes air enters into the gas line because it is at such a low-lit flame that it dances along, stuttering amongst the circular head, and isn't completely ignited. Like Ace, who is in disbelieving gasps, with too many thoughts circulating through his mind, thinks there is no way that Jacob will be able to handle a bow because of his injury and the scent of his blood. Do the chances decrease now that Jacob seems defenseless to Stalker, who has stepped up in his progression? First and utmost, you have to turn off the flame and take in a deep breath to release tension; then, you can ignite it into a full flame of rage to burn off the oxygen, like Ace has done, and he starts his journey into a maze of heroism. With two wolves at hand, it is essential to set a medium-high flame to the burner, depending on how much you can manipulate; called "multi-tasking," a must for survival in opposition to the wolves and cooking! As I said, Stalker is now watching Jacob, who is very discreet in his actions, keeping his eyes on Stalker so as not to show his true intentions. Ace has been able to see things from all perspectives since he was walking between the three with a centered focus on the boys, but that excludes Stalker. Ace is now in the loop and continues over to Jacob, not to change the action that has set its course. It is time to rise up, all men of faith! Jacob slowly sets his blade in a striking form, with the tip of the blade between his three-finger grip, in a hunter's expectations of the chemistry and revolving things into motion's courage and faith of the others! Then he roars at the top of his lungs, "Down, boys," and before he can even say the first spoken word, his knife is propelled into a spiral velocity, "cutting into the wind," giving it all that he has left in strength, which sparks a separate action amongst all; the boys do the command correctly, while Rolette decides to spring into action toward Duke, who at this precise moment is glancing over his shoulder to see what Jacob is up to, and seeing the blade come directly at him. So, with his mouth open wide, he is able to turn his head just in time to have the knife split his hair and then catch Rolette into his neck's jugular vein, falling hard onto Duke's back, trapping him momentarily. Stalker is stunned at first because, *How can a man who is still gazing into my eyes throw a blade with so much accuracy? Just amazes me. Wait, is he now unprotected and incapable of pulling back on his bowstring?*

Such is the life of the sauté cook, having to use the entire stove top, adjusting flames as needed, and sometimes sharing burners with smaller pans onto the large grates, with the goal of completing his task quickly, while the middle back burner has dispersed and moved into other locations to serve their purposes. Hunter is in search of more than just food; he seeks to preserve a legacy, knowing that failure could bring shame upon his name as the wolf who lost a proud paradise during his reign. Not a care in the world that his whole pack is about to be shattered as such is the faith in their little god. Leaving behind the fatal scene, he rushes up the flight of stairs as his hope splinters to shards, and he realizes that the gate to a quick entrance in the sanctuary is closed tight.

Hunter thinks out loud, "Whoever designed this frigging botanical garden thing made sure those who visit would walk completely around the sanctuary's secluded grounds to enjoy life in full bloom, with limited entrances and too many thorns and structure to break through a painful shortcoming in patience."

Yes, Hunter, you will witness the mayhem of your pack's lifeless bodies scattered amongst the garden and yet so close to the cemetery's entrance. But the kicker is kindling the fire is that Hunter can see the two perpetrators through branches of the crape myrtle trees; oh, such beauty of a rich lavender color in bloom. The glaring of the two defenseless snouts looking in his direction as Hunter's mind visualizes the two of them glaring into his eyes in laughter that can fuel the fire inside of him!

POISON IN THE POT

In a prophetic vision of the future, during the time of Elisha, men of faith will gather in the timberlands of Gilgal. They will come together to celebrate the heritage of their forefathers and rejoice in the presence of their gifted and blessed sons. The men, throughout long conversations of the glory to God in exhausting details, enjoying the fellowship after some time, become famished, and what a better way to celebrate than to have a feast out in the manly, man woods, to ignite a campfire and bring out the cast iron. Each is in search of something that will enhance their salt-preserved protein. Knowing that God will be faithful in providing for nature's provisions. Now, these men are very knowledgeable of the word of God, placed upon their hearts, but not so much about wild herbs and certain fungus. But they manage to gather an assortment of root vegetables and potatoes from the earth's deep offerings. As others will begin to arrive at the woodlands, Elisha, the guest of honor, shall be amongst the men who sit and simmer with the morsel aroma of the stew at brew. Where a stench breaks wind as if chitlings were amongst the ingredients in the pot, there will be such a disgusted look written on the faces of these men that have never been seen before in the woods of Gilgal. One shall announce that something has died in the pot, for there is the smell of death! Elisha, a blessed man in the hands of our God, will suggest stirring flour into the pot of the unsettled broth and, out of faith in what the God of Abraham has placed into the pot, it shall be served to the hundred or so men who have gathered to satisfy the hunger of all. So shall the times of the Engarlands Way, for this same vision has been stewing in the mind of Ebenezer for some time since God had revealed this calling but kept it hidden in the depths of his very soul of Alymore's testimonial discovery. Both circumstances shall come to pass, but for now it shall be the time for the two creatures of faith to respond and be faithful to follow through with their purpose and calling this hour.

Ebb walks over to the stone pillar where the clay and mortar are starting to decay as the rain washes off the sediment of sandstone. He looks in disbelief that lost souls would put their faith in such a worthless altar as this with no particular shape at all, just a slab of stone discs, not in any type of unity but pieced together to make a single unit of mass, and opens up the conversation, "What benefits does a composer have from a piece with no rhythm at all with no meaning or purpose of the lyrics, written within and just noise of our drenched, forgotten souls? A ritual to another humdrum day, like a piece written on rice paper that would crumble at an abrasive touch or could ignite easily. That's if there was a flaming heart in its presence. For there is no breath within the words written on these stone objects of desecration. Even if you illustrate the beauty of a rose in lyrics, with no truth other than to worship that object of affection, you still have nothing. Especially if you place your faith and whole beliefs in this object as the wolves have done. God is not an object of affection, He is a living, interactive, loving Father and does miraculous miracles, for faith is the key element of our God. In just believing what we cannot see or touch, but he dwells in our hearts as so much does his living word. For who can see in which way that the wind blows. So would you have come if I told you all things, Aly? You could have stayed with David, and I would be just fine, but you are a key element of the puzzle. Your destiny was to fulfill all the circumstances of this day's outcome, Aly. Be thankful that God is blessing you in His goodness in your life!"

And a song of prayer deep within the passages of his heart bruises the petals of a heart's crying rose, releasing a fragrance into the air with the pouring of God's reign. The rain begins to fall upon the Engarlands Way like no other rainfall has ever fallen before.

Ebenezer looks up into the heavens and the rainfall of this day.

"Lord, I have come with clean hands, for You are the truth in which I shall seek and praise. My reward is to serve a loving God wholeheartedly and keep Your word hidden in my heart and active in my mind. Help me to be of good courage and grace your laws upon this wretched body, which is a vessel for the living waters, and the blood flows in purity, withstanding strong in You. Help open my eyes into Your sight of righteousness to guide and lead me into Your pathway, Lord, my God."

The sound is so magnified by the cluttering and falling of metal pans flung across the kitchen by an angered cook, who has had the worst reviews on his heart-felt entrée, bashed by the guest. As the Lord brings on the thunder, the earth trembles like popcorn, popping in an open container, not being contained with the shifting of its very foundations. Lightning strikes and splits the atmosphere with the destructive words of an angry chef in disappointment in his staff and pride! Shaking the ground with the sounds of revival is the God all so powerful.

"Now is the time, Aly; see, the well is an activated volcano of churning waters. You must open the sachet of natural gatherings and place the bark and cypress cones, then the fresh herbs and sap of the sycamore tree, and most importantly, the dredging of natural ground flour without being stirred. All great recipes have to be sprinkled with patience and timing for all the ingredients to mature, but will there be enough time with the enemy approaching?"

(45)

The Left Back Burner

Well, I guess I mentioned earlier about timing that it is everything; with Jacob's releasing of the blade, Stalker was already making up ground for the distance between them when Jacob shouted with so much hostile intensity that it impassioned the behavior of Stalker into a craze of adrenaline that catapulted him into a tackling of hard contact, flattening Jacob onto his back and releasing all of the oxygen out of his lungs, allowing Stalker to become a beast of chaotic, ravishing release of revenge. Thankfully, Jacob is able to react in all the dismay by covering his head and tucking in his chin to guard any major arteries, but his forehead takes on the penetration of Stalker's blood-stained pearls. But help is on the way with Ace, who is now riding on the back of Stalker by his neck, just enough to take hold and break the skin but not enough to cause any catastrophic damage. Kicking like a rodeo bucked riding cowboy on a bull named "Rampage," in a circular pattern of this way and then that way, Ace is on the ride for his life, with back legs trying to wrap around the inside of Stalker's lower ribcage, anything to hold on. But he ends up flipside, flopping to the underside of his belly; he loses an important three-point contact and tumbles to a dead stop in front of Stalker's front feet, allowing Stalker to gouge into the right front lower chest of his ribcage, puncturing and shaking his head back and forth, tearing an open wound into Ace's side.

He gives just enough time for Duke and Rocco to roughhouse Stalker into a ball of paws, feet, and neck sticking out like a whirlwind. This helps the recovering of the breath of Jacob, who is in reach of his quiver of arrows and grabs an arrow by the tip, then rolls on top of the tumbling timber wolf and jabs the arrow deeply down the inside roof of his open mouth, stopping Stalker's panting immediately; all his muscle tension goes limp with the collapse of Stalker's lungs.

You see, the back burner is always a good functioning tool to keep the main courses' productivity, but sometimes, we alter a technique that may have an entirely different outcome than expected. For we really will never know the aspects that a day will bring all in God's mercy and grace our lives are caught up in the moment of intensity that we take the little things for granted. Each of them gathers themselves and evaluates for damage control of the closure and bringing things back to a simmer.

"Listen, boys, Ace is hurt really bad; he needs *antiseptics* to address the *wounds,* do you remember the widow, *Isabella, up the road* with the *natural garden* off the side of the *road?* Why am I talking to a dog? Yes, Lord, I am being obedient to Your voice, but really? Anyways, we need aloe vera *plants* and lavender and honey, but we can use the sap from the sycamore tree and lavender out from the cemetery entrance *to help heal the wound.* Now hurry up and go! Go and get the aloe vera plant from your favorite *rabbit-chasing* area in this neck of the woods! Then head toward home; after I bandage Ace, we will head back to *Jesse.*"

This brings us to another kitchen term of a system of single-used words to bark out orders that are understood with very little communication involved but with ultimate results because of understanding the two departments understand in code. In the hands of the kitchen, "Expediter," the command center. Using keywords like, "*Pick up speed* to table seven," "Hold the *lavender oil* on the *greens,*" or "86 the *rabbit* stew," or funny slogans like, "Are you *chasing* the chicken to get to the eggs?" Anyway, you get the point; the cooks are on their own without the expediter guidance for a smooth ticket turnover and to get the meals out right, on time, and hot. Such is the communication of a shepherd and his smart, loyal sheepdogs in gathering what they do best gather sheep on the call! So, yes, they do understand Jacob, but will they be on time to get there and back, with Jacob proceeding homeward to Jesse?

Jacob breaks down and cries because he is a man of compassion for all things that breathe and has taken the lives of many, all out of defense, and this may be the loss of a long-time companion and loyal friend. He's exhausted by the reigning elements of God, the confusion of Ebenezer and Alymore's fate or whereabouts, and mostly all of his strength is well spent to the last cell of his flesh.

He opens up in prayer to his loving Father and the reviving of his spiritual well-being!

"Lord, You see the chain reaction to all of fate's aftermath and the outcoming destruction of my enemies in the annihilation of their existence. My enemies have pursued and almost overtaken me and the boys, but by the strength and Your covering, we quieted their snarling snouts and placed them under our feet. With the sharpness of my arrows and the flint of my blade, I have gouged their necks and pierced their sides in the anointing of the Lord; You settled the battlegrounds of destruction. The yelps of their wounded souls fell silent to the dust of the winds magnified to an intensity that even the great oaks could not withstand. But my soul melts within for the recovery of Ace and the boys who are in search of Your healing plants. Let them be quick and understanding of the necessities required to save Ace. And bring the relief of anxieties of Ebenezer and Alymore for their unusual disobedience that will bring forth a blessing in disguise, for You have a purpose for all things. Amen."

Lighting illuminates the sky in the darkness of the cloud covering and blinding rain of a passing shadow moving along the outer shrubs of the sanctuary. Trying to be unnoticed in his background retreat route, a lone wolf scuffing away in his grand illusion of slyness in the sight of Jacob's peripheral vision. But more importantly, in a full-frontal view, Jacob witnesses an animated Ebenezer, bobbing his head around loosely, back and forth, he-hawing away loudly, as the rain and thunder stop momentarily so that Jacob can hear him. This is good for Jacob but also bad because now Hunter can pinpoint their whereabouts, exactly where he thought that the two TV dinners would be located, back to where the wolves have once called home!

The state health department requires certain safety items on hand to take care of any accidents that may occur in the kitchen and the mishaps are numeral due to the surrounds involved. A first aid kit, materials to clean up blood-spilled areas, and, of course, to cover wounds of a lesser occurrence such as small cuts and burns. Anything other than that, they send you to a care unit where they can provide attention to serious injuries. And for those, you do whatever you can with the items on hand until medical attention is on hand if it is really serious or someone on the staff drives you to medical attention. The latter situation is the circumstance Ace is involved in, with only the care of Jacob, who has limited supplies on hand but has a leveled head on his shoulders and will do his best.

Jacob comforts Ace, holding him closely to examine the wound in more detailed attention, as Duke comes over to lick his friend's deep wound and whimpers as he realizes that there is not much that he can do here. There is a natural instinct that dogs have to know when situations are in extreme demand of attention. Anything from broken daily routines, when they are going to be left by themselves for a while, your emotions, aches, pains, and life-threatening occurrences that place them into a defensive mode of "I have to do something" attitude!

Rocco acts on the command barked out by Jacob, knowing exactly of his destination and the plants and herbs required of him to receive. Duke follows Rocco to the entrance and stops suddenly at the sycamore tree. Under the shelter of the tree's massive limbs and the hollow caved surrounding at the base, a faint, familiar voice of the timberlands speaks forth, "Are you fearful of your circumstantial incident? Has it overwhelmed your spirit that it has awakened my desire to assist in the etiquette of the woodlands? My roots are deeply embedded in the substance you are seeking, my friend. Take from my torso the bark of two substantial pieces and place them at the base to collect the sap seeping within my channels, and then enclose the sap between the two pieces and go quickly before the sap sets!"

Duke gathers the sap and brings it to Jacob. Apparently, Jacob has been busy gathering the lavender in bunches of blessings of the herb as he, in a rocking motion with his knife, uses the length of the blade to bruise and extract the essential oil into a piece of his torn robe. Josephine's body has been placed across the wounded area, providing pressure to the wound and the warmth of her fur since the blood flow has drained from her cold body. Ace is lying still in a half-dazed awareness, wetness dripping from his nose and his tongue panting for the coolness of the rain. With the return of Duke with much-needed supplies, Jacob removes the lifeless body from Ace and the blood-soaked robe piece, which has stopped the bleeding until the pressure is released, but the congealed blood has clotted in the area and has slowed down dramatically.

"I am grateful, Duke, for your tender heart and understanding of the provisions you have supplied," Jacob says, as he begins crunching up the sycamore leaves that are somewhat sticky as he blends in the stems of the lavender herbs to make a pack of goo and places it on top of the wound with splintered bark, more of the sap, then the fresh herb oil-soaked robe material, and smears more sap on the whole cloth placing it back onto the wounded area. "Now, Duke, snuggle up across the wounded area, keeping pressure on it, and use your body as a blanket of comfort. The lavender oil should help in comforting and relaxing the muscle tissue to decrease the spasms. You take care of him, Duke, until I get back with Betsy. Maybe by then, Rocco will be back with the essential aloe vera plant for later use, and then the four of us will transport Ace back to Jesse and the comfort of home."

Attitude is everything in troublesome outlooks in life. Jacob and the dogs manifest an understanding of the chaotic situation, but they all have an awareness that everything is in the Lord's hands. It doesn't mean you don't have the right to feel the emotions racing through your mind, but what good is it if you don't have clarity? This cues in on Hunter and his grand entrance into the floral pathway into the pleasure of his domestic quarters. Listening to the donkey conclude his ritual disorder, as the atmosphere unexpectedly quiets and all is still, that you can detect the peculiar sounds of carbonated water near the well. Hunter remains motionless and quietly talking to himself, observing the volcanic eruption of the swelling of the living waters.

"Why isn't the well flooding over? Such a hypnotic sight to witness, the bark dancing inside the well, hmm, rising up and down! The powdery substance on the herbs and cypress cones bound in a dust of flour puffs suspended above the mixture adrift. Could this be the all-powerful God that Shadow had mentioned in his teachings? A feeling of melancholy controlling my mind and actions? How can this be?"

Secured in a trance for now, Hunter listens into the conversation of the two colorful figments of his distorted imagination as the wise mule speaks into life, "Okay, Aly, now let's back up out of the way things could get wiry here!" The thunderous sounds of the gates of heaven dawn in the magnificent light descending from the sky, the vocalizing and proclaiming of the approaching angel of the Lord.

*Come all who are thirsty to the living waters and the blessings of God,
Praise God! And to the one who settles in his own anguish and
desiccated the well and this altar,
in an attitude of ungratefulness,
shall witness the revival of the well and the destruction
of this pedestal, in which you stand and dedicated as your faith,
shall be cursed this day!*

(53)

"*For whom is God, except the Lord? And who is a rock except our God? 'A stone is heavy, and the sand weighty; but a fool's wrath is heavier than them both' (Proverbs 27:3). Has not the shadow cast against your beliefs, Hunter, teaching the word of God to your restless heart in the homeland of your own pack? Yet even you questioned the one who brought the good news to your soul and rejected his words; not his word that came to the inner being of your life's breath, but My spoken words implanted and embedded in Shadow's knowledgeable mindset. Shadow's life is just a vapor of moisture, now, in the rain that I shall pour down and is no more, although My reign shall be everlasting. This day, as the lightning strikes in tremendous force from the skies and the dark clouds become as the night, shall the frost of the hailstones and coals of fire ignite this altar in your sight? And your heart shall strike with grief three times, and it will be witnessed by the living waters, the destruction of the altar of this stone pillar, and the freedom of the two chosen ones who shall walk away with a monumental stone anointed for the purpose. Shall your soul come to rest or ever so be in a living fire and destruction in your last breath taken in these times? Your choice shall be an apocalyptic quest for the horsemen of the end of time!"*

Ebb's eyes get really wide, as do Aly's, being shoved into the covering of the well. "This is not good, Aly, God…" and that is as far as the conversation comes to an end to the thunderous thunderclap as the atmosphere in the vicinity turns a bitter cold that you can see the breath of Hunter as he exhales his life's breath, and only the whites of the eyes of our two companions because of the sudden darkness of the skies. The frost places an icecap over the stoned-pillar altar from the top to the very end; all other surfaces remain the same. Then fires ignite from the well of the living water as it has been hit with a lightning strike reflecting off the well's substance and bursts into flames on the pedestal, once a god to the wolves, which stood proudly, starting a splintering of the stone from the inside and vertically, due to the extreme temperature change in the immediate climate. But most importantly, the lightning strikes the stone, which is impacted by three consecutive lightning webbing, causing the altar to explode into fragments. Aly pokes his head up and picks up a fragment with his teeth off the fully intact well's edge as Ebb and Aly begin to depart. The rage of Hunter has awakened, and with leaps and bounds, he acrobatically jumps obstacles, springboards onto the stone benches onto the well's edge, and hurdles forward to try and clear the…

An Archer's Point of View, from the Eyes of Jacob

The arrows in the sessions of three consecutive pulls of the bow are released quicker than Jacob has ever managed to do so as Betsy stays stable so that his aim will be true. The arrows play follow-the-leader, past the mockingbirds, through the crape myrtle's low-hanging branches and the shadows of the great oak trees, finally coming to their destination, all three lounged into the backside of Hunter. Seemingly, Jacob was never able to look his opponent in the eyes due to Hunter's backside posture of cowardliness! Spoken words fill the emptiness of the sudden deliverance of the storm's end, and Jacob thanks God for his clear vision of the location of Hunter due to the elements of God's awakening!

The guidance of the wind, with the arrows overtaking in flight, as the three feathery shafts pierced their destination point and impelled into the Exodus of new foundations at heart into the life force of the Engarlands Way. A conclusive settlement between man, beast, and the altar shattered by the strength of the Lord. Jacob, with an expression of affection, caresses Betsy's glossy coat in appreciation of the calmness in her spirit. The uncertainty of fate is a concern from a heroic measure by a gentle disposition in Ace. Comforting him into Jacob's arms of security, delicately lifting him into a rig using the saddlebag as a harness, up toward the knob of the saddle and Betsy's mane. Using the leather straps from the quivers to confine Ace. Heartstrings have been tugged on as an emotional Betsy glides through the forestry underbrush in a barrel race for time. Weaving so delicately but ferociously, Ace's life depends on her. Jacob crouches and holds onto Betsy's mane to keep from getting bushwacked by entangled twigs. The narrow path starts to widen to where the rubber hits the road, sort of speaking! The sunlight intermingles with the upper branches, assisting them into the departure of the timberlands and into the freedom to a roadway home to Jesse.

(46)

Arise Lord,
Comfort him with Your hand placed upon his very soul.
For he is one of Your many treasures and a blessing to me.
Show me the path of life for this little one that is hidden in my heart.
As we take flight to the homelands, secure us in the
cradling of your mighty hands.
The Lord lives and is my rock.

ANOTHER BACKBURNER EXPEDITION

(47)

The backlashing events at the well of the living waters continue and are in progress as we return to the fermenting water of the well under the view of our two anointed companions! The sound of Jacob's voice startles the two creatures of faith through the humongous thud of the thunderclap. As our meek sheep, that is, Alymore, is cluttered with the sounds and sights, his heart begins to race with thoughts going through his mind like a flash drive connected to a computer's intake. The shout of Jacob's cry, "Wolves amongst us!" has been heard by Ebenezer and the flock many times by David in the night's watch at the midnight hour, as the boys are back in town to ward the wolves and send them rearing into the covering of the night! Or in the pastures, at the peak of dawn, where they peek from the hollows with shoulders crimped and ready to spring into action on a wandering sheep. Now, the second command is one that can strike fear into the flock when the shepherd raises his voice, "Take cover!" We are dependent on the utterings of the man in charge.

Utilizing their time wisely, with the announcement being sent by the Lord and Jacob's warning, all mayhem breaks loose; it is probably best to crouch and be under the protection of the well's shelter. Stunned in the same trance that Hunter is in, fascinated by the soothing aroma of the fragrance of pine and lavender that has a calming effect deep down to the soul of things, but he can see in Ebenezer's eyes the reflecting lighting web striking the altar. And then the silence, after such a destructive incident sets forth coarse fragments into flight.

A moment's hesitation, then the growling in the monstrous sounds of snarls from Hunter, "Who are you to take away the god of our ancestors? Do you not know of his wonderful powers and capabilities? I laugh in your faces! Our god is unaffected and will not slumber just because the proclamation of the true living God has made foolish remarks toward our pack, and most importantly, you made a bigger fool out of me, you imbeciles!"

The sober sounds of rustling feet trying to balance in areas where paws aren't meant to be placed. Listening to the wolves muttering, Aly needs to shout it out loud, so he shouts out, "Who's calling whom a fool? When you look in at yourself, that's all you will ever see, you self-centered goon!"

Then comes a swift sound of arrows in flight, three thuds making a detestable sound of contact, and the shrieking of a lone wolf collapsing in front of them, a lifeless body dangling on the edge of the well. There's gurgling and then separation of the natural offerings as he stands up to witness Hunter being devoured by the waters of the well!

Ebenezer, looking up from the covering of the fountain, says, "Well, how was that for a dramatic scene, Mr. Alymore? Did you get the stone? Any piece will do, for it is purified, and then we can go!"

Coming down from the well's edge, Aly says, "Ywwews, whight beenwt my chweek an ummms!" Aly spits out the unique stone that falls to the ground, "Now what, Ebb? Jacob is just over there in the floral garden. Maybe we should just head that way and go with him; it would be a whole lot safer, don't you think?"

Ebenezer stops dead in his tracks and turns to look toward the whimpering sounding voice, "Aly, Aly, Alymore, and your silly questions of now, or then, or where, and why, or tell me of all the wonders? Aly, do you want that to be your legacy of one who didn't complete what God has called you to do, and what might have been if only I did this or that?! Are you going to crumble and give way to your insecure thinking? I can't tell you everything will be all right, but what is the point in going this far and then leaving on the flip of the coin, sorta speaking!"

Alymore shows his sensitive side as the words sting his very eyes, "Oh, okay, Ebb, but how are we to get this stone to David? Don't you think it will look like a sheep just passing a stone or something? It will not make any sense to him, Ebb!"

Ebenezer is happy to hear a positive explanation from Aly, well, close enough to one. "Aly, we are called only to be good stewards of the blessing, and God will open the doors to wherever, however, and whenever of the matter; faith, my air-dried lamb. You almost became lamb chops, Aly, with a cremini mushroom and merlot sauce to compliment your delicate cuisine, Mr. Alymore, so what do ya see, big fellow? Are you in for the ride of your life like Noah, hanging on the high hopes of the waves breaking?"

Alymore looks into the direction that the voice was thrown from, "I can see Jacob is a broken man loyal to his calling and the responsibility of bringing a lost sheep back home, but he is over there for some reason, Ebb, to keep him from pursuing after us, don't you think, Ebb?! Oh, by the way, I take that as a compliment of meal choice, for who the heck would want to eat an old stubborn, he-hawing donkey anyways!" Both try to get the best view possible, absorbing all details, to see the matters holding Jacob back from pursuing his purpose, when they see Jacob scooping down, picking up a wounded animal, and Duke whimpering loudly.

Jacob has the heart-aching sound of a man who has lost someone dear to him and quietly announces, "Ebenezer and Alymore, return to David, for many things have happened this day, too many strange things, all for some divine purpose at hand. Things are complicated for this calling, but my purpose has been fulfilled here in the eyes of a loving God. Go forth is His word to me, for your ears to hear. Are you listening?! Now, go forth! I must leave you in the safety of the Lord, for Ace is hurting something fierce on his side and needs proper medical attention. May God's will be done for the three of you. There is safety once again in these timbers, and remember, our God is still the same!"

Now that Jacob has placed Ace harnessed onto Betsy, he gently sits down on the saddle, comforting him, and then gives his commands to Betsy, with the sounds of crickets clicking in fast sessions, letting Betsy know that means *pronto!* And then the quickened pace of silence satisfies the hunger of the Engarlands Way.

The sadness of Alymore sets in the tragic misfortune, and finally, he has a chance to just breathe in the air without all of the despair as he mentions, "Listen, Ebb, the forest is awakening, I hear it in the birds a-chirping, the crickets crickety-cricking and the gratitude of the trees. So where to now, my fellowship of the donkey kindred spirit? There is definitely clarity in the voice of Jacob, but first, we must see the sycamore tree. Out of all due respect, then do we look for Penny or just go directly to David?"

Ebb, shaking his snout and snarling his lips, says, "I know you get this; it's here at rock bottom with this stone, my friend. Did you know where the wind blows in finding this stone? Sure, the Lord gave me input, but the where and how, were they not the answers that the Lord would show in His timing alone? Let's just walk with a carefree attitude and trust in the one who has given us life!"

The two swagger around for the first time in a while, bringing drive into their strive, for the energy's intensity is a mesmerizing wave throughout the forestry floor. Daylight's beams show the way to exit through the cavity of the great sycamore tree! Aly is the first to speak, "Thank you for your guidance of the ways of the woods, Mister, ah, hmm…"

As a tree limb graciously sways and waves as if saluting Aly, the hollow voice speaks authoritatively, "You may call me Seymour; all my friends do so. And you will always be welcome as my guest of honor, my little one. Finally, redemption has been served with new beginnings to start! The comfort of the rain flourishes deeply into our heritage roots, growing and bearing underneath the surface; our past is now our Lazarus! The restoration duration has already commenced with the circulation of moisture and photosynthesis of the new buddings and fresh sprigs of grass. A new day is shining through, and springtime is like the old time by and by!"

"Well, praises be to God, and you will see us again in our wanderings down the old beaten road, my good friend indeed!"

A little skip in their walk is very apparent in Mr. Ebenezer and Alymore of the green pasture's flow. Aly opens up his mind, heart, and soul into a declaration of the evergreening forest.

(48)

From the depths of the hollows and the peaks of the forest floor,
to the streams of the brook,
a path taken, one end to the other, full of thistle and briars
once sufficient,
over the years of dissolution.
Arise as You lift these spirits up to the heavens,
swiftly as the deer once again enters these same woods,
in Your shelter and lifted from the shadows of despair.

THE MEADOWLANDS

*Not once did my feet slip, and with my head lifted high,
You enlarged my path amongst the highest ancient oaks,
to the tenderness of the crape myrtles.
For this is the season and dawning of our anointed king,
who shall be loved and hated by those who keep him
within arm's reach.
The one who comes before the true beloved king,
One of a great deliverance,
and all shall bow down before Him.
And shall anoint the reign of David while
conquering many nations in bloodshed,
while he shows mercy to others.
To the reign of David and
his descendants forevermore!
As another displays compassion, denying His rightful reign,
Christ our Savior!
As I give You thanks,
So be it!*

(49)

— Chapter Eight —
CHRIST AND SPRING

"In B-flat"
As David Is in the Audience!

In the distant past, his two lost companions have started their journey back to the loving arms of David, who has begun to interact with the acceptance of nature to occupy his time wisely. Repetition of figure-eight and whirly birds in flight, as a solo bumble bee ignites in a joyous sentimental journey around the anatomy of David and the laughter of spring, declaring, "Surely goodness and mercy shall follow him all the days of his life, and he will dwell in the house of the Lord forever. And he shall be anointed with oil in the presence of his enemies! Hallelujah! There shall be a new hermitage, a dynamic haven brought back to the parched lands of Tavor Oaks and mankind, as nevermore forsaken because of the sanctification of the well of the living waters for all to receive this day! Quickly, go tell the others of the great news and proclaim to every creation my winged friends of the airways! For the third stone is in the grasp of our tender-hearted lamb, Alymore of the green pastures, and Ebenezer, the wise ole mule!"

THE MEADOWLANDS

As the general begins to pack his hammock and tidy up a little, he announces to the eyes on patrol, "All right, ladies, that's our cue; we need to vacate the area and announce this report to Penny and the others!" The squad begins to gather and redirect their navigational devices and search out new landmarks to identify their location on return for calculating purposes. A twisted trunk and the overhanging drapery of the corkscrew weeping willow tree will do sufficiently for the trio to remember as our bumble bee continues in song,

God, You created all things,
all things to perform for me,
Your beauty influences other lives,
In a craftsman's skill of adequate finesse.
As the seasons change to spring,
Your intense colors of life,
dawning light to a magnifying,
a glorious name.
From a heartbeat and a soul-searching sensation,
seeking of His beloved people, my love,
The Lord loves you just the same.
Spring is a new awakening,
budding the blossoms of life
from the written promises of Your word.
Planting the seed
For the Lord to nourish a future and hope,
a promise harvested for you and me.
Watered with the rain,
and then the radiant rays,
springtide flowing through the stems,
life given by the warmth of the sun.
God, our Father,
springtide flow through our veins,
nourishing eternal life through His Son.

"My little bumble bee friend, how delicate is your word toward the Engarlands Way. Now that the forest floor is in order cleared of all of the hindering debris, all mankind is called to clean the household of their minds and replace the clutter with the life of My spoken word, giving birth to a newborn fragrance of life, setting forth of a true sacrifice to seek Me first, kept in the bosom of your heart, to hear and know My voice in the springtime and winter of life's unpredictable circumstances of your enemy within.

"A child being born will change everything, a couple's blessing of a newborn's life placed in the arms of uncertainty. Nourished in love and understanding, caring for the heart's desires to see the developing personality over time's open window. So shall be the life and birth of a child born in a manger.

"He will be born to place My word in order that will set the captive free, open the eyes of the blind, and draw Me closer to those who believe and send those to seek and save the lost at heart's turning confession of faith. But there will be a division of families and loved ones over the coming of a Savior whom people see Him as a new ruling king to end the rule of those who rule over them. Every mankind will have their own giants to face throughout life, but through this Man, those battles shall be conquered! Such will be the life of David. Let me embed this vision into your beautiful markings of life, deep into your heart to what is to become and shall pass in the times of another ruling emperor of a Roman empire, a king."

The bumble bee ponders on all that has been spoken to his heart and mind, almost too much but is overwhelmed by the love of the Father and understanding of His hidden word brought to life, to this animated life of a bumble bee. After reasoning on his chosen hymn, in the translated words of nature's calling, for even the stones shall cry out His name, and begins to sing in B-flat…

The pages of these leaflets ascribe the cry of the day's awakening. The rising of our exalted Lord and anointed, reigning King, while a flask of bitter wine, a token,

THE MEADOWLANDS

poured out like waters flowing.
For no limbs were broken,
all of them are still intact.
His strength was taken and surrounded,
by the sheep in wolves' clothing, at the well of the living water.
The day is sprinkled with the dust of death,
Exclaiming, where is He in whom you trust,
the one who satisfies and delights,
in your soul.
You know, your anchor in the storm.
Taking my last breath
of freedom granted at birth,
freedom taken in captivity,
now lies still embedded in the earth.
For the trouble is near to the heart,
the nailed pierced hands are now set in
place, east to west and worlds apart.
Someday we shall see the blossoms of the flowers,
from the frost comes forth the new prism-colored leaves.
Now He is uncovered, unrobed,
for the casting of lots in the breeze.
Removing and casting away the stone
And speaking forth to God, our Father,
You have answered me.
I cannot count it at a loss, the debt which I owe,
The sin in which was worn is now covered with dirt,
in this tombstone grave, a price paid in full,
in which I will never own.
Then he heard my cry, for all eternity to hear,
and saved me the cost,
of the grave that was calling my name.
The deaf will hear, the blind will see,
the poor shall be satisfied.

ALLEN W. LEAFGREEN

Proclaiming across the nations,
the name above all names,
do not let it hide,
or keeping it safe in the dark,
but to seek and find what has been lost. As Christ lives in me.

To the next generations who will come and declare the good news of His righteousness' calling to those who will be born again that He has done all this for all; you are invited, so just come and believe!

THE PATH TAKEN
(50)

The tune is catchy, and David begins to hum the sound of the buzzing buzz and the rhythmic rhymes in the intake, tilling to the steps of his cultivating feet to the thoughts of the green pastures. Content in knowing the heart of a shepherd, allowing him to walk and graze near the still water flowing in the time of the lazy sun upon his shoulders. How much that he doesn't realize that his beloved four-legged friends literally walked through the forest valley in the shadows of death that followed each step taken. With the comfort of no fear, aware that the Lord has the setting of life, all in the placement of His will, knowing he has the good Lord watching over them, for maybe the Lord has slowed the flow of the day for His purpose in time. A sudden silence has filled the air, for where has the chirping of the birds following him in the air gone and the bumblebee leading the way away from boredom? Each step takes him closer to his destiny, all the days of his life!

SHELDON'S FAREWELL
(51)

"The crew of three lands on the landing strip near Penny, where the good news of all that has been told by the bubbly bumble bee and all that has and shall come to pass. The finding of the stone, the reigning of kings, the importance of the birth of David, and the coming of another who has to suffer for our well-being.

"Penny's eyes light up like bottle rockets taking flight in the darkness of time when she hears the mention of a bubbly bumble bee, saying, 'Oh, you mean Clarence, the gleeful seer! I thought I might have heard him before we left the ceremonial tribute to the fallen soldiers and Delora! Always in a hurry; that's my thorn in the side. Do you want to see my scar? I know, never mind, maybe some other time then.'

"Sheldon slowly throttles over to a hyperactive hare named Penny, hoping to find grace in his chosen word scheme as the birds chirp away with whoever shall listen, for some things are not easy habits to break when it comes to social behavior; anyway, better now than never… as Penny speaks forth saying, 'Tell me what Sheldon, what needs my grace? You do realize that you have been saying this out loud since the time you noticed the girls and the general's arrival, right? So it has to go on record now, so please, proceed on, Sheldon.'

"A sad Sheldon clears his throat and takes a drink of water from the calming brook, still attached to his rigged harness, and Gretchen caters to his call so that she can listen into this conversation to get an earful and, of course, be productive for Sheldon.

ALLEN W. LEAFGREEN

*Penny,
This is the time,
this is the place,
and this is the day.
Where the rudder on the boat,
meets the water's flow,
and in my mind,
this counseling inside
that I can conceive,
for I know this is the day!
I must set sail,
the brook is calling my name,
I must answer.
Don't you know,
this is the day?
To the season and its purpose,
I must go for this is the day!
For there is a seed, a budding,
embedded in the deep end of thought
inside of me.
Clutching the stem,
watch the thorns,
or you might just get them in your side.
For this is the day!
It's sad to say,
break it down,
it's all the same,
built it up along the way.
For a cheer, a kindred heart, a silent gesture,
and belly-busting laughter,
for such as little as an embrace,
igniting a caring spirit,
for this is the day!*

THE MEADOWLANDS

Watch over the stones,
one on my backside,
and on Gretchen's chest,
in a tangled web of life's uncertainties,
but this is the day!
No time to gain,
no time to lose,
as seconds begin to count the minutes,
and the hours become days,
keep it all in the present time,
in time spent wisely,
don't throw it away,
utilize it accordingly,
amongst the ones you love,
for this is the day!
Speak your mind in a rhyme,
don't stay silent in your love.
Peace out, my friends,
let hate be detected and not infected in the mind,
replaced, my beloved, with forgiveness;
keep things straight and intact,
and don't sweat the little things,
keep it all in perspective
but pay attention to the wildfires!
For this is the day!
And until the setting sun,
all will be done,
on my way,
where the lily pads drift away,
and the bullfrogs call out their dismays,
as they drop and plop from one lily to the other,
just to get there, get up, and go along the edge of life.
I guess that's all I've got to say,

when the draft of wind is just a call away.
Lean on the general.
Carry on, my sisters,
as I rest on another bank
of the river's amazing grace.
Will you answer His calling?
That's all I got to say,
when today is the day.

"I, Sheldon of sound mind, declare and transfer the rights of possession of carrying this anointed stone, for my yeses have always been yeses and my nos have always been nos, for there is no grey area, to the safety of its calling to where I relinquish my rights to a journey's way back home. I am also going to another calling requiring my utmost attention, where my faith is deep and stronger in the presence of my Lord. For this is Officer Sheldon, who has had the honor to serve in the army of God. You are free to serve! At ease, sir!"

Penny's Calming
(52)

"Sheldon, this is a ghostly apparition, and I am riding on a horse named 'Nightmare' clutching the very soul that I cling on to. Gretchen, tell me that I am still in a dream! Will you help me over here, Gretchen? Tell him he is making a wrong decision. Keep him suspended; don't you dare release him to the ground, not just yet, girl; I need time to think, for I am like a person waking up from sleep!"

Sheldon is rockin' back and forth as if he was swinging on a swing, with his stubby legs trying to make contact with the earth's edge. Gretchen watches the tension in the line, doing what Penny has asked her, knowing better that it isn't quite the right action in the matter, but she does not want Sheldon to part ways from them, spinning like a top due to the emotions of the two.

She says, "I'll keep him suspended, girl, against his wishes. Look at him, Penny; you're lucky he is trained for situations like these, girl! I can't do anything for you, girl, and you know that it is true! Who am I to interfere with God's purpose for him? You know my dame well, by his character alone, that he is being led elsewhere; it's as logical as, why did the chicken cross the road, don't you think, Penny!"

As Sheldon dog paddles in midair to the beat of the drums in his own head, Gretchen gently places him on the ground in a rhythmic stride of pitter-pattering in an oscillating gesture. Then, he is released from custody, giving him free will to carry on.

"A soldier salute, ten-hut; officer at ease, you are dismissed! A soldier does not look back into his past, always taking notes on improving skills and procedures and applying them to advance to new horizons. Penny, Amber, Nicole, and Gretchen stand still, stiffened in their joints, not to catch them off guard in their emotional collapse. Sheldon approaches Gretchen and asks for her assistance in removing the stone from his backside and giving it to Penny so that the transaction goes smoothly. The general swings down in front of Penny, asking about the placement of the stone and where it shall take place. In the midst of my heart and cover it with my fur, then you can spindle your webbing to keep it intact. Rebounding quickly as the general, Penny, and the others watch Sheldon walk the line, chest proudly protruding out in front of him, squaring off into the flowing upward calling to the stream of things to come!"

Penny watches the last ripple across the surface of the brook as Sheldon materializes further upstream, paddling in the current with his head moving side to side in wonder. All is so surreal, and Penny authentically tries to grasp anything logical in this tall tale. Emitting rays of light shining bright, a profile image can be seen walking on water, or is it a mere reflection?

Then an angelic voice speaks forth, *"Wake up, Penny! Wake up from your sleeping stupor, for a stone has been recovered and rests in the hands of two of your dear friends now in transit to their return to David. For I have made my presence known in the Tavor Oaks in the purification of the well and destruction of the altar, an idol to the timber wolves in Engarlands Way. In the annihilation of that very altar, a stone of refinement from the scattered fragments has materialized and anointed to be gathered and collected with the other two stones in the chosen carrier's grasps. Now, about Sheldon, my lovely woman, what is that to you? Let there be no anguish hindering or any doubts cast upon our shelled friend, for his time has come, and you shall see him no more! The whirlwinds of time shall embrace our little one in a peaceful rest in the hands of the Lord and shall not see the grave. Let your minds be at ease and listen; from the foundations of the earth, the two remaining stones have been placed in the hands of others, collected for keepsake, and released at predestined timing!*

"For Penny, many times you have entertained into the paradise patch, west of Eden, of the fresh vegetables and of its fruits, in this tilled nourished soil that is planted of your favorite delights. Amongst and between the two gold-painted pipes of the known widow, 'Isabella's Haven,' a place of refuge and hospitality. But don't abhor your timely matter of the small things from the guardian of the garden, Murlene, a fine, furry Günther's vole who is fiery at heart. Her domain is near the heightened capstone, in the cabbage summit of life's pleasantries. Do you not know of this location? For your interest, another stone is to be acquired for this quest. Between the two olive trees, a fragrance of the blue orchid blossoms will guide you to the river rock bedding that provides coolness to the fragile roots. Amidst the river rock, look closely and ponder in and in between. There is a honeycomb-shaped stone formation of seven sides in a geometric shape; it cannot be mistaken when identified.

"No expenses have to be paid, for there is no set price on the materials she has required in possession over time. You mustn't whittle her down, for she is very wise and choose your spoken words carefully; they will have

a strong influence on the decision at hand! Only one action will set the stone free, locked with a key of admiration and her passion for a hobby's fancy. You must find that key to open her heart before any transactional trade or bargains can be apprehended. Look into the western skies as the powder puff clouds float peacefully within the calmness of the wind."

From the stillness, you would find it hard to believe that a severe thunderstorm had made its way through other than the gully-made potholes and a maze of dirt-dodging mess. The general is just a-swinging between the ears of Penny, as she has them erect so that she can listen to all that the angelic voice has to say, as his silence swallows the air in the atmosphere and the angelic attendant of God departs from the water's edge.

The girls are a-bebop, flip-flopping along the roadside, weaving in and out to avoid any disturbances and the mud, anxious to settle at Penny's side to verify the voice that they heard. Amber, in a gleeful tone, says, "Did someone say that we are going to go on a shopping spree or a rummage sale? And who is Marlene? Is she the host of the yard sales?"

Penny glances over to Amber with a harsh look of disbelief and asks, "No, it isn't anything like that, didn't you hear? The purpose is for a geometric-shaped stone that we have to be wise to obtain and figure out her heart's desire. For she is the guardian and very intelligent! I have accompanied her on several occasions bartering for the trade of vegetables, so we are going to have to be clever. We're not too far from the entrance, but you have to know what to look for because if you blink, you can walk right past it, giving it no mind! The low-lying shrubs of the broom trees are at the entrance, having to go down into a ravine area that hides the view of the access gates where the signage of her calling. You can easily go down into the gully and be distracted by a bright light appearing in your vision as things begin to accelerate into oblivion, and you notice..."

— Chapter Nine —
THE AWAKENING OF GLENN ALYMORE AND A DONKEY WITH HIS SHEEP

Suddenly, as if Rocco had gone through a universal portal, he enters into this dimension of the reality of things to come. And the four-legged critter is engulfed by the bright light rays as the spotlight is directly in his face…

I'm lost in a daze of things as if awakened from a long winter's nap, with the heater on full blast and wrapped in a blanket in security. A stern voice, one that is familiar from the depths of my mind, but I can't put an image or even a face to the heart of the matter. I'm laid out in a gown with IVs connected to my arms with what looks to be water and some kind of plasm because there is a burning sensation going through my veins. Confused by these circumstances, I try desperately to speak forth, "What the…" but I have no muscular control of my mouth.

A man in a white jacket leans over to look at my vital signs on the beeping monitor and replies, "Are you awake, Glenn? Your mom is right over here to your left. She hasn't left your side in quite some time. You have a blessing to have her as your parent. We are going to have to put you back to sleep so that your brain will be able to get proper rest and heal. You will be fine. I'll let you see your mother for a little time, but it is crucial to let you get proper rest, my young man; you're a fighter at heart; be strong and of good courage!"

As he opens the door, he looks at Penny and says, "After you've gotten him comfortable again, I will discuss the prognosis and what we will have to do in this next stage, Mrs. Alymore. Oh, so sorry, you're right. I'm going to call you Penny; my bad."

Penny comes into the room, trying to wipe any signs of crying, although her glands along the eye show other than that, but it could be put off as lack of sleep. She says as she approaches Glenn, "Son, you have had a serious incident. A weak blood vessel in your brain has caused a hemorrhage and burst when you hit your head, which has put you in a sleeping stage. I am right here and will be reading your favorite stories, talking, praying, and crying, but you are strong. Now close your eyes and rest, my child. You will always be my little Glenn at heart."

Then, the awkward silence, drifting, tumbling into unconsciousness. Am I gonna be okay…?

"Hey, Aly, are you okay? You're looking a little sheepish here, pardon the pun, but are you doing all right? We have been through quite a bit, and I could understand if you went into shock-ill-nation here. Speak to me, boy… aw, come on, don't give me the silent treatment; I can handle all things, but not that!"

A concerned look crosses over Ebenezer's muzzle. Aly stands still with his knees a-knocking in a drum solo, with the strobe lights flashing, slowing down the natural body movements, making a particular style, looking sporadic, while the rockers go wild at his rhythmic antics. He opens up the conversation, "Oh, were you speaking to me? I feel lost in a daze and a little confused, sorta drunk in hysteria, I guess, but I'll be fine. I think I heard something about Penny and the archangel that we saw over at the well, but I am lost for words, and nothing makes sense at this point. My blood sugar must be very low!"

The look on a donkey's face is hilarious already, with their deep black eyebrows bringing out their big brown, olive green shades. Then there is the mane, which looks like a mohawk cut, the floppy ears, add the silly grin showing the molars, and you got Ebenezer gleefully announcing, "Let's go get something to eat, we can stop off at, 'Isabella's Haven,' chat with Marlene, and get something on the sweet side; it's along the way, but a way's down the road. Whatta ya say? I'll introduce you to her; she's a big hoot for such a small being. Let's go!"

"Let's go over here, Mrs. Alymo... I'm sorry, Penny, but I want to give you some privacy. Okay, I'm not going to sugarcoat the circumstances here; your son, Glenn, is in a serious, life-threatening situation, and my anesthesiologist is medically inducing a coma at this very moment to keep his brain activity at a minimum. This will help keep minimal swelling of the brain but is not a solution; time is essential and could go on for a long period. We will continue monitoring his brain activity; at first, it will be silent, but as the anesthesia increases, consciousness and awareness could broaden during this time period. When you go back in to see him, he will be on a ventilator because he cannot breathe on his own due to the type of injection he is receiving. If you have any questions about the medication being used, you may speak to Marlene; she can tell you about the medicine and its effects, for I must be going to check on others. I trust her guidance and will back up anything she advises you on; she already has a history with your son. Penny, your son has a very strong spirit about him and is a fighter. Let's pray for his situation anytime you need to, and when I can make myself available, I will do so with you if you are comfortable with that! Oh, here's Marlene now; don't worry, we have staff watching and monitoring him at all times. Let me introduce her to you; she's a hoot with a big personality for such a, well, you'll see."

Penny turns around to see a short, round melon ball strolling down the hall, gleefully greeting all whom she passes. "Dr. Robertson, all's good with our little soldier at heart. He's counting sheep, and brain activity is minimal; he has a big ole grin on his face, which is understandable. To whom do I have the pleasure of meeting, sir? I've seen her in the halls, so this must be the mom. He resembles a lot of your features and is very handsome, Ma'am. I'm Marlene; I just left your son in very good care…"

Dr. Robertson excuses himself from the whirlwind that Marlene is able to create. Just give her a topic on any subject matter, and let's just say she is Jeopardy contestant material with a strong British accent.

"Oh, okay, Dr. Robertson, so tally-ho and good day to ya." She walks over to Penny and offers a gentle handshake with an embrace around the shoulder to encourage Penny to come over to the lounge chairs at hand and sit next to her, "Any questions for me?"

Penny sits down and adjusts her clothing out of nervousness, "Yes, since Glenn has been unconscious for many hours, he has been able to breathe on his own, but the doctor says that he will be on a ventilator during the whole duration. Will he have any pain when he regains consciousness, and during his unconsciousness period on this medication, will he be able to at least hear and comprehend our conversations with him?"

Marlene, a mountain of joy in her voice, says, "I do say so; these are very good questions, Penny. Let's see; two to make a partner, a dosey doe. The first question is, depending on the recovery time, the longer induced it is, the longer it may take to regain functions. The more serious complications of this procedure are weakness in mobility and hallucinations, with the possibility of blood clots due to inactivity. The nurses will help blood flow, massaging legs and arms. Also, a blood thinner will be given through his IV. Minor symptoms will include agitation, anxiety, and confusion. There could be discomfort, and some do experience pain; they should pass in due time, but we are a long way away from home. Now, the second: yes, and this communication and interaction with him will stimulate his senses and help with the healing process. Anything that he has of interest, bring it up in your conversations. I see that you carry a Bible, and it is well used by the look of it; it gives it life and character; it's probably all written up inside with notes and all, cool! Do you read from it and apply it to your life? I know the answer already, but I think it is time for you to testify because I could ramble on for hours, especially about the word of God!"

Penny feels the tension leaving her body, finding out that Marlene is a Christian. "Oh, you are so kindhearted, Marlene, and yes, I do read the living word to Glenn; he is on the borderline of accepting and is very knowledgeable of scripture. I have been reading to him about the matters of the ministries of Jesus and Paul, the importance of accepting Christ, His resurrection, and what must be done for salvation. So, he already understands all of this; I've seen him studying the Word on his own at times but haven't pushed the matters on him, and now look at this…!" Penny breaks down in the comforting arms of Marlene, who is doing her best to comfort her.

"Yes, Glenn has been on my heart ever since I knew of his entrance into the emergency room, and I have been checking in on him on several occasions, praying over him, talking with him, letting him know that he is with the best surgeons, and the master surgeon of them all is Christ Jesus. The battles that he must face of his mind and physical wellbeing!"

"Marlene, I try to watch and guard my mouth of negative input for Glenn, but I have been speaking things out loud just to clear my thoughts of these whole circumstances; he is still my baby! We're limited in the number of visitors; is there any chance that the amount that he is able to have in a room beforehand will increase? I try to alternate people in and out so that just maybe he would wake up from his trance. They read to him as well; at least there are a lot of Christian role models in his life that have always planted seeds in his spirit."

"Penny, since he is in ICU, he will be limited in the amount of people at one time and visiting hours. You are the only one able to be with him as long as you don't mind sleeping on this little couch; that is bound to give you a crick in your neck and…"

"Ebb, does the creek over there seem to be swelling? Maybe because of the storm. I just don't feel all so well all of a sudden, I just need to stop and catch my breath before we go meet Marlene. Her name alone soothes my spirit as if I already know who she is. There's a richness that, by all costs, will never be attainable, or a set price could talk me out of how I feel, knowing that a loving God is watching over us. My soul has been searching for quite some time, and as strange as this sounds, this is the best thing that could have ever happened. Maybe I'm closer than I think. I think more than rain has fallen on my spirit. My fleece seems white, whiter than snow! While I'm standing here face to face with a stubborn ole mule as my companion, can this get any better, Ebb?!"

"Oh, Aly, you have yet to witness all that God's glory will reveal to us on this journey's way back home!"

Somewhere between here and there, Clarence, our glee-bee in

the glebe land of enriched soil, knows that a strong British accent is about to greet many visitors listening to a voice of gab. Our social, hairy, kaleidoscopic-eyed, multitasking, prophetic, pollination fanatic and filled with the love of Christ sings of all to *bee*.

Don't be worried about the price that was paid,
that day at Calvary,
where many had gathered in His name.
A price for a plot of soil
was to become His open grave.
They did not understand the power,
of His chosen spoken words,
until the empty tomb,
and the stone that was rolled away.
The callused and nail-driven, scarred hands,
now come to the broken-hearted and the enriched soil,
where his footprints lay across the land.
To each and every one
for each and every man.

CHAPTER TEN
THE LIVES AND FRIENDS OF GLENN ALYMORE

"Glenn has always been that typical teenage boy. The only strike against him, and it was huge, was the loss of his father at the age of eleven. They were close-knit together in a nightly game, around the age of five or so, which became the birth of the "night-night game," consisting of anything and everything to do with arts and crafts, like putting stickers in their appropriate places throughout a superhero's storyline sticker booklet.

"Sheldon Alymore, a dedicated father and a military man in the Air Force, worked on electrical generators throughout the years. Talented in pencil and charcoal drawings to where he started drawing again, gaining confidence from his lovely wife, Penny, an adorable woman who is very encouraging and has an open hotline to the Lord. It all started with the drawings of an early day off and him picking up his son beforehand from his Aunt Susan. Glenn had a fascination with huge cardboard boxes, so to personalize the box, Sheldon drew animated cartoon characters. A donkey, a rabbit, and a meek-hearted sheep, with characters of other natural settings, anything from bumble bees, one named Clarence, to birds flying in the air; you name it, it was on there, in the Engarlands Way, a mispronounced word that was meant to be "The Acreland Woods," the name Sheldon gave to the scenery because of his brother who lives in a small town in Albany County, New York. It is a vacationing spot that they went to yearly and stayed in a cabin out in the middle of nowhere. A summer vacation spot of open relaxation and getting caught up with the family. Anyhow, that's neither here nor there, just rambling. But back to the night-night game, it's worth mentioning the creativity of his son; he developed art drawing skills and would come up with some ingenious, imaginary topic matters, one being a war theme. This was where the famous "Call of Doody" had taken place, drawn by his father; it was a picture of a very poorly drawn gorilla sitting on a commode, which was a gut buster to Sheldon but not so much from other family members, especially Glenn. Glenn's drawing was military and tactical. It had newfound and named weaponry, with its proper use shown in action and with lines representing gunfire and explosives. Over time, the drawings became more detailed, the themes more complex, and they included the addition of video games for more hand and eye contact, well, for Glenn, not so much for Sheldon; as a matter of fact, he was very poor in any technological skills of the video world. Sheldon had an artistic hand for drawings and would draw many of Glenn's favs for the timeframe of his interests, keeping them in paged portfolio magazines. They had family nights of card games, three-way video games, you name it. They had very close-knit family ties.

"Well, all was typical in this blessed household until that fatal day of an ordinary day when they received a call from Sheldon's Officer Abbot about a severe accident that his father had been involved in. A crucial fall from a considerable height led to uncertainty for the intertwined family of three. One of the darkest nights of Glenn's early teenage years if it wasn't for the family's youth pastor, Pastor Harold Ebenezer, who they were fond of, calling him Ebb because it sounded cooler than Harold.

"Glenn was just beginning to have some curiosity about the spoken word of God after making several good friends from that ministry. He especially had a crush on Amber Hillington, a cute moonstone-blue-eyed girl with thick satin brown hair. Nicole and others were Amber's tag-along friends in the faith; speed dialing and long conversations of gab were their specialty. Glenn's best friend at the church was David, whose relationship became a wildfire of overnighters and inseparable, tied at the heart for life. And then that escalated in the 'Magnificent Seven': Rocco, a given name because no one liked the name Rudolph for this fearsome seven; Ace, he loved any kind of card game imaginable and his real name is Fredrick; Jesse; Duke, also a given name instead of Daniel; and the only girl, Amber, who had a wicked frog punch to the arm. And, of course, Glenn's nickname would become Aly, although he would just rather be called by his full last name because of the coolness of the pronunciational rhythm. Well, David was just David, but he was the spiritually inclined one of the group, leading all to the Lord and tugging on Glenn's heart at the time before his serious accident. Thank God for those boys who became a great inspiration and helped heal a gaping wounded heart. And Ebb, who became a very young father figure to Glenn, became an open invitation to whatever was on the young man's heart.

"One of Glenn's passions was creative writing, with which he gifted a long, story-based poem to his mother, a school project. The topic had to be school- and family-related, and then the kicker to make it more difficult was that it had to intertwine with a projected job career and their first remembrance of going to school. He so much wanted to rat out the bullies in his life, especially Hunter and Destin; these two were definitely destined to fall if things didn't change drastically for their cruel pack of mischievousness, and it seemed to be increasing in number of fellow grime participants as the months went by, but he couldn't find a way to fit it into the storyline. Anyway, his mom illuminated it in a small paperback printing, glossy and everything, like a real hardback book; that was very cool to him. Anyhow, this is how it went down, and we realized he was gifted at such an early age.

"But my only question to myself is, did he just write this as a piece of literature or a true confession of heart, for this is the only time he had written the words 'in Jesus' name'? Did I fail as a parent not to follow through when the opportunity was standing there before my face with an invitation so pronounced? It just seemed strange that in passages, he wrote out a spoken prayer for myself but not for himself; as the teacher, maybe I'm overthinking it, but I have let doubt rule in my mind, but what does my heart say? I put myself in this predicament!"

With trembling hands, Penny picks up the glossy book cover and begins to read the short story that Glenn had written, which had brought her comfort and made her very proud of Glenn's accomplishments.

"An Apple for the Teacher" The Good Ole Days

"Do you remember the good old days? Walking those country miles, barefooted along the grassy contoured road, in the direction unknown, to those who just pass through in this very small town, inspired by the townspeople, bringing life anew.

"The sweet smell of the cornfields in each diagonal role of our lives, running parallel in the morning breeze, finding ways to pass the time while kicking a can or dispersing the morning dew and singing a good old country tune.

"Laughing in the warmth of the afternoon, just happy to be, like two peas in a pod, as we walk each county mile, flocking like birds of a feather, who flock together, happy to belong to this bunch, an inner circle, as best friends for life. Even through our trials.

"Like the summer's breath, taken away by the heat, has passed, so has our midsummer amusement come to an end.

"Tomorrow brings a fresh new start to the beginning of our school year. New faces, old friends, and a new schoolteacher.

"The morning sunlight rays now awaken and tickle my ten toes, bringing joy deep to my level of understanding. The silence is kind of strange, especially to start the day, as Dad springs up from the other side to take my breath away, only to be received by giggles, grins, and giddy songs to make you chuckle, like 'give me some of that bacon, give me some of them beans, and we will fart out a song, just you and me,' one of our favorite melodies. Oh, Daddy-O, you're so silly, willy! A high five exchanged between the two, and as quick as the light's reflection brought him in, he has vanished into the shade of the day.

"So, I missed Mom's wake-up call that usually lightens up my day. She's not in here in the kitchen. Or the laundry room, down through the hallway. The dingy glow of sight sets the mood into the duskiness as I hear a familiar voice weeping through a closed window of time. I do not like to see da-momma cry or interrupt her whenever she is talking to Him.

"I just want her to be happy, for then I feel secure. I listen to what my beating heart says as I listen at the door.

"'Lord, You know I am easily frightened at this time of year. I know you go before them and are always by their side.

"'I pray for your mighty protection as my son begins his journey to school this very day. Watch over him and his friends; I pray he never wanders off alone. The choices he takes of the safest way from here to and fro, along the creek beds where he likes to play, the trees he feels that he must conquer, to the many hidden dangers that are kept in the secret. Lord, I ask for Your comfort in these times of unease. That his heart settles into the light You provide, to draw closer to you, and his comfort in You will be his humbleness on his knees. Send others that will guide and love in the ways that You provide. Bless him in his school education and to grow strong. Allowing those who direct his path in the direction of encouragement and understanding to help him find out where he truly belongs. A prayer for the principal, the staff, and the new schoolteacher.'

"As I listen in, I can hear a familiar joy in her song. One that needs no words but must come straight and directly from her character and personality. As I enter, I know she realizes I was listening in, for she gives me one of her uplifting smiles, the one she has after talking to Him.

"Gliding across the room swiftly, her hair sways like a musical tune and she gives me an enormous bear hug, so tightly, but lets me know that I am loved. Every heartbeat of her pulsing life's flow transfers to me, making it so much harder to let go. Bending down so gracefully, her eyes are alive with so much delight, and she kisses me on the cheek, brushing my hair that flows over my forehead so she can witness my baby blues. The time is essentially ticking away the time spent together, as I think to myself, *She has always demonstrated true love, but even more so, she shows me more after she talks to Him.*

"Walking me to the door in the comfort of her embrace, as one of my best friends indeed. Another quick hug and a goodbye, as my lunch is placed in my hand with an apple in the other, to give a smile, the apple, and a welcome as you meet and trust the hands of a new schoolteacher.

"Past the meadows, over the bridge of the crystal-clear brook. Down a path of hardened dirt, the short and narrow way Mom allows me to go. Past the timberlands of the thick evergreens, and never to go inside their mocking calling. I hear the ringing of the school bell calling, in that loud thunderous kind of clang. Safely gathered amongst the sheepish faces, I blend with some of my friends and some who assemble as wolves in sheep's clothes. A new face awaits us at the double red shepherd's wool framed door with a tender guide, a reassuring smile, and a soothing 'hello.'

"Approaching him nervously and shyly, my heart tells my mind it's okay to return a comforting smile. I begin to wonder if he talks to Him.

"Doubts, shyness, delays await, fighting my clinging fears. Encourage, sure, rest assured when reassured, remembering, showing yourself friendly, then others will be friendly. Always to do with love and understanding, for love will open many doorways that will lead you directly to their hearts; giving your name and then returning their given name will lead them along the way to a friendship that will continue with no end. Strongly saying, 'My name is David,' with a gentle smile to welcome them with this caressed, sweet gift of an apple. He introduces himself as Glenn and thanks him in Jesus' name. And that is when I realized that the new teacher talks to Him.

"The room is filled with anticipation as we all have been seated in an orderly fashion, as we begin our first day.

"A friendly gesture to the darkness of the chalkboard, as the screeching chalk dispersing in a powder puff cloud indeed, a rolling chain of words of expression, making himself known as a name, has been introduced to his face for all to see; Glenn Alymore is the flow of all things to become, and all that I can be. Calmness in the quietness of the room as a burst of excitement dances in the air of the electrical current of our new schoolteacher, now with grace, to bow our heads to say a prayer in Jesus' name. I pledge allegiance, and a child leads in prayer after the school bell rings. Lessons to learn, Math, English, History, things to help us on our way. Finger painting, play-dough, watercolors, expressions from each child's heart. Compliments, encouragements, correcting in a kind way, a seed planted, a seed nourished, in each and every child's heart. Recess, lunchtime, more lessons to learn. Six hours of a day, fun and gone. Oh, how easily time slips away. Cleanup time, organizing, with a closing prayer. The school bell rings, and a smile opens the door, excited about coming back tomorrow! Super speed. I cannot wait to get home! My heart is pounding faster than a freight train and seems to skip a beat, with palpitations, because deep, deep down, I am very happy deep down inside of me. And I cannot wait to see my mom so I can tell her all the reasons why my heart is exploding with love. She asks how my first day went, as if her heart tone wants to sing, as she places her hand on my shoulder in comfort. 'Come on, let's go inside so you can tell me everything!' She places me on the countertop so I can see deep down into her blue eyes. Her beautiful, reverent hair shining in the light. Her life lights and sees every expression on my soothing face as she anticipates each precious little word. That lets me know that my little life counts, as she is concerned about my beliefs.

"'Mom, I had so much fun throughout this day; school is really great. I am learning all kinds of new things in a different, special kind of way! The apple given was accepted with a firm handshake. His name is Glenn Alymore, and he's a man of God, sent to watch over us. Mom, this may sound a little bit unusual and a little bit strange, but he talks the same way as you!' And I can see she is a little confused because of the expression on her face. So, I try to make it so clear with my little chosen words. And although the words are very simple, 'Mom, Glenn talks to Him, like the way you talk to Him,' she gasps for air as if it were her last breath given, as her eyes begin to swell with tears, her tenderness inspired that I want to be comforted, expressing to me that everything is still okay. Her gentle hand behind my neck lets me know that I have nothing to fear. Her precious eyes, the ones that can rest my soul, shift to look to heaven above, as she wraps her arms around me, which transfers her peace and love. Each heartbeat uplifts my spirit's cry as she begins to speak; each word vibrates to her vibrant life waves.

"'Lord, no other peace have I known than in an answered prayer. To show You're walking with me, in Your special ways You've shown to let me know that You really do care. Thank You for those people placed into my child's life, and thank You for the new schoolteacher for being another guiding light. Amen.'

"Now I think I can understand where my mother's love and joy come from, the love and peace that surrounds her heart. A heart that is filled with pulsating life that can support our family tree. Praises of joy continually, sweet as fruit on the lips. And I can feel my heart every day growing in this love so divine. There is a confidence in her that I cannot explain, but it is where she is loyal and in trust. And although she may look meek, she is very strong, that is why she talks to Him!"

We all know that the Lord,
He works through us in many different,
mysterious ways.
By His will, to answer our prayers,
and to help lead us along our way.
And it is sometimes
strange and hard to comprehend.
How the Lord can make things happen
suddenly.
God always gives direction
if it is in His plans,
for there is always hope and purpose
in all that He provides.
Although sometimes
we find it hard to understand,
He will always answer prayers,
ask and you shall receive.

THE MEADOWLANDS

*Even if it appears through an apple
given to a new schoolteacher that day!
Just believe.*

Penny takes a trip down memory lane and can visualize his delicate blue eyes looking up at her, and she tears up about praying for him and his friends and many of their outdoor adventures, for there were many in the past. Wading creek beds to find little schools of fish and turtles that he kept in his little red wagon. *Once, he confessed to me about an old wooden raft that was out in a moss-covered pond, just a little way out so that he could possibly walk out and not get wet. Thank God for angels watching over him because, at that time, he didn't know how to swim. Speaking of the time, he almost drowned with his Uncle Fred, who was able to grasp his arm to pull him out of a sinkhole that made the water's edge go over his head when he went down in it. There are other incidents that he made known to me years past, such as events that show God being faithful to the prayer coverage. So, where's his angel for this particular event?*

Her mind drifts and is able to subconsciously pick up the news telecast on a muted TV with the captions still on as she slowly keeps up with the flashing words as they read:

"Now, for a local breaking news event that just happened and is in the process of notifying parents of their loved ones, where friends of friends walking through the well-known Tavor Oaks area came across a collapsed scenic route, a terrace that overlooks a valley brook at the Northern Outlook after heavy flooding jeopardized the foundation structure causing damage to the reinforcement beams extending above the red oaks' massive trunks where the balcony intermingles with the extending branches. Local city inspectors are trying to bring clarity to reasoning to see if the structure has been updated to compliance coding and to determine the access damage to the support system, but they believe they have narrowed it down to the erosion of the ravines' valley incline. Further investigations are underway. As local teens gathered at this popular hangout spot, a social disturbance abruptly took place by two acquaintances and became a public disturbance, where witnesses say shoving occurred as one unaccompanied individual was pushed by more than one into the railing. Other associates tried, by rushing over, to break up the disturbance when the balcony collapsed, and most plunged down into the abyss. Witnesses say as many as seven fell in the collapse, but the number and injuries have not been defined at this time. Police officers are still questioning witnesses at the scene, but in addition, any other information has been foreclosed to the media or public until all information is gathered. Once again, for those just tuning in, a terrace at the Northern Outlook has collapsed. We have been notified that Mayor William Nameberry is due to address the public and media for updating and questioning. The mayor has set a time for 5:30 p.m. An estimated eighteen years have passed on the timeline since the foundation and structure were built, and it has been inspected yearly for the public's safety. Now for some good news…"

Ebenezer is concerned that his four-legged walking mop head is a little out of whack due to the fact that he has been able to hit the majority of all the potholes along the way, "How are you doing, Aly? It looks like your legs aren't rattling anymore. How about some good news, Mr. Alymore of the green pastures? Penny knows where the fourth stone is in the midst of the area, and that's when you kind of blanked out on me for a little bit, and my signals for some strange reason got lost in translation, if that makes sense or not, who knows, just saying!"

A bewildered Aly says in agreement, "Yeah, I'm fine, it just seems like my heart rate is a little low, maybe just allergies kicking in or something. That's good about the stone; we need a little pick-me-up in this neck of the woods!"

Ebenezer listens in because Aly keeps glitching in his conversation, so it is hard to tell if he is finished or not; then he says, "And I saw Rocco, heading west with aloe vera foaming in his mouth, he muttered something which aggravated the plant making matters worse, his appearance was like a rabid dog in the heat. The complications with open wounds that deep can cause infection, which is not good for Ace; it could obstruct the healing process! I sure hope that he will be all right; he is such a good ol' boy! Anyway, we will probably run into Penny before we even get to David."

The cold hard facts of the local newscast have set deep in her mind, penetrating thoughts of discouragement that they didn't even mention anything about David, but then again, he is a minor, and that information cannot be disclosed until parents are notified. *I am definitely sure David was by his side, just like in school.* As another memory of Glenn enters the passage, waves of her inner thoughts are spoken out loud.

"While in school, he excelled in the art institute's skills and the technological path, he has good manners, and he is reading at a college student level, so why, then, would he even think about doing the one thing that landed him in the intensive care ward?"

Penny speaks outside the closed door, thank God, in a whisper; this is exactly what she doesn't want to do in front of Glenn, so she exits the room and ever so gently closes the door. She turns to see a rounded face wearing spectacles as wide as her joyous smile.

"Marlene, so good to see you!"

"And the same here! Just wanted to stop by and see the boy before I leave for the evening; he is doing good, so the staff and I will leave so that you can have privacy…"

Penny interrupts Marlene before she can finish her sentence,

"Oh, will you stay to talk just a little? If you could, it would be great, and I need a broader scale of social outlet other than talking to myself and listening to the newscast outside the lobby!"

Marlene nods her head in agreement. "Well, I have some great news to tell you. I wasn't able to get you more visitors in the room, but after talking to Dr. Robertson, he agreed that the youth pastor, Ebenezer, may stay an hour after regular visitation time because of your social activity with the Lord and that it would be good for Glenn to hear familiar voices! If you like, Penny, we could get started here by opening our hearts to Jesus, where to begin, or picking up where you left off because God is in the house!"

The Key to Marlene's Heart: In The Beginning of Wisdom, There Are the Proverbs

The general, in a demanding command, tries his best to smack Penny a couple of times for good measure to break Penny, fuzzy tale, out of being a space cadet, or at least snap her out of this comatose stupor that she is in as he yells out, "Wake up in there already, *Penny!*"

And out of nowhere, she does and screams, *"God is in this house!* I am in an emotional commotion that will not get out of my frazzled mind! For there is something that goes down deep into a man's soul of the taunting words that destroy the mind, for it is like poison to the soul, settling in your spirit and setting up for the kill. Let there be no compromises, for there is no room for doubting, pray without ceasing, and Satan must flee. Isn't that what You say, Lord? That we are to cast all burdens upon You, for Your love sets us free. There are wolves in sheep's clothing everywhere we go, especially further down the stream and past the bridge by the brook of uncertainties, for when we enter through the wooden gates with the wood-framed, red doors, we enter the enemy's kingdom. Greetings from the new teacher, Marlene, full of wisdom, who will be introduced to a boy named Glenn as he has the key to David's heart stone. And through the friendship of many, the last two stones will be recovered and placed in the brook's stream, where destiny will be found this very day, for the thunderous clanging of the bell and destruction of the altar is all out of whack. The cost of many lives is due to the haunting of juvenile actions, but one's very soul is a fighter for his life and, more importantly, for his very soul in a quest, for the rest and assurance of a mother's love."

Then, silence, as everyone just stays away and stares wide-eyed in Penny's direction. The silence is interrupted by Penny's last spoken words, clearly summing up everything.

"Who am I?"

Glenn Alymore is peacefully sleeping in the comforts of his own dreams as the accompaniment of music on the monitor leaps, bleeps, and skips a beat on the heart monitor of life. The rasping sounds of the ventilator fill the room. Penny opens up the pages of her life changes and concerns when a loving Briton listens and counsels in, "I understand you want to rest assured, as any mother's love would want to do so. Penny, no matter how many seeds we plant and water with the Word of God, each and every individual has to make their choice on their own, all in God's timing. Sometimes, those who haven't even known them reap in the blessing of the harvest others might have planted. We are called only to be faithful and believe. Now let's pray the serenity prayer and…"

Penny, seeming a little surprised, says, "But I am not an alcoholic or go to any of the meetings?"

"No, but the prayer covers and defines what you can control

and what you have to let go and give to God, it is good counseling even for such a strong faith in the Lord that you have! See how that prayer calms your soul? I told you, Jesus is here when two or three gather, and if I did my math right, there are three in this room right now, maybe more if you count the spiritual beings, but that is a whole different ballfield or battleground! Let me pull out my little KJV holy hand grenade that will set out an explosion of wisdom on your tuchus! Give me a sec. Okay, here we go."

My son, forget not my law; but let thine heart
keep my commandments:
For length of days, and long life, and peace, shall they add to thee.
Let not mercy and truth forsake thee: bind them about thy neck;
write them upon the table of thine heart:
So shalt thou find favour and good understanding in
the sight of God and man.
Trust in the Lord with all thine heart; and lean not unto
thine own understanding.
In all thy ways acknowledge him, and he shall direct thy paths.
Be not wise in thine own eyes: fear the Lord, and depart from evil.
It shall be health to thy navel, and marrow to thy bones.
Honour the Lord with thy substance, and with the
firstfruits of all thine increase:
So shall thy barns be filled with plenty, and thy presses
shall burst out with new wine.
My son, despise not the chastening of the Lord;
neither be weary of his correction:
For whom the Lord loveth he correcteth; even as a father
the son in whom he delighteth.
Happy is the man that findeth wisdom, and the man
that getteth understanding.

— Proverbs 3:1–13

"Now Penny, apply that to your own life; we sometimes get spiritual amnesia and forget how powerful His name and word can be; a devotional to our lives. See, I can see the peace of God all over you, girl."

Penny takes in the spirit of fresh, clean air three times, in and out, and announces, "Yes, God is good all the time, and your British accent brings the living word to life with your pronunciation as well!"

Marlene takes in the compliment. "Yes, some people say that I should do a series on Proverbs doing the Bible narration on the commentaries because they are the key to my heart and to all wisdom, anything, and everything of life sources! You'll see; just you wait and see!

The general, Amber, Nicole, and Gretchen stand in amazement at the word of God flowing out of Penny's spirit and such powerful scriptures as Gretchen speaks of the incident. "Wow, the wisdom flowing through you and the path we are to take because I haven't a clue to where you are going with all of that… that scripture, and where did the British accent come from, Penny?! I am very concerned here. Are you having a bad hare day due to the passing of Sheldon? I mean, we all loved him and his antics and all, and he kept us entertained. Are you just giving things a new twist or something? Penny, Penny, are you listening at all to me?!"

An anxious hair is sticking up on our furry little hare, who says, "Come on, ladies and gentlemen, and get your thinking caps on, for there is more at stake than just these stones and David; there is a whole lot of faith riding on this quest of this fellowship, my friends!" The British accent slowly fades away halfway through the first stanza. "Are you ready? Well, people, get ready! Just you wait, just you wait and see!"

Our Clarence, the bumble bee, flying solo, oh, it's not good to be alone. He humbles in the presence of a rising king, *buzz*, *buzz*, *buzz* of nothings in the prelude of David's ear and sings him a song of a company's greetings that shall be. Just you wait, just you wait and see!

"There is the inevitable acquaintance in this obscure fellowship that will chaperon this distinguished, unheralded occurrence of chronology. But whometh to speaketh and whometh to accord in this longevity affair? Simplicity in modesty. With an accent from the homeland!"

Translation:

"Everyone, sooner or later, no matter the personality's indifference, is going to hook up and get the job done, but how long will their actual relationship last? Is it just a fleeting glimpse of common grounds that has brought these individuals together?"

The standard version translation of the King James version.

With a British accent!

Now let's let Marlene put some wisdom together with a jaunting through the King James version and the Proverbs!

THE VISITATION

Something has begun to change in the atmosphere in this room, as the spirits roam freely amongst all in the room, but there is a barrier, a covering over the three humans, trying to penetrate the spoken words of the living Bible. Darkness is trying to overtake the flame that is burning in the hearts of the conscience. But the one they want is vulnerable in the weakness of the mind and heart, for he is still questioning the truth that can set a prisoner free. Definitely not because of the lack of knowledge, for he has searched the word out and has entered his mind, but for what purposes is the intent of his heart? Satan has acquired that same knowledge but has been cast out, and rightly so, for his rebellious spirit, taking those who followed him down with him as well.

And oh, so diligently, they want the soul of Glenn Alymore, who is suspended between heaven and Hades but still alive by the grace and mercy of God. However, he cannot be touched, for he is in the covering of the Lord, and his mind is at free play, to all to possess and control or uplift, independently acting on his own free will.

Lurking and clinging to the walls and ceiling that transforms this metamorphic structure in the darkness of the imagination? Therefore, in the spiritual realm, there are hideous interconnections of agony and despair, where past forms of life or death have lingered here in the questioning of their final destinations. In reality, these same walls and ceilings support this cubic interior and are just mere shells of projected images that have become their fantasy, medical illusions. If it was only physical suffering, most people can tolerate a painful injury with the assistance of medication, but there is a demonic terror that is responsible for taunting the minds of these individuals to insanity, and the medications only increase the horror within. And it is as if they are in a dream, or "Did we forget to wake up and have become that same evil within?"

The animal paw prints, one set forward into motion, the other set heading back, for isn't that how we perceive things in our minds, always looking in the rearview mirror? Both sets are lodged in the beaten pathway of our minds that induces fresh thoughts in the minds of Ebenezer and Alymore; that harmful situation is deeply embedded into the realization of the element, as their hooves leave current progress and leave behind all the hindrance of what will become yesterday's news. Rocco is long gone and on his way home to the safety and comfort of Jesse and soon to be with Jacob, who fought so bravely with Ace.

Oh, to be bound in a furrow of misery, just wanting to feel comfort again, but there is no comfort for Aly as he says what troubles are on his mind, "Ebb, why do the mountains rise so high, and the sky, so blue, only to be swallowed into a massive gully that veers into a sea of loneliness? This transformation deep within is definitely like a wildfire of emotional dependency, from one extreme to the other, this ill-effect madness enclosed by the urge of laughter! Why must my soul fight for its own independence so far away from this God we serve? But who am I to say, and what's the difference between knowing and believing? The tree is being shaken, and I am the leaves about to fall!"

A baffled look similar to a jigsaw puzzle with one piece missing to offset a work of art crosses the face of Ebb, confessing, "Awww, come on, Aly, don't wig out on me now, just breathe, take in some fresh air because what you're saying is what comes out your back end! Relax, you're still feeling the effects of our experience on the timberlands, and now that your adrenaline has ceased, well, there you go, you're all over the place, silly goober!

"Look, since you have carried the stone of purification, you've been acting weird. Where have you placed the stone, Aly, up your…?!" Aly rudely interrupts Ebb before he can finish what needs to be said; Aly halts him before the sentence can be relayed.

"Don't you dare complete that sentence, Ebenezer, and by the way, I've entangled the stone in my wooliness next to my heart!"

The room is quieted by the souls of all hearts that beat as one, in a eurythmic cure for all that is in despair, for once again, the atmosphere has shifted as the heavens of the heavenly begin a transformation of attitudes, and the angels sing to the spoken words.

THE MEADOWLANDS

The scriptures pin the demons to the wall, where they are forced to listen to the truth be told by Marlene, a rolling ball of joy who proclaims, "'A merry heart maketh a cheerful countenance: but by sorrow of the heart the spirit is broken' (Proverbs 15:13) and 'A merry heart doeth good like a medicine: but a broken spirit drieth the bones' (Proverbs 17:22). Girl, you just have to find ways to keep your mind occupied. His glory will shine through you; just be you and watch what the Lord can do! Keep the scriptures close at hand, and you will never be alone in His word!"

A cheerful smile crosses the face of Penny as she reaches down into her lovely bag of specialties, a hobby that she so much loves to do to relax. "Yes, I do so with this, my crochet hooks, a skein of wool, and for every stitch made, the word of God is spoken life into this blanket for Glenn, a multi-colored Joseph-kind of color rays!" Then there came a rapping. Who could that be knocking at my door? "Come on inside, 'Where no counsel is, the people fall: but in the multitude of counsellors there is safety' (Proverbs 11:14). The door is always open, and bring your Bibles."

Two men walking in stride come through the door with lovely grins on their faces. Youth Pastor Harold Ebenezer and Doctor Robertson open up the conversation. "We should have known that God is in this house and that the Lord always takes a direct line! We're running a little late, but we had a drastic alert of one of the casualties related to the same incident. He is doing better, but I am sorry that I brought it up, for this is the only information that I can give. I would like to bring it up in an unspoken prayer of divine healing because that is what it will take!"

"Such a tragedy for both lives at such a young age. How is everyone? It looks as if all is calm with Glenn, well, at least with the monitors, but they are subject to change. Have they?"

Marlene, always smiling, says, "His brain activity has been on the rise, but whenever we speak the word of God, the changes are drastic; I just wonder what he could be thinking. Penny and I have been quoting scripture while she is crocheting away on a blanket for Glenn to cover him in prayer."

Penny chimes in on a random thought that reminds her of Glenn in the process of each stitch crochet, as she proclaims proudly, "Yes, I even taught Glenn how to crochet a single square patch and how to piece each piece together to make his own blanket, which he did and gave it to me on Mother's Day when he was twelve!"

Pastor Ebenezer, mentally thumbing through the pages of the living Word, says, "Wow, very impressive, and I think that this is a fantastic ideal. Reminds me of the days of the Apostles Paul and Peter. How are you holding up, Mrs. Alymore? I love the concept behind your blanket, and I think we should pray over it for the purpose of healing your son. Let's do so; the enemy will flee in the presence of a holy God! Let us enter His gates of praise!"

The four of them join in unity, hands placed on the blanket for security as the scriptures flow like honey from a honeycomb.

The demonic screeching of agony and affliction has crazed their unnatural character into a frenzy of rage and fiendish attire. "Release us from our own despair. The truth is being told as the saints gather in unity, and do our souls burn with grief for the remainder of our fallen souls! Do not cast us out, for we will be a disgrace to our kind! Let us enter into the cockroach, searching for an exit of this sanitized arena, then we shall begone from your sight, for the barrier has extended into the eternal living God, and the angels are legion and come armed to our defenseless existence! Let us exit the way that we entered!"

Then silence arises!

The overwhelmingly silent but adventurous pack is walking in a tight closeness in the solitude of the day, with their eyes glued to the ever-so-changing scenery. The moisture in the air is being sucked into the vines, roots, and greenery, bringing new lives and leaves budding to the gathered saplings along the road. The monstrous clouds that stalked each and every one on this route have calmly subsided into the thinness of the air, dispersing in a circular pattern of nothingness, as Penny gleefully states to the group, "Looky here, fresh paw tracks of a domestic animal, someone entered, someone exited, and over to our right is the broom tree, its deciduous nature a land marker for our entrance. Down through this furrow at the vanishing point of our existence into the seclusion of Isabella's Haven, how sweet!"

The crew is grounded and *hip hop*, their spiky little legs into the hidden paradise's calling, as the General sways to gravity and the magnetic force of Penny's thudding as she moves into leaps and bounds. The fragrance of cabbage and broccoli distributes the earthy smell of fresh vegetarian produce. The ripeness of the pomegranate and apple trees of the orchid are plentiful and ready to pluck. Figs from the tree are amongst the timberland's flooring, ready to become a newton to someone's sandal or a quick appetite for the ladies as they cannot resist. And from the midst of a huge hollowed-out cabbage, an image emerges from the core of perfection: two beady eyes and wiggly whiskers, twitching to see who her companionship or repertoire of performers are who have made their existence known to her where there are no trenches or foxholes or battle cries, only the peaceful tranquility of Marlene chewing on some remains of cabbage. And so, the battle of the proverbs takes place in the quest for this heptagonal stone.

— Appendix —

1. Numbers 33:1

2. 1 Samuel 16:7

3. Psalm 68:33; Psalm 70

4. Acts 16:14, 23:14, 23:27–29, 24:9–10

5. Ezekiel 37:1–14; Matthew 5:6

6. Matthew 5:6, 13; Isaiah 43:19

7. Mark 8:18; John 21:18; Luke 6:47; Ephesians 6; Jeremiah 29:11

8. Judges 6:36, 7:13; Psalm 44:21, 25

9. Proverbs 14;16; James 3:16, Galatians 5:23; 2 Peter 2:6; Romans 7:25, 8:27, 34

10. Romans 7:25; 1 Samuel 13:14, 15:35; Psalm 55

11. Romans 15:3; 1 Samuel 13:14, 15:35, 16:19; Psalm 55

12. Mark 1:1–3; Psalm 69:7–11, 13, 16

13. Numbers 22:23–29; Psalm 8:2; Psalm 68:9

14. Deuteronomy 30:19–20, 31:36, 33:46; Numbers 13:2, 20, 30

15. 1 Samuel 17:1

16. 1 Samuel 16:12, 13
17. Job 29:15, 16, 24, 25
18. 1 Samuel 17:24
19. Ezekiel 17:21; James 1:5–8, 14–17; Proverbs 16:25; Hebrews 11:6
20. Numbers 22:23–26
21. Judges 4:4, 5:10, 15
22. Jeremiah 23:23, 28–29, 24: 6–7, 25:4–5, 10, 32, 26:1, 9, 18, 19, 27:5–6, 22, 28:4, 29:7, 12–13
23. 1 Corinthians 13:1–2, 13; Numbers 9:1, 2
24. Romans 3, 5:15, 20, 6:14, 22–23
25. Psalm 90:12–17, 91:1, 11
26. Revelation 1:7, 11
27. Luke 15:11
28. Psalm 3:3
29. 1 Samuel 2:10
30. Luke 16
31. Isaiah 40:31
32. 1 Samuel 2:35
33. Psalm 18:1
34. 1 Samuel 2:35
35. Psalm 17:3–8, 1 Samuel 2:33, 35

36. Psalm 18:16–19

37. Psalm 18:17–15

38. Job 39:3, 4, 8, 16, 21

39. Psalm 139; Jeremiah 1:18

40. Isaiah 4:5, 5:8–30, 6:2, 7:23

41. Psalm 18:7–15, 25–32

42. Habakkuk 2:1–20; Psalm 18:17–42

43. Habakkuk 3:13–16

44. 2 Kings 4–40; Psalm 18:20–24; Habakkuk 2:18–20

45. Psalm 18:37–43

46. Psalm 16:11, 17:13,14, 18:46

47. Psalm 18:33; Psalm 36:4–5

48. Psalm 18:47–50

49. Psalm 22:12–22, 30, 31, 23:5, 6

50. Psalm 23:1–4

51. Ecclesiastes 3:1 8

52. Zechariah 4:1, 6:8–10

53. Psalm 18:12–14, 31; Proverbs 27:3

54. 1 Samuel 17:8